SOULMATES FROM THE PAGES OF HISTORY

SOULMATES FROM THE PAGES OF HISTORY

FROM MYTHICAL TO CONTEMPORARY, 75 EXAMPLES

OF THE POWER OF FRIENDSHIP

JACK ADLER

Algora Publishing
New York

Library of Congress Cataloging-in-Publication Data —

Adler, Jack.
  Famous and fanciful friends: the book of friends / Jack Adler.
    pages cm.
  Includes bibliographical references and index.
    ISBN 978-0-87586-981-0 (soft cover: alk. paper) — ISBN 978-0-87586-982-7 (hard
cover: alk. paper) — ISBN 978-0-87586-983-4 (ebook)
  1. Friendship—Case studies. I. Title.
  BJ1533.F8A35 2013
  177.62—dc23
                            2013011603

Front Cover: Athena and Poseidon.

Printed in the United States

With gratitude and fond memories to past and present friends

Table of Contents

Introduction

Fascinating and illuminating friendships between luminaries have existed over the years running from mythology, classical antiquity and the Bible to contemporary times. These friendships takes many forms, but there are some common themes in what brought and kept the pairs together; in some cases in what disrupted the friendship; in the impact each friendship had on the individuals' lives and careers; and their collective influence on the world.

The sinews of friendship are not unbreakable. Yet, as the profiles in this book suggest, there are many touching stories that illustrate how strong the bonds of friendship can be. Few elements of life are more universal and constant than the need for friendship, and we are driven to search for friends. Many guidelines have been written, but there are no real rules. Hopefully, this book can serve to illustrate some of the powerful values that have secured memorable friendships throughout the ages.

In the following chapters, seventy-five outstanding friendships are explored, from Enkidu and Gilgamesh in Babylonian annals and David and Jonathan from the Bible to the criminal exploits of Al Capone and Johnny Torrio and the political harmony between President Franklin Delano Roosevelt and Harry Hopkins.

With the stories of these friends we will find ourselves mingling with individuals of great talent: writers like Herman Melville and Nathaniel Hawthorne and Franz Kafka and Max Brod; poets such as Lord Byron and Shelley, as well as Samuel Coleridge and William Wordsworth. Philosophers take in Adam Smith and David Hume, with Auguste Renoir and Claude Manet as painters. Warriors are represented by Achilles and Patroclus and Alexander and Hephaistion. Key friendships among musicians include Maurice Ravel and Claude Debussy, and Sergei Rachmaninoff and Vladimir Horowitz. Other extraordinary friendships include Voltaire and King Frederick the Great and Tchaikovsky and his patroness, Nadezhda von Meck.

Distaff friendships include Susan Anthony and Elizabeth Stanton, two women's rights advocates; Helen Keller and her mentor, Anne Sullivan; and Gertrude Stein and her lifelong companion, Alice B. Toklas.

Many factors go into exploring the nature of friendships. Among many comments on the subject:

> "If a man does not make new acquaintance as he advances through life, he will soon find himself alone. A man, sir, should keep his friendship in constant repair."

> —*The Vanity of Human Wishes*, Samuel Johnson

> "What is the secret of your life?" asked Mrs. Browning of Charles Kingsley. "Tell me, that I may make mine beautiful, too."

> He replied, "I had a friend."

> —Related by William Channing Gannett about Charles Kingsley (an English clergyman and novelist)

Chapter 1. Gilgamesh and Enkidu

"Gilgamesh and Enkidu," an ancient epic written on clay tablets several thousand years ago in Mesopotamia, is one of the earliest known works of literature. It's also the story of a friendship with universal themes of the natural and pure man versus a more sophisticated and civilized counterpart. Additionally, it illustrates the perennial search by mankind to escape the clutches of time and to achieve immortality. The pair, and their adventures, have found their way into the Old Testament, subsequent mythologies and epics like the *Odyssey*, and no shortage of later works of art. Even computer games show their continuing influence and presence.

A Possible Representation of Enkidu

Scholars have noted parallels to the story of Adam and Eve in the Garden of Eden, as both "books" include reference to a man being created by the gods or god, to a woman who comes along to influence the man, and even to a serpent. References to a great flood inundating the earth are eerily close to the story of Noah and the Ark. Gilgamesh has become a cultural icon and symbol of man's continual quest for answers to the mysteries of life and death.

Different translations have been made of the work, which probably emerged from combining various Sumerian legends. One of the opening lines gives a hint of the search to understand life's mysteries: "He Who Saw the Deep."

Gilgamesh is the young and somewhat brash king of Uruk. Many in his kingdom are unhappy with his rule. Complaints range from his conscripting men to work on building his favored projects and variously taking advantage of everyone below him. The people pray for deliverance and Anu, leader of the gods, comes to their aid.

Enkidu is created from clay to eventually become a strong and equal counterpart to Gilgamesh and to serve as an instrument to change or moderate his headstrong ways. However, Enkidu's appearance and persona is so natural that it's raw. He's a hairy and unclothed wild man living like an animal in the fields. The two are direct opposites, with Gilgamesh more the urbane warrior-king. Shamhest, a priestess from the Temple of Enlil, is dispatched to civilize and educate the primitive Enkidu.

Gilgamesh and Enkidu, who is brought to Uruk, quickly clash. Enkidu is enraged by Gilgamesh trying to have his way with a young bride, and he blocks Gilgamish's way into the bridal chamber. They fight, and though equal in strength, Gilgamesh is the victor. Nevertheless, they bond and become fast friends, vowing to always protect each other.

Ninsun, Gilgamesh's mother, even adopts Enkidu while also asking Shamash, the sun-god, to protect her headstrong son. Bolstered by the presence of his new and close companion Gilgamesh is eager to seek greater glory and renown. Though warned by Enkidu of the dangers involved, the pair set out to the dread Cedar Forest to slay the ogre, Humbaba, who reigns over the region. Humbaba, in no way frightened, threatens to disembowel Gilgamesh and Enkidu and feed their flesh to the birds. In the ensuing struggle, said to make the mountains quake and the sky turn black, Humbaba is defeated by the combined efforts of Gilgamesh and Enkidu. The monster then pleas for his life and Gilgamesh is tempted to spare him; but now Enkidu argues for them to complete their mission, a decision that comes back to haunt him.

The duo cut down a large tree to build a new gate at the Temple of Enlil as well as a raft to sail home to Urak on the Euphrates River. The severed head of Humbaba, proof of their bloody deed, is also on the raft. Perhaps too sure of himself now, Gilgamesh rejects the advances of the goddess Ishtar, distrustful due to her lethal treatment of former lovers. This doesn't sit well with Ishtar, accustomed to getting her way, and she appeals to her father, the powerful god Anu, to send Gugalanna, the "bull of heaven," to Urak to avenge this insult. The fearsome words are issued: "I shall bring up the dead to eat food like the living; and the hosts of the dead will outnumber the living!" The bull is very effective in creating devastation whereby reed beds and marshes are destroyed, lowering the level of the river in the process. A terrible drought follows and the people suffer.

Gilgamesh and Enkidu now have another mission. They come to the rescue of Urak and kill the ferocious bull. Enkidu, in an indelicate gesture showing his disdain, even tosses parts of the bull's rear end at an image of Ishtar. Furious, Ishtar appeals again to Anu to redress the killing of the bull as well as the slaying of Humbaba, and Enkidu's insult.

Led by Anu, the gods meet and decide that either Gilgamesh or Enkidu, their own creation, should die. It's deemed that the pair had no justification for interfering with the will of the gods. Judgment is passed despite the appeals of the goddess Shamash who asks for leniency.

Statue of Gilgamesh, University of Sydney, Sydney, Australia

Enkidu is the one sentenced to die. He bewails his creation and the attempts to civilize him which have led to his downfall. But then the goddess Shamesh scolds him, saying that he should better appreciate the benefits of civilization, including his great friendship with Gilgamesh. At his end Enkidu comes to terms with his fate and no longer bemoans having been born. Stricken with a fatal malady, Enkidu finally dies, lamenting that he couldn't at least have died heroically in battle.

Gilgamesh mourns the death of Enkidu whom he terms as "the sword in my belt, the shield for my front." He calls for all the elements of nature — mountains, rivers, forests, fields and animals — to join him in lamenting the death of Enkidu. In addition, Gilgamesh commissions a statue of Enkidu to be built and he offers gifts to the gods to ensure an honorable reception for his departed friend in the realm of the dead. In his grief Gilgamesh holds off the burial of Enkidu until he spots a maggot emerging from his nose. This scene, perhaps an epiphany for Gilgamesh, spurs him to seek to escape the finality and bodily humiliation of death and to seek eternal life like a god.

Subsequently, wiser and more mature, Gilgamesh goes on to many other adventures in the worlds of life and afterlife. But his main motivation now is to escape the ultimate fate of death, visited on his dead companion, Enkidu, and to discover the secret of obtaining immortality and eternal life. He finally seeks his ancestor Utnapishtun, said to be the solitary survivor of the Great Flood. Both Utnapishtun and his wife were granted immortality by the gods. But first Gilgamesh has to overcome various dangers such as lions and scorpions, en route. Finally a marine goddess tells him the way to the Island of the Blessed.

Gilgamesh learns about the fateful deluge from Utnapishtun, who also informs him that no others may achieve immortality: "The life that you are seeking will never be found. When the gods created man they allotted to him death, but life they retained in their own keeping."

Gilgamesh returns to Uruk. While he has failed to gain the secret of obtaining eternal life, he is still the stronger for now he has the precious knowledge of his own mortality. This knowledge enables him to more properly worship the gods and to be a king loved by his people. However, he is probably honored more in posterity through the famous epic of his life and struggles than was likely the case during his lifetime.

CHAPTER 2. RUTH AND NAOMI

Naomi and Daughters-in-Law

The story of Ruth and Naomi, from the Bible, is one of the most touching and loyal friendships ever recorded. Though the time period has been set around 1000 to 900 B.C., and credited to the prophet Samuel, the circumstances in the tale may well have been much later. As the perspectives of the two women dominate this section of the Old Testament (which is hardly the case for most of the Bible), some scholars believe it may have been written by a woman.

During a famine a Jewish family — Elimelech, his wife, Naomi, and their two sons, Mahlen and Chinion — decide to move from Bethlehem to the nearby tribe of Moab. Settling in, Mahlen marries Ruth, a Moabite woman; and Chinion marries Orpah, another woman from the Moab tribe. Then a triple disaster happens. The three men in the family all die, and Naomi is left alone with her daughters-in-law.

At this juncture Naomi decides to return to Bethlehem where she still has family ties. She tells her two daughters-in-law to return to their own mothers and find new husbands. "May the Lord deal kindly with you, as you have dealt with the dead and me."

Orpah does opt to leave Naomi after a tearful farewell but Ruth elects to stay behind and says, in words that have been immortalized: "Entreat me not to leave you, or to turn back from following you. For wherever you go, I will go. And wherever you lodge, I will lodge. Your people shall be my people, and your God my God. Where you die, I will die, and there will I be buried. The Lord do so to me, and more also, if anything but death part you and me."

The two women thus stay united and then return to Bethlehem at the time of the annual barley harvest. Ruth converts to Judaism. Boaz, a relative of Naomi, is a well-to-do farmer, single and childless. Naomi is unhappy with her lot in life and calls herself "Mara," or bitter. But she sees a chance to perhaps improve their situation. She has Ruth go to Boaz' fields and pick up the bits of grain left after the harvest which are offered free to the poor. Boaz spots Ruth. He learns about her devotion to Naomi, and he is very impressed.

According to the laws of the Jews at this time, a widow at her husband's death is still considered to be part of her dead spouse's family. But a male from the family, considered a "kinsman/redeemer," has to marry the widow to keep the widow's property within the family.

Shrewdly, Naomi has Ruth apply perfume to her body and to don her best clothes one day after collecting grain in the fields. Thus prepared, Ruth goes to the threshing house at night where Boaz is sleeping. Under the customs of the period, when a woman seeks marriage to a man she "uncovers his feet." Some scholars have interpreted this gesture more anatomically.

"Who are you?" Boaz asked, surprised to be so woken.

"I am your servant, Ruth. Spread your garment over me, since you are a kinsman-redeemer."

"To spread the cloak" was another expression attributed to this sort of marriage proposal; and it worked.

Naomi might have hoped for this outcome, or Ruth may have been especially audacious. Boaz is actually second in line to become the "redeemer," but he convinces a less distant relative to stand aside. Boaz, considerably older than Ruth, is possibly smitten with her. But he is very cognizant of his familial responsibility and readily agrees to marry her. This assures a measure of security to both Ruth and Naomi. In time, Ruth gives birth to a boy, Obed, whom Naomi helps raise.

One woman of Bethlehem, doubtless expressing the opinion of many, told Naomi:

"Blessed be the Lord, who has not left you this day without next of kin. May his name be renowned in Israel! He shall be to you a restorer of life and a nourishment for your old age. For your daughter-in-law who loves you, and who is more to you than seven sons, has borne him."

What is more, eventually Ruth becomes the great grandmother of the future King David

The story of Ruth's steadfastness has been given many interpretations — from both academic and religious circles — of love, loyalty and faithfulness.

CHAPTER 3. JONATHAN & DAVID

These two biblical men, one a shepherd boy who became king of the Isra-elites and the other a prince who might have been king, are forever linked as illustrating one of the strongest ties of friendship. Their expression of love for each other underwent many turns that demonstrated the strength and durability of their mutual regard.

It's in the nature of things to wonder if their relationship had a physical side to the emotional attachment. Many religious figures as well as academicians have taken sides in this issue, some seeing an erotic aspect to their friendship while others view their trio of covenants as a platonic combination of mutual affection and political compromise.

Regardless of one's belief their story, as described in the Book of Samuel in the Old Testament, offers lyrical testimony to the capacity of two men to forge a friendship for the ages.

Some background is necessary before Jonathan and David meet. At this time Saul, from the tribe of Benjamin, was anointed by the prophet Samuel as the first king of Israel. Jonathan, Saul's eldest son, was next in line for the crown. Israel was faced with a running war against the Philistines who threatened to over-come the small collection of tribes that composed Israel. Samuel was the major prophet and his word, considered to be interpreting the will of Jehovah or God, had great impact on all the Israelites.

I SAR. XX.

Iam Ionathas animum novit, furiasq parentis,
Davidemq monet jacta sagitta fugæ.
Mutuo nunc sibi cor suprema per oscula tradunt;
Sic quoq cor duplex verus amicus habet.

Prinz Ionathan kennt schon des Vatters Grimm und Herzen,
warnt David mit dem Pfeil, daß er nicht länger bleib.
Und redlich geben Sie mit einem Kuß die Herzen:
So kriegt ein wahrer Freund zwey Herzen in den Leib.

Jonathan Embracing David

Jonathan and David meet at a battle against the Philistines in the Valley of Elah. David, the son of Jesse from the tribe of Judah, has been sent to the field to bring food to his brothers who are in Israel's army. Jonathan is in full armor while

David is dressed as a shepherd, his only weapon a slingshot. However, David, accustomed to protecting his flock of sheep from wild animals and human predators, is quite handy with that simple item.

The Philistines bring forward their champion, Goliath, a giant of a warrior, to challenge the Israelites to a one-against-one battle. Whoever wins will be master of the field, and the Philistines are confident their man will triumph. The name "Goliath" has since gone on to be used in speech and literature to depict a huge and powerful man. King Saul and his soldiers apparently have no one who is willing to confront the hulking Goliath.

The king offers one of his daughters to any man who will fight and kill Goliath, but there are no takers and panic is setting in among the Jewish army.

It's at this crucial moment that David takes it upon himself to accept the challenge. Bravely, he steps forward to confront Goliath, and we can imagine the taunts and jeers from the Philistines seeing a mere boy, armed with just a slingshot, coming to meet their mighty champion.

The result is well known. David coolly takes aim well before the two can clash, and unerringly the small rock crashes into Goliath's forehead. He falls to the ground, dead. The Philistines are astounded and then they run in a disorderly retreat, pursued by the Israelites. Many Philistines are slaughtered.

Meanwhile, David — in the custom of the times — cuts off Goliath's head and brings the proof of his unexpected but thrilling victory to King Saul. This is when David and Jonathan first meet. What then happens has also been subject to different interpretations. King Saul, some contend, had fallen into some disfavor among the people and Jonathan sees the writing on the wall. He feels he is not destined to succeed his father. But he is much impressed by David, his junior in years. David is brave and loyal and true to the tenets of their religion, worshipping a deity that is unseen but all powerful, while the Philistines and other tribes worship idols.

Accordingly, a bond quickly forms between the prince and the shepherd. In a symbol of his recognition of the coming prominence of David — destined now, Jonathan seems to suspect, to rule Israel, Jonathan sheds his armor and gives it to David. This union has political and religious aspects to go with the feelings of friendship that spring up between the once unlikely pair.

David is taken into the king's entourage and becomes very much the fair-haired boy in the court constellation. King Saul, recognizing David's capacity for leadership, gives him command of the Israelite army. David also receives the hand of Michel, one of King Saul's daughters, in marriage. Jonathan was also married. David goes on to win signal victories, further cementing his popularity with the people.

But his growing popularity sows the seeds of fear in King Saul's mind. His throne might be at stake, as well as his line of succession. While Jonathan may be willing to surrender his rightful role, Saul wants to retain his kingship and he perceives young David as a threat.

Consequently, even as the friendship of Jonathan and David continues to flourish, King Saul plots to rid himself of David and he makes several attempts. Sent into the front lines of battle, where his life is most in danger, David not only survives but also brings more glory to himself. A sudden thrust of a javelin at court goes awry. On another occasion Michel helps slip David out of a window before the king's assassins can reach him. She even makes up David's bed to deceive the attackers by installing the shape of a figure under the blanket with hair from a goat on the pillow.

Jonathan is clearly stuck between father and friend, and he chooses his friend. His father, Jonathan feels, is vain and overbearing. David, moreover, is innocent of his father's claims of plotting to wrest his crown away. "Wherefore shall he be slain?" Jonathan argues with his father. "What hath he done?"

But King Saul is unconvinced. "What more can he have but the kingdom?" Saul worries. He sees David as continually growing in stature. Finally, Jonathan feels compelled to warn David that it's no longer safe for him to stay at court.

David flees into the wilderness. But Jonathan knows where to find him, though he professes ignorance to his father who is eager to send soldiers to hunt David down. The king is furious and upbraids Jonathan.

After a while King Saul relents and Jonathan sends word that it's safe for David to return to court. Some measure of reconciliation takes place between King Saul and David. But then the same fears return to bedevil King Saul, and David's life is again in jeopardy. Warned by Jonathan, David seeks sanctuary again in the wilderness. Jonathan finds ways to keep David abreast of conditions at court through couriers. On one occasion, he uses archery practice as a means, telling the courier that if his arrows fall to the right of the target, it's safe for David to come back; but if they fall to the left, there is still danger. Some time passes and despite opportunities to kill King Saul David desists out of respect and reverence for one anointed by Samuel in obedience to the Lord God Jehovah.

When Jonathan goes himself to see David at his refuge in the wilderness, they clasp onto each as long lost brothers. They swear again to stand by each other. David will someday be king and Jonathan a loyal second-in-command; David, as the ruler, will protect Jonathan and his family, insuring that the succession of Saul's house won't be cut off. Without their knowing it, this is the last time the two will see each other. As the bible records this session, Jonathan said to David, "Go in peace, since both of us have sworn in the name of the Lord, saying, 'The Lord shall be between me and you, and between my descendents and your descendents for ever'."

Thereafter, Jonathan and his two brothers Abinadab and Malchnishua perish in a battle at Mount Gilboa. Grief-stricken, and again in disfavor with Samuel for disobedience to the tenets of Judaism, King Saul commits suicide. Jonathan has left a crippled five-year-old son, Mephibosheth, whom David protects and places at his royal table when he becomes king. Thus, King Saul's line is preserved. Jonathan is not forgotten as David, who becomes Israel's second king, laments: "I am distressed for you, my brother Jonathan. Very pleasant was thy love for me, passing the love of women. How have the mighty fallen, and the weapons of war perished!"

Chapter 4. Theseus & Pirithous

In Greek mythology both Theseus and Pirithous may have had a god as their father and a mortal woman as their mother. In other similarities, they were both kings and considered brave and strong warriors.

Theseus, easily the most famous of the pair, is credited with being the founder of Athens and its later king. Poseidon, the god of the seas, was considered to be his father. Theseus is also renowned for venturing into a fearful cave in Crete and slaying the ferocious Minotaur, half-bull and half man, who terrorized the kingdom of King Minos. Theseus is helped by Ariadne, the king's daughter, who gives him a spool of twine that he secures to the entrance of the labyrinth. After dispatching the savage brute, Theseus makes his way out of the dark cave by following the thread back to daylight. But his success is marred by forgetting his arrangement with King Aegeus, his mortal father. He was supposed to set white sails for success, but black sails if he failed. As the sails were left black, King Aegeus threw himself off a cliff in grief when he spotted the fateful ship returning to Athens.

Pirithous was said to be a son of Zeus though other accounts have him as the son of a king, Axion. Pirithous ruled the Lapiths, a tribe of horsemen in Thessaly. Having heard of Theseus' prowess, Pirithous wanted to see for himself how he stacked up against such a famous and rival warrior. Accordingly, he made off with some of Theseus' cattle or oxen. Theseus pursued Pirithous and the two were set to fight each other. Instead, in a mutual show of respect. they put their arms down and vowed to become lifelong friends and brothers in arms. According to *Plutarch's Lives*, Pirithous was the first to offer peace and to pay Theseus for any damage; but Theseus released him from any liability.

Theseus Slaying the Minotaur

Subsequently, Pirithous was ready to marry Hippodamia, a princess. Centaurs, mythic half men-half horses, were invited to the wedding feast. But the centaurs, unused to wine, became drunk and some even tried to rape women at the party, including Hippodamia. A fierce battle ensued, made famous in different oral, written and pictorial versions. The centaurs were defeated and expelled from the party as well as Thessaly. Theseus was said to have slain Eurytion, the leader of the centaurs, himself. In Ovid's *Metamorphoses* Theseus kills the "fierc-est of all the fierce centaurs."

Discussions in the *Centauromachy* suggest that the battle symbolized civi-lized versus untamed behavior and mankind overcoming mythical monsters that might even be in their own make-up. The Greeks considered it a sign of civiliza-tion to dilute wine with water, reducing its potency.

Later, the two warrior-kings — each with a possible god as their father — vowed to each marry a daughter of Zeus. Theseus selected Helen from Sparta who was then a child and not ready for marriage. But he had to abduct Helen first. With this mission accomplished by the duo Theseus placed Helen in the care of his mother, Aethra, in Athens, until she grew older. Pirithous was less modest — he wanted to wed Persephone. The problem was that Persephone was already married to Hades, god of the Underworld, where she was queen. Ironi-cally, Persephone — daughter of Zeus and Demeter, both gods — had previously been abducted by Hades and brought to his underworld domain.

Both Helen and Persephone were believed to have had godly fathers. Helen, who was rescued by her twin brothers and brought back to Sparta, went on to be abducted again by Paris, thus setting off the Trojan War.

Undaunted by the challenge Theseus, as a loyal friend, accompanied Pirithous into the underworld. In one version of the myth, Theseus and Pirithous rest on rocks on the outskirts of the Underworld. But then they found they couldn't rise and were attached to the rocks. Suddenly they were beset by a screaming band of horrible looking Furies with snakes protruding from their hair and whips in their hands. Theseus and Pirithous were taken prisoner and condemned to live in half-darkness as eternal punishment for their impudent plan to take possession of Persephone in the Underworld.

Another account has Hades pretending to welcome the pair and setting up a welcome feast. Hades pointed to special seats — known as the "Chairs of Forget-fulness" as one would forget everything henceforth — for Theseus and Pirithous to sit in. But when they sat snakes suddenly materialized, fastening around their legs until they couldn't move. Again, punishment forever was to be their joint fate.

In still another variation, Theseus and Pirithous threw lots over who would have Helen as his wife, with the loser to help his friend obtain another wife. Pirithous wanted Cora, the daughter of the Molossian king. But when this ruler discovered that Pirithous wasn't there to court his daughter but to make off with her, he had both Pirithous and Theseus imprisoned. Subsequently, the Molos-sian tyrant had Pirithous ripped to pieces by the king's very large and very savage dog named Cerberus.

Legend then has it that Heracles (Hercules) passed through the Molossian kingdom. It was too late to do anything for Pirithous but he managed to get

Theseus released as a special disposition. A different version also has Heracles coming to the Underworld as part of one of his tasks and securing forgiveness from Persephone for Theseus. However, when Heracles sought the release of Pirithous, the Underworld shook. It was then deemed that Pirithous had gone too far in his desire for Persephone, a married queen no less.

So Theseus was restored to the upper world while Pirithous remained bound in the kingdom of the dead, his fateful friendship with Theseus essentially ended.

The life and feats of Theseus have been the subject of many novels and plays, and his friendship with Pirithous has also been a frequent reference in literature.

Chapter 5. Damon & Pythias

There's little doubt that the legend of Damon and Pythias is the greatest testament to the loyalty, trust and devotion that can exist between friends. The legend has been the subject of many works of art, both by classical and later writers and poets. In this ancient Greek legend, dating to the 4th century B.C., the young pair are both followers of Pythagoras, the Greek philosopher and mathematician. Best known for his mathematical theorems on geometry today, Pythagoras also contributed other teachings including strictures on religion. There was a brotherhood privy to various esoteric dictums and Damon and Pythias were followers if not members of this group.

As it turned out, the two youths had reason to visit Syracuse, in Sicily. The city was ruled by King Dionysus I, who was considered to be a harsh ruler. Pythias apparently made some less than respectful remarks about the king's cruelty to his subjects. The king, learning of these comments, considered it an instigation to unrest and perhaps he even suspected a plot against him. Pythias was hauled off to prison and sentenced to death.

Surprisingly at peace with this sudden threat to his young life, Pythias petitioned the king for a chance to return home and settle his affairs, which included making arrangements for the care of his elderly parents. The king naturally turned this request down, sensibly indicating that once released, Pythias would never return. Here is where Damon enters the scene. While Pythias might have initially demurred, he finally agrees to let Damon ask the king if he can be held as a substitute.

Illustration of Pythias Arriving To Save Damon (courtesy of the Baldwin Online Children's Project)

Surprised by this odd arrangement, the king agrees as, after all, he still has a hostage, and one subject to death if Pythias — as expected — never returns. A month and day is set, and if Pythias doesn't return in time, Damon's life will be forfeit. Only Damon believes that Pythias will come back. But he suffers numerous taunts and jeers during his month long imprisonment over his supposed naïveté.

The crucial day comes, and goes; and there is no Pythias. Damon is led to the place of execution which varies in the legend between crucifixion, beheading, and being hanged. At the last moment, when Damon is about to be killed, a breathless Pythias rushes in.

The usual tale has Pythias explain that pirates attacked his boat, and that he then swam ashore, and ran to Syracuse. Other misadventures, including being robbed by thieves on the road and tied to a tree before breaking loose, have also been ascribed to his desperate return to Syracuse.

Damon, it was also told, was still willing to die for Pythias; but Pythias refused. King Dionysus took charge now. He was so impressed by this dramatic show of true friendship that he pardoned Pythias, released Damon, and made them members of his court. They were subsequently much valued, both for their counsel and as role models.

Chapter 6. Orestes and Pylades

Orestes and Pylades are figures in Greek literature symbolizing friendship so devoted that they were willing to die for each other. Their relationship has been the subject of many paintings, and the tragic story of Orestes, which figures in the Odyssey, an *epic* poem attributed to Homer, became the theme of famous plays by the ancient Greek dramatists including Aeschylus, Sophocles and Euripides. Each playwright came up with his own version of the doomed family which has a wife murdering her husband, and then her son, Orestes, killing her in revenge.

Orestes was the son of Agamemnon, the leader of the Greeks who fought in the Trojan War, and Clytemnestra. To secure fair winds on the voyage to Troy, across the Aegean Sea, Agamemnon is willing to sacrifice their daughter, Iphigenia. Clytemnestra is furious and motivated to then have an affair with Aegisthus. Neither Agamemnon or Clytemnestra knows that Iphigenia, who was supposed to be sacrificed at Aulis, was instead saved by the god, Artemis, and spirited away to Tauris.

Meanwhile, young Orestes is sent away during his mother's continuing infidelity to Phocis where he was raised by King Strophius along with his son, Pylades. The two youngsters, around the same age, bond like brothers and vow to become lifelong friends.

Pylades is depicted as protecting Orestes stricken by a spell of madness

Then Orestes learns that his mother has murdered his father. The fact that Agamemnon returned from Troy with his concubine, Cassandra, a Trojan princess, only added to Clytemnestra's motives for killing her husband. Orestes consults the oracle at Delphi and feels impelled to seek revenge. Pylades accompanies Orestes back to his home in Mycenae, with both young men disguised as messengers. They meet secretly with Electra, also one of Orestes' sisters. She too seeks to avenge her father's murder. The trio proceed with their plan to kill Clytemnestra and her lover, Aegisthus. Clytemnestra, while perhaps accepting her own fate, pleads for Orestes not to take on the guilt of killing his own mother.

But the deed is done. This act by Orestes, in connivance with Pylades and Electra, was praised by some as a justified act of revenge in the age-old tradition of executing a murderer, while it was condemned by others as the incredible sin of matricide. In the aftermath, both Orestes and Pylades seek to escape retribution. At first Pylades returns to his home at Phocis, but he is exiled by his father for his part in the murder of Agamemnon. Pylades then returns to Mycenae to help Orestes avoid execution. The pair attempt to murder Helen, the wife of King Menelaus and the woman at the forefront of the Trojan War, when Menelaus doesn't help to protect Orestes. But this plot, supposedly stopped by the intervention of the gods, is foiled. An attempt to kidnap Hermione, daughter of Menelaus and Helen, also comes to naught.

To avoid arrest and possible execution for their various crimes, the pair go to Taurus. In one version of the myth they are ordered by Apollo, the god of love, to retrieve a wooden statue of Artemis, the goddess of the hunt, which has fallen from Mount Olympus, the home of the gods, and to bring it back to Athens.

Once in Taurus both men are seized. Under the customs of Taurus, strangers were subject to be sacrificed to the gods. In prison, Orestes has what might be considered a manic attack. The myths depict him as being pursued by the Furies, female spirits of justice and vengeance who drive men mad for their misdeeds. In one contemporary report Pylades, treating Orestes more like a father than a brother or friend, "wiped away the foam, tended his body, and covered him with his well-woven cloak."

It turns out that the high priestess at Taurus, who will be in charge of the sacrifice of Pylades and Orestes, is none other than Orestes' sister Iphigenia. Of course she doesn't at first recognize her long-lost brother. Nor does Orestes know that his sister is still alive, believing her to have been sacrificed under his father's orders. Even so, Iphigenia does take pity on them and offers a deal: one can go free if he delivers a letter, in the form of a tablet, from her to Greece while the other is left to his fate. The decision on who goes free and who stays to die is up to them.

Pylades and Orestes wrestle with making this horrible decision. Each wants the other to go free. In another contemporary account, Orestes asserts that Pylades is far more worthy to live, saying the "slaying of this man would be a great grief to him as I am the cause of these misfortunes. Give the tablet to him. As for me, let anyone kill me who so desires it."

Finally, Pylades gives in, and he receives instructions on delivery of the tablet.

But then before Pylades leaves and the sacrifice made, Iphigenia finally realizes that Orestes is her brother. Now the trio — with brother and sister reunited after many years apart —all flee from Taurus, taking the statue of Artemis with them.

Little is known of Pylades after this point in the story. Does he reconcile with his father, or even succeed him as king? One version has him marrying Electra. Orestes, we know, returns to Mycenae where he takes over the kingdom, killing Alete, Aegisthus's son, in the process. Still burdened with the enormity of having killed his own mother, he may have married Hermione around this time. Subsequently, Orestes was said to have died from a snake bite in Arcadia, with his body taken for burial back to Mycenae.

References to Orestes' act of matricide and the familial revenge surface often in later literature, besides the plays of the ancient Greek dramatists, while the mutual trust and loyalty between Orestes and Pylades makes them iconic symbols of the bonds of friendship.

CHAPTER 7. CASTOR AND POLLUX

Castor and Pollux were twin brothers in both Greek and Roman mythology, but accounts of their birth aren't clear — ancient writers differed in their accounts, telling us either that both were mortal or that one might have been divine.

Their mother was Leda. Castor is often considered the mortal son of Tyndareus, the king of Sparta. Pollux, on the other hand, is regarded by some as the divine son of Zeus, leader of the Greek gods, who visited Leda in the form of a swan.

In one account both boys were born from an egg together with their twin sisters, Helen and Clytemnestra. Another version has that Leda was impregnated on the same day by Zeus in the daytime and at night by Tyndareus, her husband, and as a result produced two large eggs containing two pairs of twins. Helen and Pollux were the children of Zeus, and Clytemnestra and Castor the children of Tyndareus. The two boys, however, were regarded as sons by Zeus and became known as the Diascuri. But the goddess Aphrodite was angry with Tyndareus for failing to make the requisite offerings to her, and she showed her displeasure by marking both his daughters for future adulteries.

The brothers are often depicted on painted ceramic vases wearing skullcaps as the remnants from the egg they were hatched from. They're also shown as excellent huntsman and horsemen, often wearing helmets and brandishing spears. The two brothers, both heirs to the Spartan throne, may account for the later political system in Sparta which was the only city-state in ancient Greece to be ruled by a pair of kings.

Depictions of Castor and Pollux wearing characteristic skullcaps besides their horses.

Inseparable, the brothers always acted in concert including venturing forth on the famed voyage of the Argonauts in search of the Golden Fleece. During that expedition Pollux defeated King Amycus of the Bebryces, a savage if mythical tribe in Bithynia, in a boxing match. More importantly, they helped save the crew in a storm that led to the legend about St. Elmo's Fire. St. Elmo's Fire is an electrical phenomenon that can occur in the highly charged atmosphere of a storm or a volcano, whereby sharp, tall objects like a boat's mast can break forth with a stunning ball of light accompanied by a loud noise. Castor and Pollux became, in due course, the patron saints of sailors who believed the "fire" represented Castor and Pollux as a storm warning. The brothers, as helpers of mankind, could also be called upon to produce fair winds. For landlubbers, their skill as horsemen/hunters led them to also be patron saints of athletes.

When their sister Helen was abducted by Theseus, they invaded his kingdom at Attica and brought her back to Sparta. Subsequently, they kidnapped two women, Phoebe and Hilaeira, who were already promised to their mortal cousins, another set of twin brothers, Idas and Lynceus. The women bore a son for both Castor and Pollux. Resentment over this situation spilled over into a dispute over the disposition of some cattle the four cousins had appropriated in a raid. Idas and Lynceus, who thought Castor and Pollux had stolen their cattle, set off in pursuit. They left Helen alone with the Trojan prince, Paris, who was then visiting Sparta. Another abduction took place, with Paris stealing Helen away. The long Trojan War was soon to begin.

Catching up to Castor and Pollux, Idas managed to ambush and then kill Castor. In quick revenge, Pollux slew Lynceus. In turn, Idas was about to do away with Pollux when Zeus, the leader of the Greek gods who was watching the violent scene from his home on Mount Olympus, hurled a thunderbolt that killed Idas and saved his son, Pollux.

Now Pollux was faced with a choice. Should he assume his divine role and live on Mount Olympus or give half of his immortality to Castor, his mortal brother? Pollux chose to share, which would enable them to stay together, living sometimes on Mount Olympus and sometimes in Hades. In recognition of this strong bond, Zeus placed them as bright stars in the heavens, where they became known as the Gemini ("the twins") constellation.

In time, Castor and Pollux were incorporated into the Roman mythology as well, with a Castor and Pollux Temple located in the Roman forum. Their names, emblematic of touching friendship and fidelity, frequently crop up in literature through the ages.

Chapter 8. Achilles & Patroclus

Questions about the relationship between Achilles, the legendary Greek warrior famous for his role in the Trojan War, and Patroclus, also a soldier of renown, have intrigued writers and academicians for centuries. Even the *Iliad*, the epic poem generally ascribed to the bard Homer, leaves it somewhat ambiguous. The ancient Greeks greatly admired the male body, and physical relationships between men and men, and men and boys, were common.

Men, however, were expected to marry and produce children, preferably males. Achilles was the son of Thetis and King Peleus of Phtitia. Even as a youth he was considered outstanding, and he killed his first wild boar at the tender age of six. His mother Thetis, as the legend goes, dipped him into the river Styx to make him invulnerable to spears and javelins; but she held him by his left heel, which was to be his ultimate undoing.

Patroclus, the son of Menoetius, was Achilles' cousin. In an argument over a game of dice, Patroclus accidentally killed his friend, Clyson. Subsequently, he and his father go into exile and seek refuge in the land of their kinsman, King Peleus. The two boys — near the same age, with Patroclus a few years older — meet and quickly bond as virtual brothers. As was the custom of the period, King Peleus sent both youngsters to learn to survive in the wilderness. They were to be raised there by Chiron, the king of the centaurs, and trained to be strong leaders and warriors. The boys, hardy in body and spirit, were fed on the bone marrow of bears to generate courage and the marrow of fawns to instill fleetness of foot. Both Achilles and Patroclus excelled in all aspects of their tough and arduous training.

Achilles bandaging the arm of Patroclus

As a mature man, Patroclus became one of the suitors of Helen, a beautiful woman of noble lineage. But she eventually chose King Menelaus of Sparta to be her husband. All the rejected suitors swore a solemn vow to protect Helen from harm. Subsequently, Paris, the son of Priam, the king of Troy (a land believed to have existed in part of the area that is now Turkey) was traveling through the Greek city-states and met Helen in Sparta. How deep the attraction was between Paris and Helen is not particularly clear, but the upshot was that Paris took Helen away with him as he returned to Troy. Menelaus sought the aid of his fellow Greek rulers and leaders, calling on them to stand by their oath — which they did. A naval fleet was organized, with Patroclus contributing 10 ships. Warriors were assembled and the armada crossed the Aegean Sea to Troy, situated near the coast. This sailing led to the famous line about the beauty of Helen as "the face that launched a thousand ships."

The war raged for nine years with neither side able to claim victory. Both Achilles and Patroclus fought bravely and well, killing their share of Trojan soldiers. The two men lived close by in tents and faced the Trojans on the battlefield together.

Under the rules governing the spoils of war Achilles was awarded Briseis, a royal Trojan beauty, who had been captured. She became his favorite slave. Subsequently Agamemnon, the principal Greek general, became furious when he was denied a similar prize. In a fit of anger that he later regretted, Agamemnon took Briseis away from Achilles and for himself.

This didn't sit well with Achilles. Now he sulked in his tent and declared that his fellow Greeks would have to fight on without him. The war had been dragging on for so long that morale was very fragile, and the Greeks knew quite well that the Trojans would take heart when they heard that the greatest Greek warrior had decided to go on strike.

The tide turned in the Trojans' favor, and now they were threatening the Greek boats. Some vessels were set on flame. Every ship the Greeks lost meant no ride home for that many soldiers. They would be stranded, left behind, and subject to the mercy of the victorious Trojans.

At this point Patroclus stepped up and suggested that he don Achilles' armor and pretend to be him, and thus stop the Trojans from burning their boats. Reluctantly, Achilles agreed, but he secured Patroclus's promise to stop fighting in his place once the Trojans were driven away from the boats. "Seek not to press the Trojans without me, lest thou add still more to the disgrace already made," Achilles said.

But the Trojans, seeing the mighty "Achilles" in the field again, quickly retreated, and in the heat of the battle Patroclus got caught up in seeking more glory. The result was fatal. After killing over 50 Trojans, Patroclus suffered one grievous wound and then was finally killed by Hector, the son of King Priam, the greatest Trojan warrior. Soldiers protected Patroclus' body on the battlefield until it could be recovered. (If a body wasn't buried properly, under Greek belief at the time, it might not be able to enter Hades.) As the story is told in the *Iliad*, the god Apollo comes to the aid of the retreating Trojans by having Patroclus lose his armor, and thus he was slain. Dying, Patroclus asserts that he would have left the battlefield in full honor if he had only had mortal foes to contend with.

Once back in Greek quarters Achilles mourned the loss of his closest friend. At first he held off the requisite burial during his grief, smearing himself with ashes and fasting. Some believe an apparition of Patroclus appeared in Achilles' tent, urging Achilles to do what had to be done, as he couldn't enter Hades without a proper cremation. Achilles sheared his hair and sacrificed 12 captured Trojans before placing Patroclus' body on the funeral pyre.

Even Thetis, his mother, urged Achilles to put aside his grief and avenge the death of Patroclus — despite having been warned by the gods that such an action would cost her son his life.

Returning to combat with a fury, Achilles sought out Hector, and in a furious battle killed the Trojan champion. To shame the Trojans, Achilles dragged Hector's body behind his chariot in the dust around the walls of Troy. Initially, Achilles wanted to prevent the vanquished Trojan from having an honorable burial. Later, however, after getting ransom gifts, he relented at the plea of King Priam and released the body so the Trojans could give their fallen hero a traditional burial.

To honor Patroclus, Achilles organized a mini-version of the Olympic Games including javelin and discus throwing, archery, wrestling, chariot and foot races.

But then the prediction of how Achilles would die came to pass. Paris, advised of the one place in Achilles' body where he was vulnerable, shot an arrow into Achilles' left heel from the ramparts of Troy. Thus perished Achilles.

The ashes of Patroclus and Achilles were mingled in one golden urn so that the two, inseparable in life, would remain close in death. One report has the urn buried in a common tomb with the location unknown. Another version, not in the *Iliad*, has the urn buried on Leuke, an island in the Black Sea.

Chapter 9. Harmodius and Aristogeiton

In 514 B.C. Hippias, aided by his brother Hipparchus, held power in Athens. (In those days, "tyrant" meant someone who had seized power in an illegitimate way.) Two close friends, Harmodius and Aristogeiton, decided to end their tyranny — with tragic results initially and then with enduring fame. Harmodius was a teenager. As a contemporary wrote, he was "then in the flower of youthful beauty." Aristogeiton was older, probably in his twenties, and from one of the city's aristocratic families.

The situation was brought to the tipping point when Hipparchus, accustomed to getting his way, made advances to Harmodius. Aristogeiton was far from pleased. Rejected, and angered by Aristogeiton's attitude, Hipparchus sought revenge by questioning the virginity of Harmodius' sister, who had been picked to lead the celebrants into a major festival, the "Panathenaic Procession." Custom required that the girl selected for this honor to be a virgin.

Provoked by this personal quarrel but also wishing to end the savage reign of the ruling brothers, Harmodius and Aristogeiton, together with some others, planned to assassinate them at the festival. They carried daggers concealed in ceremonial myrtle wreaths. When they saw one of their co-conspirators greet Hippias in a friendly manner at the foot of the Acropolis, they felt betrayed and rushed into action, ruining their original plan. Before being stopped by the royal guards, they managed to kill Hipparchus. But things went quickly awry and Harmodius was killed on the spot by royal guards. Taken into custody, Aristogeiton was tortured to reveal the names of co-conspirators.

Statues of Harmodius and Aristogeiton

One account has it that during his ordeal, monitored by Hippias, Aristogeiton feigned a willingness to betray others in the plot. But first, he insisted that Hippias must clasp his arm as a guarantee of his safety for providing this information. But as soon Hippias agreed and clasped Aristogeiton's arm, Aristogeiton taunted the despot for clasping the hand of his brother's killer. Furious, Hippias had Aristogeiton immediately slain, sparing him further torture.

Tradition has it that Aristogeiton was also in love with a courtesan, Laena. She was suspected of being involved in the plot, and so she was also tortured at Hippias' orders. She died without revealing anything. One version of the legend says Laena bit her own tongue off in fear that the torture might break her resolve to stay silent.

Hippias didn't stay in power much longer, and he was expelled from Athens in 510 B.C. Harmodius and Aristogeiton were then elevated to the status of heroes and patriots as well as martyrs. Public statues of them were raised, and that was the first time that Athenians had considered any of their fellow countrymen worthy of such sculptural honor. Coins were struck with their images. They were called "liberators" and "tyrannicides" who put their desire for a just government over their personal lives. A law was enacted that prohibited anyone from criticizing the pair. Their descendants were given privileges including meals at public expense and front row seats in the amphitheatre for performances of plays and other events.

The pair became a symbol of how democracy evolved in ancient Athens, and writers and artists have made frequent references to them. They even inspired a popular drinking song in Athens:

> I will carry my sword in a myrtle bough
> Just like Harmodius and Aristogeiton
> When they killed the tyrant
> And made Athens a place of equality under the law.

Chapter 10. Alexander and Hephaestion

Alexander the Great conquered a good deal of the world, and he was renowned as a great warrior during his lifetime and throughout the ages. He had a lifelong friend in Hephaestion, a fellow Macedonian nobleman who many consider his alter ego. Macedonians, who had their own language, were considered cousins to the Greeks. The main focus of Alexander's life was military conquest and integration of the conquered lands into a sort of Greater Macedonia; and the driving force of Hephaestion's life was Alexander.

Consider this description by ancient historians when Alexander reviewed the conquered Persians at Susa. The Persian queen Sisygambis kneeled before Hephaestion to plead for her life and that of her retinue, thinking he was Alexander. Hephaestion was taller than Alexander, around the same age, and they wore the same attire. Mortified, the queen apologized for her mistake. But Alexander, standing nearby, consoled her. "You were not mistaken, mother. This man is Alexander, too."

Their story together began in the 4th century B.C. in the Macedonian court in northwestern Greece and ended in the Asian hinterlands, when both died less than a year apart, still in their early thirties.

Hephaestion was from an aristocratic family which secured him a post as a page in the Macedonian court at Pella. Prince Alexander was the heir apparent to his father Philip, who had successfully defeated the independent Greek city-states and made Macedonia the master of Greece. The two boys met, shared secrets, and bonded. The early friendship they forged enabled Hephaestion to survive court intrigues. During this period, Hephaestion was probably being taught by Aristotle, with Alexander and other students, at the Temple of the Nymphs at Mieza. Schooling was somewhat like a boarding school, with the subjects including philosophy and morals, logic, medicine, and art.

Alexander in battle

Hephaestion fought in various battles on the Greek mainland including the pivotal battle of Chaeronea in 338 B.C. This victory gave Philip mastery over most of Greece. Alexander commanded one division of the Macedonian army.

Subsequently, Alexander succeeded Philip, who was murdered. He was twenty and eager to conquer the known world. Hephaestion was with Alexander as he embarked on his ambitious campaign to expand the Macedonian empire. When they visited Troy — they both were familiar with the *Iliad* by Homer — they paid homage to Achilles and Patroclus, even running a race to honor their dead heroes. The parallel of their friendship and that of Achilles and Patroclus was not lost on them or many of their contemporaries.

In 334 BC, he invaded Persian territory, and in a ten-year campaign in Asia, Alexander kept seeking new tribes to conquer and territory to be added to a Greater Macedonia. He placed more and more responsibility on Hephaestion. While some question Hephaestion's military capacity, he is generally rated an excellent engineer, organizer, and diplomat. He supervised the construction of bridges to cross major rivers, such as the Euphrates, and commanded the fleet that provided supplies which enabled Alexander to sustain his campaigns. He also created forts and new settlements.

In this fashion, Hephaestion became a second-in-command and one Alexander could rely on to carry out his wishes while still showing initiative. Hephaestion also became joint commander of the Companions, a special cavalry unit that served as Alexander's personal bodyguard.

While the soldiers found glory and more practical rewards in the spoils of war through Alexander's continued success, many disagreed with his policy of integrating the Greek and Persian cultures. At one point Hephaestion helped thwart an assassination attempt against Alexander by disaffected members of his command structure.

Alexander took Stateira, a daughter of the deposed Persian King Darius III, as his wife, after the crucial battle at Issus in 333 B.C. Meanwhile Darius had escaped from the victorious Macedonians, leaving his wife and daughters behind. At the same time Hephaestion wed Drypetis, another daughter of Darius. Apparently Alexander wanted future heirs to come from the same lineage. Thus, Hephaestion became a member of the royal family. Alexander also appointed him a chiliarch or vizier that reinforced his role as second in command.

Hephaestion was now Alexander's brother-in-law. Much earlier he had been the torch-bearer or best man when Alexander wed his first wife, Roxana, a Bactrian princess from an eastern province in the far-flung Persian empire. Roxana was believed to be a marriage for love, while Alexander's marriage to Stateira was politically motivated. Hephaestion's marriage was also determined by the requirements of diplomacy.

Meanwhile, the military campaign continued as Alexander and his army reached the Indus River, with all of India to be conquered. But there were grumblings from his soldiers, who were weary. Apparently they had come to the gateway to India during the monsoon season and the steady downpour was difficult to endure. Hephaestion had survived one spear wound during the many battles. But now he was struck again at Ecbatana, where some of the appropriated Persian treasure was kept, this time by what might have been typhoid. Some suspicion of poison has also been posited. According to Plutarch, Hephaestion disregarded the orders of his doctor, Glaucias, to avoid indulging himself and "sat down to breakfast, ate a boiled fowl, drank a huge cooler of wine, fell sick, and in a little while died."

Hephaestion lay, beset with fever, for seven days. Alexander was summoned, with Hephaestion's life in the balance. Hephaestion seemed to be about to recover, but then he died before Alexander could get to his bedside. Still in his early thirties, Hephaestion had only been married four months. Alexander was beside himself with grief. One contemporary account has him lying on Hephaistion's corpse until wrested free. "This is the friend I valued as my own life," Alexander said.

Soon, Alexander petitioned the oracle at Siwa to grant Hephaestion divine status, and so his dead friend was revered as a divine hero. A period of great mourning ensued with Alexander shearing his hair and fasting. In an ancient mourning custom, he ordered the tails and manes of horses and mules to be cut off. Flute playing and other music was forbidden for a while. Glaucis, the physician attending Hephaestion, was crucified for not having taken better care of Hephaestion. Alexander also had a tribe called the Cossaeans massacred as an offering to the spirit of his departed companion.

Hephaestion's body was taken back to Babylon where a magnificent (and expensive) funeral was arranged. This solemn event was followed by games in honor of the Macedonian leader. Alexander even drove one funeral carriage for a symbolic period. In a signal honor, previously reserved only for a king, Alexander ordered the flame in the temple at Babylon to be extinguished.

When Alexander's horse Bucephalus expired — said to have happened when he was around 30 — Alexander erected and named a city, Bucephalia, after his favorite steed. Alexander died a scant eight months later, still far off in Asia, and still planning more conquests and monuments to Hephaestion's memory.

A representation of Hephaestion

Chapter 11. Julius Caesar & Mark Anthony

Julius Caesar and Mark Anthony were friends, close colleagues politically and militarily, and cousins as well. Both are linked forever in history and the subject of countless literary works, with Shakespeare's play *Julius Caesar* the most famous of these outpourings. Antony (his name was actually Marcus Antonius) was born in 83 B.C. He was Caesar's cousin through his mother's side. His life was a trajectory of well-recognized military valor, though this capacity was weakened in the public eye by his steady carousing.

Antony was married five times, and had children, including twins with his last wife, the Egyptian queen Cleopatra, who had previously been a paramour of Caesar. Caesar, who was born in 100 B.C., had also had several wives.

Anthony's military career began at the age of 26 with campaigns in the Middle East. He acquitted himself well and became a staff officer in 54 B.C. with Caesar's legions in Gaul, now known as France. He served Caesar capably and received more and more responsibility and higher and higher ranks. In the process he also bonded with Caesar, becoming probably his most trusted confidant.

But Antony was instrumental in the crisis Caesar faced when he was summoned back to Rome to answer various legal charges. His great successes in Gaul and England were not enough to grant him immunity before the law. Roman law called for him to first divest himself of his military rank and political command of the province of Gaul. At the time, he was locked in a fierce rivalry with Pompey, another great Roman general and leader, and Caesar was afraid he would be at the mercy of Pompey's soldiers without his legions to back him.

Accordingly, Caesar crossed the Rubicon River in northern Italy, signifying he was defying the Roman Senate. In this action, he thus set off a civil war between him and Pompey for control of Rome and the far-flung territories that Rome's disciplined and powerful legions had won.

Bust of Caesar

While Caesar was off defeating Pompey in Spain in 47 B.C., Antony was left behind and made administrator of Italy. However, by most accounts he was ill suited to the job. Cicero, a leading member of the Senate who wrote extensively about the period, lambasted Antony for his wastrel ways. Caesar, now deployed in fighting Pompey's legions in the Middle East, also was upset that Antony had confiscated some of Pompey's property without making any payment. Caesar needed funds from this source to pay his troops and maintain their loyalty.

Finally, conflict arose over the general situation in Rome and Caesar removed Antony from his high post. The breach between the two men lasted for perhaps two years, but then they reconciled in 45/44 B.C. Antony might have already been sounded out for participation in the conspiracy that was being developed to kill Caesar on the grounds that he was seeking total power over Rome — which wasn't yet an empire; but according to *Plutarch's Lives*, Antony was silent.

Antony was loyal enough to Caesar to offer him a diadem, the symbol of king-ship, in 44 B.C. Caesar turned the diadem down to show he didn't intend to become the king of Rome. Instead he became the dictator (which didn't have the negative ring that it has now). In power, he initiated a number of excellent reforms, including clarification of the calendar. He was rewarded for the latter effort by having a month, July, created from his first name.

Meanwhile, the conspirators decided that Caesar really had to die, but they would allow Antony to live. Perhaps more alarmed now, Antony went to warn Caesar against going to the Senate on the fateful day — the Ides of March — but he was too late. He had been sidetracked on his way to the Senate by a diversion cooked up by the conspirators.

Caesar was stabbed to death in 44 B.C. at the age of 56. Fearing he was next, Antony fled Rome in the disguise of a slave. When the anticipated bloodbath didn't emerge, Antony returned to Rome to discuss a truce with the conspira-tors. Amnesty was declared for the assassins, and it seemed a civil war had been prevented.

As Caesar's right hand man, and family relative, it was natural for Antony to give the eulogy for the fallen dictator/general. His dramatic but rabble-rousing address, immortalized in Shakespeare's famous lines ("Friends, Romans, coun-trymen, lend me your ears....") then accused the conspirators of murder and named them. With Caesar's body on display, Antony raised his bloody clothing as proof of the multiple stab wounds.

Then he read Caesar's will, which left most of his considerable assets to the people of Rome. This was a shrewd move by Antony as it turned the tide of public opinion in the favor of the allies of the fallen Caesar rather than his assassins. The tenuous truce with the anti-Caesar faction finally broke entirely. With popular opinion now decisively in favor of Caesar, the conspirators were forced to flee.

Bust of Mark Antony

A triumvirate was then created between Antony, Octavian, and Lepidus, another general. Young Octavian had been adopted by Caesar, and he later became Emperor Augustus, the first Roman ruler with that title, when the republic was ended. Under this new arrangement Antony received the Middle East, including Egypt, which provided Rome with grain; Lepidus was given Spain, and Rome and the rest of Roman-held territory came under the control of Octavian.

In Egypt, Anthony soon caught up with Cleopatra and fell under her spell, much as Caesar had done. Meanwhile Caesar and Cleopatra had had a son, Caesarion, who was considered by many to be the rightful successor to Caesar. In due course, Antony was accused of losing his focus as he perhaps paid more attention to Cleopatra than to Rome. Their dalliance led to marriage in 37 B.C, and they spent 14 years together in a dramatic and troubled marriage.

Octavian became increasingly concerned as the growing Caesarion seemed a likely threat to his regal position; this led to the triumvirate splitting up.

Anthony was defeated in a final showdown with Octavian's legions in a naval battle in the Ionian Sea in 31 B.C., off the coast of Actium in Greece. In a display of friendship less committed than some of the examples in this book, Cleopatra precipitately fled the battle scene with her ships.

Back in Egypt, and feeling his prospects grim, Antony committed suicide in 30 B.C. at the age of 53 with a sword thrust. He thought Cleopatra had already killed herself. As it turned out Cleopatra was still alive; but she had no intention of being captured by Octavian and carried off to Rome, doomed to die in his triumphal parade. Instead she let a venomous asp do its lethal work. She was not yet 40.

The inter-related lives and shifting loyalties of Caesar, Antony and Cleopatra have received many treatments in literature and film with more probably to come.

Chapter 12. Horace and Maecenas

Quintus Horace and Gaius Maecenas were both subjects of Emperor Augustus in Rome, though they served the Roman ruler in different ways.

Horace became the leading Roman lyrical poet, with his life and work coming during the epochal change in Rome from being a republic to an empire. Maecenas was a powerful deputy of Augustus, often charged with important missions. He was also a patron to poets, whose work he admired and who he saw as a means to help the public adjust to the new regime, and his name has become a lasting symbol of patronage.

Horace's works include his *Odes*, *Satires* and *Epistles*. Far from shy, he used his own experiences in his poetry. As he showed early promise, his father spent a good deal of money on his education. In return, Horace paid homage to his father in his *Satires* which includes this passage:

> If my character is flawed by a few minor faults but is otherwise decent and moral, if you point out only a few scattered blemishes on an otherwise immaculate surface, if no one can accuse me of greed or prurience, or of profligacy, if I live a virtuous life free of defilement (pardon, for moment, my self-praise), and if I am to my friends a good friend, my father deserves all the credit. As it is now, he deserves from me unstinting gratitude and praise.

Satiric verse, it should be noted, was a literary style and genre often found in early Latin literature.

Horace, who fought at the crucial battle of Philippi in 42 B.C, was on the losing side during the war between Octavian (before he chose the name of Augustus) and Brutus, Cassius and others who had slain Caesar. However, he took advantage of Octavian's offer of amnesty given to the defeated army, though his property was confiscated. Horace even joked he turned to verse to overcome poverty, but he was able to secure a salary as a clerk in the Treasury. Octavian took supreme control of Rome soon after his victory and his reign was a long and relatively peaceful one.

Horace as imagined by Anton von Werner

In Rome Horace was introduced to Maecenas in 39 B.C. by his friend Virgil, a contemporary poet, who was impressed by his writings. He was soon accepted into the group that Maecenas supported and sponsored, describing the process as one of respect leading to true friendship as equals. Horace, though trying to maintain his independence, did provide praise of Augustus in his works. At one point, according to Suetonius, a contemporary historian, he was even offered a chance to be Augustus' private secretary. Horace, quite politely, turned down this position but he did accede to Augustus' request that he pen an epistle (a letter in verse) directed to and about him — and of course, one favorable to the Roman emperor.

Knowing of Maecenas' claim to a princely background, Horace referred to his benefactor in his first book of *Odes* as "the descendant of kings." In 37 B.C. Horace accompanied Maecenas on a journey to Brundisium, later describing their adventures in his *Satires*.

In additional to some financial support, Maecenas also arranged for Horace to get a farming estate in the countryside with five paying tenants. Being more financially secure enabled Horace to focus more on his poetry.

Horace's Epodes — long lyric poems followed by shorter poems — were published to limited acclaim in 29 B.C. His *Odes* — lyric poems — a few years later weren't that well received either when first published (they've done better since); but Augustus himself encouraged the publication of more *Odes* that firmly established Horace's reputation. His *Odes* eventually became perhaps the best admired of all his poems during the ancient period. Horace's jibes depicting the follies of the rich weren't always greatly appreciated by his targets but his talent was recognized as his reputation grew. He skirted some political issues, concentrating more on commentary and advice on how to live amid all the temptations and complications of Roman life. His satiric verses, which even included talking penises, were popular and much read.

Overall, his work greatly influenced poets of his day and future ones as well. His *Ars Poetica* or "The Art of Poetry," which suggested ways to write poems, gave many aspiring poets some guidelines.

In an epistle Horace even argued for some sort of classic status to be given to major Roman poets with the candidates including Virgil (and probably himself). In the last poem in his third book of *Odes*, Horace declared that his cumulative works had made a monument to him stronger and more lasting than one of bronze. In a self-descriptive passage in the final poem of the first book of *Epistles* Horace wrote that he was 44 years old and "of small stature, fond of the sun, prematurely gray, quick-tempered but easily placated."

Augustus also commented that Horace lacked height but not body.

Bust of Maecenas

Maecenas, perhaps influenced by his company, also wrote verse. But he was esteemed to be a better judge of poetic talent than he was a poet himself. According to Suetonius, Maecenas may have succeeded in creating a sort of shorthand writing. Reportedly, he was instrumental in introducing heated swimming pools in Rome. Despite his many accomplishments, he was forced to retire, though in considerable luxury, in 23 B.C. due a conspiracy involving a brother-in-law.

Horace, who was born around 65 B.C., died at the age of 65, shortly after Maecenas, who was about five years older. Both passed away in 8 B.C. He was buried near Maecenas' tomb at the Esqualine cemetery. As was the practice of the time, they both bequeathed their property to Augustus, an honor expected from the emperor's friends.

***

Among Horace's pithy sayings:

- Faults are soon copied.
- If you wish me to weep, you must first mourn yourself.
- Once a word has been allowed to escape, it can not be recalled.
- Force without wisdom falls of its own weight.
- He who has begun has half done. Dare to be wise; begin!

Chapter 13. Roland and Olivier

La Chanson de Roland or the "The Song of Roland" is probably the oldest work of French literature and certainly one of the best known. The epic poem is often attributed to the poet Turoldus who composed it probably around 1100. It celebrates a tragic battle at the end of the 8th century and the heroic if rash deeds of Roland and his great but more prudent friend, Olivier.

Roland is the nephew of King Charlemagne, head of the Frankish kingdom which covered most of what is now France and considerable portions of Western Europe. Charlemagne was destined to be crowned by the Pope as the first Holy Roman Emperor in 800 A.D. Roland, no doubt, was also destined to have a major role in Charlemagne's reign.

Legend has it that Roland and Olivier first met in potentially lethal combat. Charlemagne was besieging the castle of Count Gerard, who refused to pay taxes and submit to him as a vassal. But the siege wasn't going well as the count was holding out pretty comfortably behind his battlements. Finally, the two sides decided to let the matter be settled by combat between their champions, which turned out to be Roland for Charlemagne and Olivier for the count.

The two warriors met on a field before the castle. Charging with their lances, both riders were left intact. Then they fought by sword. Each had an opportunity to slay the other when they lost their swords; but chivalry was the custom of the time and neither man would attack an unarmed opponent, and so they permitted each other to regain his sword.

The battle then wore down to fighting by hand, at which time — as if by mutual consent and respect — they decided to stop fighting and declared they would be friends from that time on. The two sides celebrated lifting of the siege, and Charlemagne and the count reconciled. Roland, in due course, also became engaged to Aude, Olivier's sister.

Song of Roland in eight episodes

During this period the Moors (or Saracens) still controlled some of Spain, with a stronghold at Saragossa. Charlemagne brought his army up to the Pyrenees Mountains, which separate what is now France and Spain, with the intent to defeat the Moors and expand the territory of his empire. But he was willing to do this peacefully if the Moorish leader, Marsile, would be willing to become his vassal. In that case, Charlemagne informed Marsile he wouldn't attack and would return to his capital, much farther north, in Aachen, which is now part of Belgium.

Charlemagne sent Ganelon, Roland's stepfather, to negotiate with Marsile. But Ganelon has been described as jealous of Roland, who may have slipped in front of him in the Frankish court hierarchy. Ganelon betrayed the Franks and told the Moors that they would be able to defeat a relatively small rearguard number of solders once Charlemagne took the major portion of his army north. It's likely that Ganelon suspected that Roland, known for seeking chances to show his bravery, would be in charge of this rearguard. And indeed, Roland, Olivier, and many of the more valiant knights, also called paladins, were in this rearguard which was set up at the Roncevaux Pass in the Pyrenees.

The Franks, numbering perhaps 20,000, reportedly were beset by a much larger contingent of Moors. Many scholars believe, however, that local Basque tribesmen might have attacked and killed the Frankish detachment in search of plunder.

Here, in the heat of battle, was where the characters of Roland and Olivier came into sharper focus. Olivier, considered the more prudent of the two, counseled Roland to blow the oliphant or horn to alert Charlemagne to rush back to their rescue. Possibly, Olivier also recommended a quick retreat. But Roland refused, eager to fight and win more glory. This decision brought Roland criticism for being reckless and foolhardy while wasting the lives of the soldiers under his command in a hopeless struggle. Roland is cited in the song as welcoming the prospect of another battle, saying, "And may God grant it to us," ready to wield Durendal, his mighty sword.

The battle does ensue, and the Franks fight bravely and well; but they are overcome. In one version, when many of his troops have already been killed, Roland finally blows the horn to summon Charlemagne back, but it is much too late. In a loss of human life of vaster scale than the debacle of the Spartans' stand against the Persians at Thermopylae, the Franks are killed to the last man. Too late, Charlemagne returns but can only avenge the death of Roland, Olivier, and all the other brave paladins. Upon learning the fate of Roland and Olivier, Aude dies of despair.

For the most part, however, Roland is revered as a heroic and historical figure. He has been the subject of many works of literature and in many languages, not just French. Olivier, his friend and fellow paladin, remains in the historical and legendary background.

Chapter 14. King Edward II & Piers Gaveston

As a close friend and favorite of King Edward II of England during the early 14th century, Piers Gaveston had a strikingly varied career. He was elevated to high ranks and responsibilities and was showered with titles and gifts from the monarch. But he still suffered a trio of exiles and was finally subjected to a summary execution.

Gaveston was considered by many to be competent but brash and over-confident in utilizing the good graces of his royal friend and benefactor. His behavior, and access to royal patronage, upset many nobles who tried to limit his power and status. Meanwhile, both Edward and Gaveston married and had children.

His tale began when the young Gaveston, who came from relatively humble origins, made a good impression on King Edward I with his bearing and martial skills. Accordingly, he was assigned as somewhat of a mentor and role model to the household of Edward, the king's son and heir apparent. The two boys, both born in 1284, bonded with their friendship lasting all of Gaveston's short life (he died around the age of 30 in 1312).

Gaveston became involved in court intrigue and was exiled along with some other pages and courtiers, but his first exile didn't last long. When Edward I died in 1307, young Edward succeeded his father as Edward II and reigned for twenty years. He promptly recalled his friend, Gaveston. In due course Gaveston was made Earl of Cornwall with a rich allotment of land. The new king also arranged for his friend and confidant to marry Margaret de Clare, sister of the powerful Earl of Gloucester.

15th century representation of Piers Gaveston after being beheaded

In honor of Gaveston's marriage King Edward organized a tournament at Wallingford Castle. But when Gaveston and his coterie made off thewith the major honors at the tournament, the nobles were displeased. Subsequently, when the King went to France to marry Isabelle, the daughter of Philip IV, who ruled France, he appointed Gaveston — not a member of the royal family — to serve as regent in his stead. Now, the nobles were incensed especially with Gaveston's arrogant behavior, which included a demand that they bow to him. Gaveston also alienated some nobles by his habit of wearing purple clothing befitting a king and nicknaming some of his peers with such unflattering names as "Mr. Burst-belly," "Whore-son," and "The Fiddler."

At a coronation feast back in England, King Edward paid more attention to Gaveston than his bride, according to the nobles present at the dinner. This lèse majesté behavior to the bride was reported in due course to the French king, who was quite displeased by this affront to both him and his daughter.

In 1308, concerned over a restive public and England's uneasy diplomatic stature, the nobles, in Parliament, demanded the exile of Gaveston. The political climate had become so poisoned that some nobles wouldn't even attend Parliament as long as Gaveston was there. His continued easy access to the King was also a steady irritation to those nobles who were backed by King Philip of France, still offended by Edward's cavalier treatment of his daughter. Gaveston was roundly accused of leading Edward into exposing the country to problems abroad and at home. Questions about the draining of the national treasury were also bruited in Parliament.

Finally, under pressure despite being the ruler, King Edward exiled Gaveston in 1308; but he softened the blow considerably by granting him land in Gascony, a part of France that was under English control. This bounty was about as valuable as Gaveston's lost earldom in Cornwall. As another measure of easing Gaveston's exile, Edward also appointed him as the king's lieutenant in Ireland, where England was trying to pacify the Irish people and cement its control. By most accounts, Gaveston, not spending much time in France, was credited with an excellent performance in Ireland. His success in Ireland may have prompted a quick recall to England the following year.

Apparently though, Gaveston still hadn't learned his lesson, and he may have taken his recall as proof that the King was still very much on his side. The nobles again protested his manipulations and influence over the King. Their displeasure led to the Ordnances of 1311, a group of reforms. These measures also called for Gaveston to again be exiled — but this time with the proviso that he would be considered an outlaw and hunted down if he returned to English soil.

King Edward initially agreed to the reforms as long as Gaveston could remain, but the nobles were adamant. Obviously sad to let his friend depart, he gave Gaveston going away gifts including horses, luxurious garments, and a substantial stipend of money.

Undeterred by the resistance to his presence, Gaveston returned again to England in 1311, possibly to see his wife Margaret and their daughter, Joan. It's believed he may have also wanted to witness the birth of Amie, an illegitimate daughter. The pro-and-anti Gaveston sides were drawn, with the prospect of continuing civil and court discord. King Edward declared that any judgment against Gaveston was unlawful and he restored Gaveston's land to him. Meanwhile, the Pope excommunicated Gaveston.

In 1312, staying at his fortified castle at Scarborough, Gaveston discovered he was far from safe. He was forced to surrender to the forces of the Lancaster faction of nobles who were opposed to Edward, and to him as well. He was accused of violating the terms of the Ordnances before an assembly of nobles, which may have been something of a kangaroo court, as he was swiftly convicted. Subsequently, he was taken away to a rural spot at Blacklow Hill near Warwick. Two Welshmen serving as executioners ran him through with their swords and then beheaded him.

Devastated by the death of his lifelong friend, Edward managed to get papal absolution so Gaveston could be buried properly. The funeral ordered by the King was both an elaborate and expensive ceremony. Gaveston's body and head had been recovered by the King's men and taken to skilled Dominicans at Oxford University who sewed Gaveston' head back onto his torso and then embalmed him.

King Edward continued his reign, passing away in 1327.

Fictional portrait of King Edward II from Cassell's 1902 *History of England*

Chapter 15. Nicolas Copernicus, Tiedemann Giese, and Georg Rheticus

Without the support of friends to publish his epochal works on astronomy, the world might have been deprived — for an uncertain period — of Copernicus' theories that paved the way for the scientific revolution.

Nicolaus Copernicus was born in 1473 in Torun, Poland, to a well-to-do family of merchants. He was well educated, studying mathematics, medicine and religion at various schools and universities, in Poland, Prussia and Italy. He spent a decade in Italy alone. Early on he developed a keen interest in astronomy, even when working as a canon in the Roman Catholic hierarchy. He was encouraged in this pursuit by a close friend and relative, Tiedemann Giese, a bishop.

At this time the prevailing belief about astronomy followed the ancient theory of Ptolemy that the sun rotated around the earth. But Copernicus's calculations showed just the reverse — that the earth was just one of many planets revolving around the sun daily — and thus mankind was hardly at the center of the universe. This theory called for a major overhaul of traditional beliefs, astronomical, philosophical and religious as well.

Copernicus completed a shorter versus of his final manuscript around 1512, which he circulated only to a small number of friends. Given the religious discord spawned by the Protestant Reformation, he was hesitant about publishing his findings. There was a danger of being charged with heresy, which could be fatal, as well as experiencing ridicule. But word spread around Europe and his theories, as yet not fully refined, received mixed reactions. The Catholic hierarchy in Rome expressed interest. But Martin Luther, the leader of the Reformation, came out with a scathing comment denouncing Copernicus as "the fool who will turn the whole science of astronomy upside down."

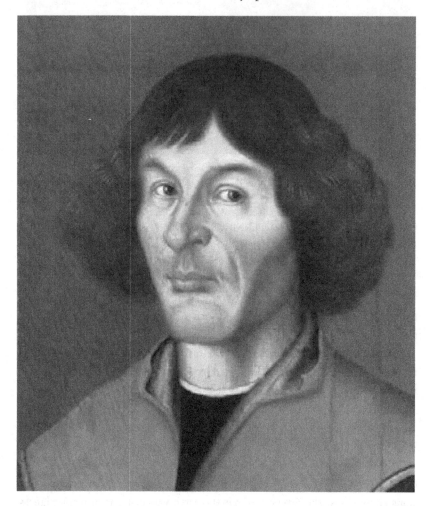

Nicolas Copernicus

Copernicus finished his final opus around 1532 but still held off publication. He resisted the advice of friends, including Giese, who urged him to take a firmer stance. Meanwhile, he did publish a booklet in 1522 on a totally different subject: how to handle inflation, basically by preserving the real value of gold in the same amount of gold and silver coins. In effect, his economic theory — hardly as well known as his scientific work — preceded by around 40 years the findings of Sir Thomas Gresham, the English financial adviser to the throne. *Gresham's Law* posits that bad money drives out good money if their exchange rate is set by law. In Poland, it's known as the *Copernicus–Gresham Law*. The concept, however, probably dates back to antiquity.

Tiedemann Giese

Finally, 25-year-old Georg Rheticus, already a noted scholar and mathematician, entered the scene. Rheticus, a stout believer in Copernicus's theory, took a leave of absence from his teaching post at the University of Wittenberg and journeyed to the cathedral town of Fromberk where Copernicus lived. Impressed by Rheticus's background and interest, as well as his gifts of books (which included Ptolemy's *Almagest*), Copernicus welcomed the younger man; but as a Lutheran, Rheticus was hardly popular elsewhere in the small town. Ultimately, Rheticus was to spend a little over two years with Copernicus. His duties as a canon were his main responsibility, but Copernicus worked when he could on his theories, using the available astronomical instruments including the "triquetrium" or "Ptolemy's ruler."

Rheticus, along with Giese, finally convinced Copernicus to go ahead with publication. He also put together a summary of Copernicus' findings in his *Narratio Prima* (First Report). In due course Rheticus took the final manuscript of *On The Revolutions of the Celestial Spheres* to a Nuremberg printer. Then Rheticus had to move to another city for a university appointment and it was left for a Lutheran theologian, Andreas Osiander, to handle the printing. Osiander took it upon himself to add an anonymous preface positing that Copernicus' work was just a hypothesis and not a true depiction of the earth's and sun's rotations.

It starts: "And if any causes are devised by the imagination, as indeed very many are, they are not put forward to convince anyone that they are true, but merely to provide a reliable basis for computation."

Many readers, however, were likely to think that Copernicus wrote the preface.

Copernicus, perhaps in a move to secure papal backing, dedicated the book to Pope Paul III. Only a thousand copies were sold, and the work — despite its enormous importance — was only reprinted about three times prior to the 20th century. While Copernicus acknowledged others for their help, he neglected to thank Rheticus, which was puzzling to many, and Rheticus most of all. Rheticus continued teaching and writing, passing away when he was 60.

The roster of seven axioms about the heliocentric theory, totally upsetting supposedly established concepts, had at its key the third axiom which held that: "All the spheres revolve about the sun as their midpoint, and therefore the sun is the center of the universe."

Copernicus died in 1543. He had never married. A touching but perhaps apocryphal story has it that an advance copy or the first printed copy of his book came in time to his deathbed and he was able to look at it before peacefully passing away. He willed his writings to Giese (who passed away in 1550) and left his library to the local church. What he left to the world was a great stimulus to further scientific investigation and to end much of the unquestioning and strict acceptance of classical concepts.

Quotes from Copernicus:

- First of all, we must note that the universe is spherical.

- Finally, we shall place the Sun himself at the center of the Universe.

- For is it not the duty of an astronomer to compose the history of the celestial motions through careful and expert study.

- For I am not so enamored of my own opinions that I disregard what others may think of them.

- I am aware that a philosopher's ideas are not subject to the judgment of ordinary persons, because it is his endeavor to seek truth in all things, to the extent permitted to human reason by God.

Chapter 16. Michel de Montaigne & Etienne de la Boétie

Michel de Montaigne and Etienne de la Boétie were two 16th century Frenchmen who had a deep friendship and whose thoughts and works have continued to greatly influence philosophy, politics, and the overall human condition.

They were only three years apart in age, with de la Boétie born in 1530 and Montaigne in 1533. Both came from aristocratic families and were well educated. They met and bonded while studying at the University of Orleans where there was significant intellectual ferment in the emerging French Renaissance. Quite precociously, de la Boétie was appointed to the Bordeaux Parliament in 1533, a year after finishing his legal studies, even though he was under the legal age. He was soon to be followed by Montaigne, where their friendship continued and flourished. Receiving such parliamentary appointments could in those days be lubricated by family connections and emoluments.

De la Boétie wrote poems and sonnets, and translated works by Plutarch and Xenophon; but he is most famous for his extraordinary and prescient work: *The Politcs of Obedience: The Discourse on Voluntary Servitude*, which he wrote while still in his early to mid twenties. In it he questioned why people gave obedience to rulers, and was roundly critical of absolute monarchy and tyranny. His themes have resonated to the present day, making de la Boétie, though not that well known, one of the founders of modern political philosophy. He laid the groundwork for future doctrines of civil disobedience and nonviolent resistance to governmental authority.

Michel de Montaigne

De la Boétie went on to become a judge and diplomat. He became ill and died at the young age of 32 in 1563. His death had a strong effect on Montaigne and many believe the loss of his close friend was a catapult to Montaigne to concentrate on his famous essays. Montaigne also saw to the printing and publishing of some of de la Boétie's works, but not his courageous political manifesto, which was first posthumously published in 1577.

Montaigne, easily one of the most influential writers of the French Renaissance, helped establish the essay as a literary genre. His essays, including one on friendship with de la Boétie as the inspiration, are still read today for their remarkable insight into the human condition. He wrote about many subjects ranging from clothing to cannibals, and was always candid, even about his intimate life.

In his ongoing tribute to de la Boétie, Montaigne wrote in one of his dedications to posthumous publications of his friend's books: "He is still lodged in me so entire and so alive that I cannot believe he is so irrevocably buried or so totally removed from our communication."

Montaigne, very much a skeptic, examined himself and the world around him with a dispassionate scalpel. One of his most famous utterances was: "What do I know?" Basically, he scrutinized the world about him with a belief in his own senses and judgment. His writing was at once intellectual but laced with anecdotes including personal references, which led to another telling comment of his: "I am myself the matter of my book." He was appalled, among other issues, by the religious conflicts of the day, such as the strife between Roman Catholics and the Protestant Huguenots. Curiously, given his lasting fame, he didn't think much of the human trait of seeking fame. Overall, his essays tend to argue against any form of dogmatic thinking, and he's considered the father of a brand of modern skepticism.

Montaigne had retired to his chateau to write his essays, but he later became mayor of Bordeaux. His essays were published in 1580 and he died at the age of 59 in 1592.

When asked about his friendship to de la Boétie in 1750, Montaigne responded: "If you press me to say why I loved him, I can say no more than it was because he was he and I was I."

Other quotes by Montaigne:

- A good marriage would be between a blind wife and a deaf husband.

- A man who fears suffering is already suffering what he fears.

- A straight oar looks bent in the water. What matters is not merely that we see things but how we see them.

- A wise man never loses anything if he has himself.

- Age imprints more wrinkles in the mind than it does on the face.

- Every man bears the whole stamp of the human condition.

- Everyone rushes elsewhere and into the future, because no one wants to face one's inner self.

- Fame and tranquility can never be bedfellows.

- Any person of honor chooses rather to lose his honor than to lose his conscience.

Chapter 17. Jonathan Swift, Alexander Pope, and John Gay

Jonathan Swift, Alexander Pope and John Gay were late 17th century/early 18th century writers, poets and satirists. They chose to have some of their works published anonymously, both for political reasons and because their jibes didn't sit well with important personages whom they roundly pilloried.

The group, whose members become lifelong friends, formed the Scriblerus Club in London around 1714; it lasted until 1745 with the death of Swift, the last living founder. The Club existed so the men could discuss their own works and use the invented name of Martinus Scriblerus for their joint writing purposes. The small bunch of writers, each with a satiric bent, wanted to lampoon pedantry, and to a large extent false fashions and tastes in learning and knowledge. *The Memoirs of Martinus Scriblerus* was written mostly by Dr. John Arbuthnut, another charter member of the club. But there was plenty of input from others. Arbuthnut is also famous as the creator of the stout, iconic John Bull figure, a national personification of England, which he used in his 1712 pamphlet, *Law is a Bottomless Pit*. Some elements of the Scriblerus "memoirs" also showed up in Pope's masterpiece, *The Dunciad*.

Pope also used the name as a pseudonym. Use of pseudonyms was not uncommon during this period when writers, especially satirists, wished to escape governmental censure and the private wrath of luminaries.

Jonathan Swift, considered one of the foremost prose satirists in the English language, was born into an Anglo–Irish family in Dublin in 1667. Two 1704 books, *A Tale of a Tub* and *The Battle of the Books*, brought him a good measure of fame. Swift was not at all averse to satirizing the corruption he saw in religion and education. *The Tale of a Tub* is a prose parody generally regarded as a satire on the excesses of established religion. There are two basic sections. The tale or narrative is about the adventures of three brothers representing different branches of Christianity, while several digressions satirize what was going on with literature, politics, theology, et al. "Tub" probably was a pun of a certain kind of pulpit though it might have referred to Swift himself as a clergyman.

Jonathan Swift

As a prolegomena or essay introduction to "Tub," Swift appended a shorter satire, *The Battle of the Books*. In this epic literary battle, books came to life in the king's library, representing ancient and classical authors as well as contemporary literary figures. They fought for victory in men's minds with Swift injecting his jibes. However, he left it for readers to ponder who the victor might be.

The two books were popular but they made Swift notorious in some circles and damaged his chances for advancement in the Church of England.

The *Bickerstaff Papers*, another satire, came out in 1708. In addition to his satires and essays, Swift was heavily involved in churning out political pamphlets. Some of his comments were put into letters and then published as *The Journal of Stella*. He supported Irish causes, which led to publication of the famous *A Modest Proposal*, suggesting a rather savage remedy for Ireland's hungry poor by convincing them to eat their own surplus babies. In a similar vein, he wrote *Proposal for Universal Use of Irish Manufactures* in 1720 and *Drapier's Letters* in 1724. Two of Swift's pseudonyms were Lemuel Gulliver and Isaac Bickerstaff.

In 1726, Swift — who had by this time earned a Doctor of Divinity degree — came to London with a four-part manuscript titled *Travels into Several Remote Nations of the World* by Lemuel Gulliver. The satiric masterpiece, subsequently to be better known as *Gulliver's Travels*, was published anonymously that year, when Swift was nearly 59. Swift was helped in this process by his Scriblerus companions. The book was successful immediately, with extra printings, and translations forthcoming into French, German and Dutch.

Swift kept writing and came out with many poems — some considered scatological — in his sixties. But his health worsened, and he finally became mentally unstable. Some thought him insane. Finally, an official Commission of Lunacy confirmed his condition and said that he had an "unsound mind and memory." In 1741 guardians were appointed to take care of him and his affairs. He died in 1745, the last of the original core of the Scriblerus Club. Most of his fortune was donated for the founding of the first hospital for the mentally ill in Ireland, St. Patrick's Hospital in Dublin. Opened in 1757, it was one of the first hospitals in the world to be created as a mental health facility, it still exists as a psychiatric and teaching hospital.

***

Among Swift's quotes:

- May you live all the days of your life.
- It is useless to attempt to reason a man out of a thing he was never reasoned into.
- A wise man should have money in his head, but not in his heart.
- I wonder what fool it was that first invented kissing.

Meanwhile, Pope — who was born in 1688 — became equally known for his satirical verse as well as his translations of Homer's *Iliad* and *Odyssey*. His fame began with his poems, *Pastorals*, based on the seasons, which were published before he turned twenty-one. He was particularly famous for his heroic couplets, many of which have been quoted over the years.

His 1711 *Essay on Criticism*, which took around three years to write, was well received. The essay discussed whether poetry should follow any natural pattern, which connoted some element of contemporary values, or follow established parameters that came from the past. It was also published anonymously. The following year he came out with the mock-epic *The Rape of the Lock*, one of his most famous works. The mock-heroic narrative poem satirized society and mocked classical epics. It was based on an incident where a dejected suitor cut off a locket of his heartthrob's hair without her consent, setting off a squabble between two families.

The Dunciad, considered by many to be his masterpiece, had three different publications. The first one was in 1728. The second version, also published anonymously, came out the following year; but Pope was widely considered to be the author and those who suffered the stings of his pen were not amused. One account has it that he carried loaded pistols with him when he was walking with his dog, which happened to be a Great Dane. He finally acknowledged formal authorship in 1735. After a considerable rewrite and extension, *The New Dunciad* was published in 1743, with a different hero. However, the book still satirized the vapidity of contemporary English culture and some of its leading figures, described as members of a tribe of dunces who worked hard to bring decay and a lack of taste to England.

One of his couplets, written about his contemporary, Isaac Newton, much renowned as a pioneer in science, was:

> Nature and Nature's laws lay hid in night;
> God said, Let Newton be, and all was light.

Other works included the *Moral Essays* in the 1731–1735 period, and *Essay On Man* around 1733. After 1738 Pope didn't write much that was new but concentrated on rewriting some material. He had never been in good health, having suffered a form of tuberculosis that affected his bone structure and stunted his growth. He was only around four feet, six inches. He died in 1744.

***

Among Pope's quotes:

- A man should never be ashamed to own he has been wrong, which is but saying that he is wiser today than he was yesterday.

- To err is human, to forgive divine.

- An honest man is the noblest work of God.

- Blessed be he who expects nothing for he shall never be disappointed.

- Hope springs eternal in the human breast.

Alexander Pope

Not to be outdone by his talented friends, John Gay, who was born in 1685, wrote *The Beggar's Opera* in 1728. The ballad-like work has been often performed. He dedicated his 1713 *Rural Sports* piece to Pope, his friend from Scriblerus. Meanwhile, Swift helped him get a secretarial post with the British ambassador to the Court of Hanover, although the position didn't last long. *What D'ye Call It?*, a 1715 dramatic skit on contemporary tragedies, didn't fare well despite Pope's aid. Gay acknowledged help from Swift in his 1716 *Trivia, or the Art of Walking the Streets of London*. The long poem provided a graphic and amusing — to some — description of London's street life. A comedy play, *Three Hours After Marriage*, still failed despite influence and support from his fellow writers. His *Fables*, however, were largely accepted and appreciated.

Gay died in 1632 and was buried in Westminster Abbey. The epitaph on his tomb, fitting his personality and lifestyle, was:

> Life is a jest, and all things show it,
> I thought so once, and now I know it.

John Gay

CHAPTER 18. VOLTAIRE AND FREDERICK THE GREAT

Friendship with a king can have its ups and downs, as discovered by the famed French writer Voltaire during his stay at the court of Frederick the Great, king of Prussia, and in their subsequent statements and correspondence.

Voltaire, the pen name of François-Marie Arouet (a name adopted in order to escape notoriety about his time spent in prison for his cutting commentaries), had already made a significant name for himself as a man of letters in Europe. He also did well through financial speculations that enabled him to be relatively independent. His acerbic wit and satiric verse, directed mostly against royalty and clergy for their maltreatment of the masses, had led to a couple of imprisonments in the Bastille in Paris and exiles in London and elsewhere.

Voltaire

Meanwhile, Frederick II of Prussia had acquired a reputation as a benevolent ruler and a man of philosophy as well as a king. He also wrote poetry and was a musician of note, composing flute sonatas and concertos. During his remarkable reign he transformed Prussia into the strongest of the various German states and principalities, laying the groundwork for eventual German unification. Through his aggressive wars, he greatly enlarged Prussian territory while making the well-disciplined Prussian army a formidable foe. No less a military figure than Napoleon rated Frederick as a tactical genius for his military maneuvers.

Frederick and Voltaire conducted a lengthy intellectual correspondence. The Prussian ruler sought out other intellectual leaders of Europe, inviting them as well as Voltaire to come to his court. Unlike other monarchs of the period, Frederick was austere in person. He spent more time with the army than with the bride his father chose for him. Frederick's austerity was also apparent in his palace at Potsdam, near Berlin, which he called "Sans souci" or "carefree."

Considering himself "a servant of the state," Frederick was a staunch believer in discipline and order. He abolished torture. He wasn't well disposed to the practice of Christianity, finding religious organizations highly dubious. Sharing some beliefs with Voltaire, the King respected the subject of the deity but not how men utilized their definitions of God. As far as his crown, a symbol of his regal authority, he described it as "a hat that let the rain in."

Finally, Voltaire accepted an invitation to visit Frederick at his castle. Voltaire, born in 1694, was 18 years older than the monarch, who was born in 1712. Things went well at first, during this 1750–1753 period, and the ruler and Voltaire were both pleased with each other's intellectual company. Frederick considered himself attuned to the merging elements of cultural and scientific enlightenment. Voltaire would generally spend some time during the day with Frederick and then attend the nightly supper parties. Voltaire received an annual pension of 20,000 francs, worth a small fortune in today's money, as well as some other emoluments. He wrote *Micromegas* in 1752 while at Frederick's court, easily one of the first science fiction books. The manuscript centered on the impressions of ambassadors from another planet visiting Earth and noting the follies and foibles of mankind.

Voltaire also annotated a 1740 essay by Frederick, the *Anti-Machiavel*, in which the king rebutted the arguments of Nicolo Machiavelli in his famous 16th century work, *The Prince*. Machiavelli advised princes that they could use immoral means to achieve their purposes, such as greater glory as well as political triumph, not to mention survival. Frederick, a believer in Enlightenment values, strongly favored the principle that princes should employ rational and benevolent policies in their statesmanship and government. Moreover, he argued, Machiavelli suggested too much reliance on machinations by princes that would, or could, end in disaster. However, Frederick was concerned that his book might offend some of his royal peers and dispatched the essay to Voltaire, who rewrote it to a considerable extent. Even so, it was not soon published.

Never at a loss for words, Voltaire quipped: "If Machiavelli were alive today, and an adviser to a prince, the first thing he would do would be to publicly denounce Machiavelli."

But then a brouhaha arose. There was a dispute between Voltaire, who was quite as interested in science as most other subjects, and Pierre-Louis de Maupertius, the director of the Berlin Academy of Sciences. Voltaire, as was his habit, wrote a satiric pamphlet ridiculing the staid director. Frederick himself took exception and the relationship with his philosopher-in-residence soured; the King had all copies of Voltaire's diatribe burned. Disillusioned, Voltaire intended to leave Prussia but he was detained at the border and stripped of his compensation from Frederick. He was also put under house arrest for a week.

Initially, Voltaire believed that given the conditions prevailing during that historic period, only an enlightened monarch could improve the lot of the people. But his experiences at the Prussian court finally changed his mind. He wrote: "I am going to write for my instruction a little dictionary of terms used by kings. 'My friend' means 'my slave.'"

Frederick the Great

The two men were frank with each other. Voltaire told Frederick that "kings use human beings for their own purposes, and the poor things don't realize it."

Frederick charged that Voltaire tended to be inconsistent in his opposition to religious superstition and the abuse of the populace by those in power, both secular and clerical. Voltaire's position was coiled in his famous statement, "Crush the infamous thing!" His target was the Catholic Church, whose abuses, in that era, included simony or the selling of church offices, accepting payment for a promise of ultimate entry into heaven, and ecclesiastical excess. Frederick, however, wrote: "You will always caress the Infamous with one hand while scratching it with the other, which is just how you deal with me and everyone else."

Finally able to leave, Voltaire found his return to Paris blocked by Louis XV, who was well aware of Voltaire's angry pen. So he went across the border to Geneva, in Switzerland, where he purchased an estate near the city. The rupture with Frederick was later repaired to some extent, but the men's relationship returned to an epistolary basis. Voltaire was not kind to Frederick's poetic output, or his attempt at composing an opera.

In Geneva, difficulties also arose under a local law banning theatrical productions. Voltaire was a playwright, among his many accomplishments. Accordingly, the peripatetic Voltaire set forth again, this time just across the border to Verney, in France, where he spent most of the last two decades of his life. Here he wrote and entertained luminaries of the day include James Boswell, scribe to Samuel Johnson, the English writer, and Giovanni Casanova who was well known in another field. He also wrote his most famous work *Candide* (or *Optimism*) at this less than modest retreat at the age of 64. This seminal work lampooned the philosophy of mathematician/scientist Gottfried Liebnitz who held that, simplistically boiled down, our world is the best possible one God could have created because the deity wouldn't have created a lesser brand if a better one were possible.

Quite popular with the ladies, Voltaire's greatest love was probably Emilie du *Châtelet*, who was a scientist and mathematician in her own right, and quite capable of keeping up with him intellectually.

Voltaire, no fan of the clergy, was a deist. Deism, as some have put it, has God as a master clockmaker who creates a clock — the world — and then lets it tick on its own without his intervention. He wrote: "If God didn't exist, we would have to create him."

But on the subject of religion itself, he adhered to the same position penned in a 1767 letter to Frederick. "Our religion is without doubt the most ridiculous, the most absurd, and the most bloody to ever infect the world."

In another famous quote, he said, "Superstition sets the world in flames; philosophy quenches them."

However, it was not Voltaire who came out with a quote often incorrectly attributed to him: "I disagree with what you say, but I will defend to the death your right to say it." This was, apparently, a biographer's effort to distill the essence of Voltaire's views on freedom of speech.

Based on his unsettling experience with Frederick, Voltaire changed his mind about the role of a supposedly enlightened monarch. He ended *Candide* with a memorable line promoting individual responsibility among other values: "It is up to us to cultivate our own garden."

Voltaire himself did a prodigious amount of literary "gardening," producing more than 2,000 books and pamphlets as well as thousands of letters. He wrote plays, poetry, novellas, essays, historical and scientific works. An advocate of social reform, human rights and religious tolerance, he attacked religious dogma and the arrogance of aristocracy. All of his writings led to his confrontations with censorship, time in jail, the burning of his material, and exiles elsewhere in Europe. His enforced sojourn in England starting in 1726 and lasting for nearly three years led to a collection of essays, *Letters Concerning the English Nation.* His opinions, which tended to applaud greater English respect for religious tolerance, didn't sit well with the French court. The letters were ordered burned and Voltaire fled.

As a writer of history — he wrote *The Age of Louis XV* in 1751 — Voltaire had specific ideas about historiography. He wrote (in Diderot's *Encyclopedia*): "One demands of modern historians more details, better ascertained facts, precise dates, more attention to customs, laws, mores, commerce, finance, agriculture, population."

In 1778, despite his advanced age, Voltaire undertook the journey to Paris to attend to the opening of his play *Irene.* Becoming ill and thinking he would die, he put down what he thought were his final thoughts: "I die adoring God, loving my friends, not hating my enemies, and detesting superstition."

However, he survived and enjoyed seeing his play performed and being treated as a hero while returning to his ancestral home. Soon, however, he became ill again and this time his condition was fatal. Details of his passing are blurry but one account seems true to his nature even if it is apocryphal. The Roman Catholic Church wanted Voltaire, as he received last rites from a priest, to retract his recriminations against organized religion and especially Catholicism. In this fanciful version, the dying Voltaire was asked by the priest to use his last moments to renounce Satan, Voltaire supposedly responded: "Now, now, my good man, this is not the time for making enemies." In a depiction of his last moments that seems more accurate, he refused to recant, murmuring to a pair of priests, "Let me die in peace." He was 84.

Years after Voltaire's death, pages were found among his papers of an epistolary novel, based on real events, that he had begun and put aside, presumably because of the problems publication might cause him. Key characters include a naïve chamberlain (which he had been at Frederick's court) who is mistreated by a difficult tyrant.

Frederick, meanwhile, continuing modernizing Prussia and composing music. He also assisted the esteemed French writer/philosopher Rousseau for a period. Well regarded by his subjects, he found one of his greatest comforts with his pet Italian greyhounds, whom he jokingly called his "marquises de Pompadour" in a sally at the royal mistress of the French king in Paris.

Frederick, who was childless, passed away in his palace study in 1786 at the age 76. He was succeeded by his nephew, who became Frederick William II.

***

Among Voltaire's many quotes:

- Every man is guilty of all the good he didn't do.

- History is a pack of lies we play on the dead.

- God is a comedian playing to an audience too afraid to laugh.

- Prejudices are what fools use for reason.

- Marriage is the only adventure open to the cowardly.

- It is forbidden to kill; therefore all murderers are punished unless they kill in large numbers and to the sound of trumpets.

And from Frederick the Great:

- Diplomacy without arms is like music without instruments.

- If my soldiers were to begin to think, not one would remain in the ranks.

Chapter 19. Jean-Jacques Rousseau and Denis Diderot

Jean-Jacques Rousseau and Denis Diderot were great friends; but they had a falling out, which might have been more over personal relationships than philosophy — though their outlooks did differ. Both major 18th century thinkers of the Enlightenment period in Europe had a significant impact on their contemporaries, with Rousseau having a much more lasting influence extending into contemporary times. Both were strong fighters through their writings against religious superstition and governmental despotism. In their own ways, they argued strenuously for social justice.

Rousseau, who was born in 1712 in Geneva, then a city-state, was a philosopher, writer and a composer whose political writings influenced the French Revolution. He encouraged more modern outlooks on political, sociological and educational values. His *On The Social Contract* and *Discourse on the Origin of Inequality* helped found the movement for social empowerment and democratic government. His *Confessions*, while shocking many with its candor, lay the framework of modern autobiographies. *Emile or On Education* delivered a potent argument in favor of creating an educational system that better prepared people for citizenship and which turned out more independent students who had the audacity to question their teachers. On the other hand, he was roundly criticized for turning his own five children over to foundling/orphanage homes rather than taking responsibility for their education. He also wrote seven operas and contributed to the musical world with his theories on composition.

Jean-Jacques Rousseau

Rousseau was somewhat of a scholar gypsy, moving to Paris, then to Venice, then back to Paris, and once more to Geneva. His religious convictions also showed some elasticity. Born as a Calvinist, he converted to Catholicism, and then went back to Calvinism to regain his Genevan citizenship.

Diderot, French-born in 1713, was just a year younger than Rousseau. He is most noted as the co-founder and chief editor of the *Encyclopedie*, an enormous project reflecting the breath and intellectual ferment of the Enlightenment. The massive work, which took years to complete, was structured to cover the full range of Gallic and European knowledge and ideas by many notable writers of the day on all branches of knowledge. There were 28 volumes issued between 1751–1772, with a new editor adding seven more volumes. He also wrote the famous book *Rameau's Nephew*, noted for its witty and satirical dialogue depicting a Parisian man about town while delivering jibes at various luminaries for their foibles. Several notable works, including *Jack the Fatalist, The Nun, and D'Alambert's Dream* were published posthumously. In addition to his famous essays, Diderot was also a noted art critic and playwright.

Rousseau and Diderot became close friends, starting around 1742 when Rousseau wrote some articles for the *Encyclopedie* on music and then later on politics.

In starting the multi-volume project in 1751, Diderot wrote: "An encyclopedia ought to make good the failure to execute such a project hitherto, and should encompass not only the fields already covered by the academies, but each and every branch of human knowledge. This will give the power to change men's common way of thinking."

While Diderot wanted to broaden the boundaries of human knowledge for most people, not just the rich and powerful, the work was formally suppressed by the authorities in 1759. The royal decree, while noting the progress of the arts and sciences, declared that the encyclopedia "can never atone for the irrevocable damage it has caused so far as morality and religion are concerned." Diderot, however, managed to keep work going in secret. The aristocracy and Church alike felt threatened by its advocacy of religious tolerance and freedom of thought. The process was difficult and Diderot lost some financial backers — and some of his eyesight, too. The last copies of the first volume were issued in 1765, marred by the bookseller/printer taking it upon himself to edit out of the proof what he thought were dangerous passages.

Diderot had actually been under police surveillance since 1747 when he was identified as the author of *Letter On The Blind*. The "Letter" posed the question of whether a person blind from birth would perceive the religious truths — such as a belief in God — that theologians considered self-evident. Ironic questions also arose on just who were the blind party. Many in the aristocracy as well as the church felt impugned.

Given these apparent affronts to religious and secular authority, Diderot was promptly imprisoned. Rousseau, his friend and ally, visited Diderot frequently in prison, at the fortress of Vincennes, near Paris (since the Bastille was fully occupied). Rousseau supposedly had an epiphany during one visit that all the arts and sciences could actually lead to a lessening of mankind's sense of worth and thus induce people to behave contrary to what he believed was their innate goodness.

At the time there was an essay contest on the theme of whether the development of the arts and sciences were really morally of value and beneficial. Rousseau's 1750 *Discourse on the Arts and Sciences* won first prize. Diderot, however, maintained that Rousseau had originally planned a different and more conventional theme, but only changed it after gleaning new insights due to their philosophical back and forth discussions.

After around three months, Diderot was released when he signed a letter of submission not to write anything lambasting religion. This meant that some of his controversial writings were only published posthumously. Diderot, while favoring more freedom of thought, reasoned that human behavior was determined by heredity. His perspective had a materialistic bent. Rousseau, on the other hand, argued that the spiritual element of man was his true nature.

In 1761 Rousseau came out with *Julie* or *The New Heloise*, an epistolary novel about two youthful lovers and their difficulties. The novel, covering elements of romance and society-imposed responsibilities, proved to be very popular. It paved the way for other novels with similar structure and content. One of his major works, the *Social Contract*, was published next year in 1762. It had the memorable opening line: "Man is born free; and everywhere he is in chains."

Vice, Rousseau held, emerged as the inevitable result of social and political organization, particularly with the rise of private property. As not everyone was so fortunate to own private property, measures were erected to protect it, thus creating in turn a false social contract based on inequality. People, Rousseau theorized, were more content before the formation of such societies and the limits that existing social/political contracts imposed. Only a more equal social contract would give people political liberty in exchange for surrendering their natural independence. Basically, man was naturally good, only to be seduced and corrupted by society. No political system, he maintained, was legitimate unless it was based on the general will.

Rousseau quickly created another seminal work: *Emile: Or On Education*. He advocated an educational system based on making sure children received the best influences, as they were starting with fresh minds and with a natural goodness.

One of Rousseau's patrons was a Madame Louise d'Epinay. She was 12 years younger than him and a woman of fashion known for her relationships with men of letters. She was also his landlady. Rousseau got into an argument with her which soon brought Diderot, their mutual friend, into the fray. Diderot sided with Madame, and the Rousseau–Diderot friendship evaporated after 15 years. Their rivalry over accomplishments was underscored by bitter letters and recriminations, and they never reconciled.

Diderot later scalded his erstwhile companion as "vain as Satan, ungrateful, cruel, hypocritical and wicked. He sucked ideas from me, used them himself, and then affected to despise me."

Rousseau, in response to a rebuttal of his article on civil religion in the *Social Contract* used a Catholic theologian as a spokesman to defend his arguments. But the vicar's creed also rejected original sin and divine revelation, which led Protestants and Catholics alike to take offense. Rousseau's books were burned and he fled Paris. Some of the banned books were published in Holland and smuggled into France using false covers and title pages.

Rousseau spent some time under the protection of Frederick the Great but when his house in Motiers was stoned in 1765, he took refuge in England with the Scottish philosopher David Hume. Rousseau had suffered a bladder infection from birth. From 1748 on his condition grew worse, necessitating frequent urination. He was forced to adjust the way he dressed to adjust to this problem, which probably didn't improve his disposition. His behavior became more erratic, including an epistolary quarrel with Voltaire and an in-person dispute with Hume whom he supposed to be in league with Diderot. His failure to learn English also didn't help; in any event, he and Hume had very different temperaments, and this led to an end of his sojourn in Scotland.

Diderot

Rousseau returned to France in 1767 under a false name. In the need to earn money, he started giving private readings of his still unpublished *Confessions* in 1771. His former landlady, Madame d'Epinay, then alerted police to these public renditions of his "shameful behavior." He was ordered to stop by the authorities, and the book was only partially published in 1782, four years after his death. He died of a fatal hemorrhage in 1778 at the age of 66.

Meanwhile, Diderot was also short of funds. He had to sell his library to provide a dowry for his daughter. No less a figure than Catherine, Empress of Russia, came to his rescue. When she heard of his dilemma, she commissioned an agent in Paris to buy the library for 15,000 livres (a tidy sum) but to let Diderot retain possession until she asked for it. Moreover, she directed that Diderot be paid a yearly salary of 300 pistoles, another substantial amount. He also spent the 1773–1775 period as her guest in St. Petersburg. When he died in 1784, his heirs sent his books to be deposited in the Russian national library.

Among Rousseau's quotes:

- He who is slowest in making a promise is most faithful in its performance.

- Never exceed your rights, and they will soon become unlimited.

- Good laws lead to the making of better ones; bad ones bring about worse.

And from Diderot:

- There is no moral precept that does not have something inconvenient about it.

- Only passions, great passions, can elevate the soul to great things.

- Watch out for the fellow who walks around putting things in order. Putting things in order always means getting other people under your control.

- Nothing is less in our power than the heart, and far from commanding it we are forced to obey it.

- I would rather be a man of paradoxes than a man of prejudices.

Chapter 20. Pierre de Beaumarchais and Joseph Paris-Duvernay

In a tremendously varied life, Beaumarchais was a watchmaker, harpist, businessman, diplomat, secret agent, publisher, arms dealer, playwright — and a near victim of the French Revolution. He's probably best known for his popular plays *The Barber of Seville* and *The Marriage of Figaro* that were turned into equally successful operas. His role in helping the American revolt against England is less known.

Many of his deeds and accomplishments came about due to his friendship with a Parisian financier and arms merchant, Joseph-Paris Duverney, some 48 years his senior. But this friendship almost led to his downfall.

Beaumarchais was born Pierre Augustin in 1732, the son of a Parisian watchmaker. Precociously, he invented a new escapement for watches. When he made a tiny ring watch for Madame de Pompadour, King Louis XV's mistress, his way into the royal court was paved. He also performed a favor to Duverney by helping him, through his connections as a teacher of harp playing (he had already improved the harp's pedals to make it easier to play the instrument) to the King's four daughters, to gain the King's approval for a new military academy he was promoting. Duverney repaid Beaumarchais with a profitable share in some of his projects, thus beginning their lengthy business association. Beaumarchais was candid in acknowledging that his mentor instructed him in the secrets of finance and how to make a fortune. He wrote: "He initiated me into the secrets of finance, of which he was a consummate master."

Pierre de Beaumarchais

Beaumarchais also made a lifelong friend in Paul Philippe Gudin, through the circumstances of a duel with another person. Gudin then became his biographer.

In 1755, at 24, Beaumarchais married Madame Franquet, a widow ten years his senior. She died a few years later. He took the name of Beaumarchais from one of her estates, feeling it suggested more grandeur. Aided by Duverney, Beaumarchais secured the title of Secretary-Councillor to the king in 1760–61, which gave him more of the "noble" identity he sought. He also adopted an elaborate coat of arms. In 1763, he bought a second title as Lieutenant-General of Hunting, which meant being in charge of the royal parks.

Beaumarchais used his mounting contacts, royal and otherwise, to further establish his new-found nobility. Subsequently, in a plan concocted with Duverney, he went to Spain with the purpose of obtaining an exclusive contract to supply the Spanish colonies with slaves. The potential deal didn't work out but Beaumarchais absorbed a great deal of Spanish culture that he put to good use in his plays. However, his first couple of plays, *The Two Friends* and *Eugenie* weren't hits like his later theatrical output. He married again in 1768, to another widow, Madame Leveque, who also died a few years later.

His fortunes took a turn for the worse when his benefactor, Duverney, died in 1770 at the age of 96. The duo had signed a statement canceling Beaumarchais's debts to Duverney with Beaumarchais to receive the sum of 15,000 francs. However, Duverney's sole heir, Count de la Blache, took Beaumarchais to court, alleging forgery. Attempted bribery of the presiding judge, Monsieur Goezman, and his wife, became an integral issue. The magistrate's decision in 1772 was to order Beaumarchais to repay all his debts to Duverney's heir, plus interest and legal expenses.

Undaunted, Beaumarchais published a pamphlet, *Memoires contre Goezman*, dramatizing his "unfair" treatment. A quote from Beaumarchais reveals some of his philosophy: "Vilify, vilify, some of it will always stick." The document brought him substantial acclaim, with the public viewing him as a champion of liberty and justice. Moreover, it helped lead to an overturn of the magistrate's verdict and his removal from his office.

The king began to use Beaumarchais as a diplomat as well as a secret agent. He helped protect the king by squelching an unflattering publication and blackmailing a certain minister.

France favored the rebellion of the Thirteen Colonies from England, its global opponent, but the king didn't want to cause a full-scale breach with a powerful neighbor. Beaumarchais, not shy about his opinions, advised the King and his ministers "to help the Americans" to prevent England from taking over French possessions in North America, including the Caribbean islands with their profitable sugar trade. His viewpoint prevailed and Beaumarchais was allowed to proceed, on an unofficial basis, to assist the colonies achieve their independence from England. Creating a fake company, Hortalez & Company, he had arms and supplies shipped to America. In what was an early example of lend-lease, he was supposed to eventually receive cargos of varied merchandise in repayment. Through such manipulations Beaumarchais steadily committed France to the American cause.

However, Beaumarchais had difficulty recovering his investment. His estate was finally repaid through a grant from Congress in 1835, with the stipend considerably less than the true amount owed.

Beaumarchais found time to write, in addition to his other activities. *The Marriage of Figaro* was completed in 1778. One innovation was adding music that made it a sort of an operetta. The king, however, prohibited its production until 1784 on the grounds the play, though set in Spain, satirized the aristocracy and diminished respect for royalty. Finally, permission was granted and the play became a big hit, with even aristocrats appreciating its humor. The work is in fact considered to have been a contributing factor to the French Revolution. The main character, a commoner called Figaro, outwits his "noble" master and in so doing becomes a symbol of the "Rights of Man" spirit beginning to sweep France and Europe. Mozart turned *Figaro* into an opera in 1786 and Rossini set the *Barber* to music in 1816.

Beaumarchais married a third time in 1786. Mademoiselle Willermaula, not a widow, had given birth to his daughter six years previously. Amid all his legal scrapes, Beaumarchais was also accused of marrying for financial reasons and perhaps poisoning a wife or two. He also published, through a German printer, banned works by Voltaire. But the project was a failure as few copies sold. He built a mansion near the Bastille, which became his prison for a while when the Revolution broke out. He was, after all, now a noble and some of his financial dealings were suspect. He was finally freed — pledging his support to the Republic — and then spent several years in exile. He only rejoined his family after the Reign of Terror ended. He began to restore his fortunes but died in his sleep in 1799 at the age of 67.

Some quotes from Beaumarchais:

- As long as I don't write about the government, religion, politics, and other institutions, I am free to print anything.

- I hasten to laugh at everything for fear of being obliged to weep.

- It is not necessary to understand things in order to argue about them.

- If a thing isn't worth saying, you sing it.

- Being right is always a crime in the eyes of power, which always wants to punish and never to judge.

- The cause of America is in many respects the cause of humanity.

- If time were measured by the events that fill it, I have lived two hundred years.

Chapter 21. Adam Smith and David Hume

Adam Smith and David Hume were two major figures in the 18th century Scottish Enlightenment that was highlighted by skepticism, a belief in reason, and a questioning of religion. Their works and philosophies have had a tremendous impact on the world.

They were about 12 years apart in age, with Hume born in 1711 and Smith in 1723. Each had a strong classical education that manifested itself in their incisive and innovative books and treatises. While their outlooks were often the same or similar, they did differ on some issues. Smith was hardly as skeptical as his intellectual companion. But their dialogues served to stimulate their creative minds.

The two met in Edinburgh in 1751 when Smith was giving a series of public lectures, and they quickly became lifelong friends. Neither ever married.

Adam Smith

Smith's *Wealth of Nations*, published in 1776 after about nine years of work, has become a sort of bible for capitalism. In arguing for free trade, instead of the then current economic system of mercantilism (the mother country gaining raw material from a colony like the thirteen colonies, and then turning around and selling them the finished product manufactured out of their own raw materials), Smith reasoned that only by allowing a free flow of commerce could the wealth of nations grow. However, while citing the need for a limited amount of controlling rules and regulations, he also foresaw potential shortcomings stemming from monopolization and excesses in free trade. Latter-day economists have been known to extol the virtues of capitalism more than the potential downside Smith pointed out.

Smith's intellectual path began with his education in Scotland and then at Oxford in England. Neither he nor Hume was particularly fond of England; their taste leaned toward France. Of his Oxford days Smith wrote: "In the University of Oxford, the greater part of the publick professors have, for these many years, given up altogether even the pretence of teaching." Though he found the teaching at Oxford inferior to that of his native Scotland, Smith did make use of Oxford's libraries to conduct research and improve his knowledge of the world's affairs.

Smith also complained that officials at the university confiscated a copy of Hume's *Treatise on Human Nature* when they found him reading the book. In this opus, Hume touted the empirical method of acquiring knowledge by using experience and observation. There was no innate knowledge, he argued. His controversial defiance of established religious principles prevented him from gaining some coveted academic posts. While it came to be considered a classic after his death, the book didn't do well when originally published around 1739. Hume wrote that the book "fell dead from the press." While Hume had some academic ambitions foreclosed to him, Smith eventually became a professor of Moral Philosophy at the University of Glasgow.

The Theory of Moral Sentiments, which Smith had published in 1759, covered the cause and range of a person's imprint on the minds of others as well as his or her own. Smith tried to examine the basic elements of accepted morality on a skeptical and non-moralistic basis. He was more interested in determining the process by which people assess whether something is wrong or right than rendering a judgment on the issues.

Meanwhile, Hume had problems with his book, *An Enquiry Concerning Human Understanding*, which led to charges of heresy. The volumes of this work, which showed Hume's encompassing and liberating insights into philosophy and morality, covered among other key subjects how ideas emerged, the element of free will, and the uses of skepticism and reasoning to comprehend spiritual subjects. Questioned as to whether he believed in God, Hume's response was simply that he didn't have enough faith in a belief that there was such a deity. He struck a better financial and literary chord with his six-volume *History of England* that came out in the 1754–1762 period.

At one point, Hume helped Jean-Jacques Rousseau get away from some difficulties in Switzerland — Rousseau was also at odds often with authorities and traditionalists — by giving him a refuge in Scotland. But the pair had a falling out, with Rousseau — not in the best of mental health at this time — accusing Hume of plotting against him. This led to Hume, against the advice of friends, penning a well-received treatise in his defense.

David Hume

Hume died in 1776 when he was 65. He managed to finish an autobiography, *My Own Life*, a few months before his death. His will named Smith as his literary executor and he provided a significant financial legacy to his long-time friend. The will also specified that his gravestone should be marked only with the usual information, his name and dates of birth and death, declaring he was "leaving it up to Posterity to add the rest." In a comment to James Boswell, the biographer of Samuel Johnson, he said, "If there is a future state, Mr. Boswell, I think I could give as good an account of my life as most people."

Smith, a friend throughout, came under criticism with a statement concerning Hume when he was dying about his stoical commitment to a form of deism. Smith wrote that his innocent revelation of Hume's mind-set "brought upon me ten times more abuse than the very violent attacks I had made upon the whole commercial system of Great Britain."

In 1779, only three years after his death, Hume's *Dialogues Concerning Natural Religion* was published. Friends had cautioned him to withhold publication when he was alive, fearing retribution. In the work, Hume challenged the notion of miracles and other supernal happenings. And indeed, the work got him in disfavor again in some quarters, but now he was safely out of reach.

Smith had his own questions about religion. He wrote about mankind's curiosity about nature and the workings of the universe. "Superstition first attempted to satisfy this curiosity by referring all those wonderful appearances to the immediate agency of the gods." Another of his sayings was: "Man, an animal that makes bargains."

Neither Smith nor Hume was considered particularly good looking. Smith referred to himself in this fashion: "I am a beau in nothing but my books."

Smith was also noted, especially in his latter days, for being on the absent-minded side. He once walked right into a tanning pit at a factory while volubly extolling free trade; and on another occasion he put bread and butter into a tea pot, drank the odd blend, and then murmured that he had never tasted a worse cup of tea.

Smith died in 1790 at the age of 67. Unfortunately, his will called for most of his manuscripts, which are believed to have been predominantly about the theory and history of governments and their laws, to be destroyed.

***

Among Hume's quotes:

- Art may make a suit of clothes, but nature must produce a man.

- Beauty in things exists in the mind which contemplates them.

- Custom is the great guide of human life.

And from Smith:

- All money is a matter of belief.

- Defense is superior to opulence.

- Happiness never lays its finger on its pulse.

- Humanity is the virtue of a woman, generosity that of a man.

- Consumption is the sole end and purpose of all production; and the interest of the producer ought to be attended to only so far as it may be necessary for promoting that of the consumer.

Chapter 22. Samuel Johnson and James Boswell

Samuel Johnson and James Boswell, two 18th-century English literary figures, are forever linked by Boswell's innovative biography of his friend in the *Life of Samuel Johnson*. Boswell's very name has entered the English language as Boswellian, a reference to someone who depicts a friend's life in candid and colorful detail. Boswell is credited with writing the first biography in a modern style, replete with anecdotes and other candid material.

Johnson, who was born in 1709, was already famous when he met Boswell in 1763. Boswell, born in 1740, was just 23 and still studying to be a lawyer. Johnson was now 54 and it's possible that Boswell might have seen his senior friend as a sort of father figure, particularly because his relations with his real father were often strained over Boswell's direction in life. The two quickly bonded, despite Johnson's distaste for Scotland, where Boswell came from. In one telling quote, Johnson quipped that oats are "a cereal given in England to horses and in Scotland to men." Nevertheless, Johnson took to the younger man and eventually nicknamed him "Bozzy."

Justly famous as a poet, essayist and literary critic, Johnson perhaps had made his strongest mark as a lexicographer. His massive *A Dictionary of the English Language* came out in 1755 with close to 43,000 entries. A few more words were added in later editions. In an interesting, and eminently useful innovation, Johnson illustrated the meaning of some words with quotations from the words of such literary stalwarts as Shakespeare and John Dryden. *Johnson's Dictionary*, as it was often termed then, didn't turn a profit for over a year. While Johnson did receive an advance fee, no royalties were involved although the book was a popular success.

Samuel Johnson

Perhaps unduly optimistic, Johnson thought he could finish the dictionary in three years. However, it took nine years. When he was told that the Académie Française had 40 scholars spending 40 years to complete a comparable dictionary of French vocabulary, Johnson tartly responded, "This is the proposition. Let me see: 40 times 40 is 1600. As 3 is to 1600, so is the proportion of an Englishman to a Frenchman."

France, evidently, was low in Johnson's pecking order, too.

Boswell eventually practiced law in Scotland but managed to make it down to London occasionally. Through Johnson he was able to join The Club, a group of wits and writers such as Oliver Goldsmith and Edmund Burke who dined every Monday at the Turk's Head in Soho. He kept a journal that aided him greatly when he wrote his biography of Johnson. Acknowledging his strong urge for sex, he also included his amatory exploits, mostly with prostitutes. The latter experiences led to many cases of venereal disease; treatments in those days often involved use of mercury, either as pills or anointments.

On a more salutary basis, Boswell wrote too, turning out some travel books featuring himself with such titles as *Boswell and The Grand Tour* and *Boswell in Holland.*

James Boswell

The two went on a trip to Scotland in 1763. Boswell's account had Johnson even wearing a kilt at one point while waving a sword and dancing a Highland jig. Johnson describes their jaunts in his *A Journey to the Western Islands of Scotland.*

Johnson also wrote the massive and influential *Lives of the Most Eminent English Poets*, which evaluated many 17th and 18th century poets. Johnson was also a poet himself; his *The Vanity of Human Wishes* is probably his best-known poem. Johnson created the poem with such speed that Boswell claimed he might have become a full time poet. His viewpoints, political and otherwise, were also registered in articles for *The Rambler*, a literary periodical; and in an *Idler* essay series.

While his skills were well noted, Johnson's behavior — including often making odd facial gestures — could sometimes confuse people who didn't know him. He was afflicted with what might have been Tourette's Syndrome, a condition not known in those days. According to Boswell, Johnson would make whistle-like sounds while bobbing his massive body back and forward.

Johnson, it should be noted, denounced any English supporters of the American drive for independence and was disturbed by the "colonists'" victory. Boswell, who favored the American cause to some extent, didn't escape Johnson's wrath on this issue. Very much indignant about the sheer audacity of Americans, Johnson wrote: "If the Americans wanted to participate in Parliament, they could move to England and purchase an estate."

Johnson died in 1784 at the age of 73. Boswell was greatly saddened and said, "My feeling was just one large expanse of stupor. I couldn't believe it. My imagination was not convinced."

However, when Johnson's will was read, Boswell was said be quite disappointed at receiving nothing. Johnson's Black servant, Frank Barber — who had been his slave for many years before Johnson released him from this servitude — received a large amount.

Subsequently, Boswell relocated to London in 1785. He practiced some law but lack of clients enabled him to concentrate on the biography. The two-volume *Life of Johnson* came out in 1791 and was an immediate and lasting success, securing the fame of subject and author.

***

Among Johnson's many sallies:

- A fishing rod is a stick with a hook at one end and a fool at the other.

- He who makes a beast of himself, gets rid of the pain of being a man.

- Praise, like gold and diamonds, owes its value only to its scarcity.

- Love is the wisdom of the fool and the folly of the wise.

- Do not accustom yourself to use big words for little matters.

And from Boswell:

- I have found you an argument; I am not obliged to find you an understanding.

- Men are wise in proportion, not to their experience, but to their capacity for experience.

Chapter 23. Wolfgang Amadeus Mozart and Joseph Haydn

Wolfgang Amadeus Mozart and Joseph Haydn, though over 20 years apart in age, became close friends and admirers of each other's notable musical accomplishments, which were mostly achieved during the latter part of the 18th century. Both men were born in Austria, Haydn in 1732 and Mozart in 1756.

Mozart, a child prodigy, started composing at the tender age of five and was performing before royalty while in his teens. His father Leopold, also a musician, was quick to recognize his son was a prodigy. Initially, he taught young Mozart and then acted as his manager/theatrical agent. Haydn similarly exhibited his superb musical talents at an early age.

The two met in Vienna around 1784. Mozart had moved to Vienna from his birthplace in Salzburg. During this period artists often had patrons from the aristocracy, though the succession of wars tended to crimp that practice. Haydn's patron, a Hungarian count, had a castle near Vienna that permitted him to make visits to the city. Under his contract with his patron, Haydn wore the count's livery, collected an annual stipend, and agreed to compose at the count's desire and only for the count unless otherwise permitted. But as the years rolled on, Haydn obtained more freedom.

In describing his experience to an early biographer, Georg August Griesinger, Haydn said: "My Prince was satisfied with all my works; I received applause. As head of an orchestra, I could make experiments, observe what created an impression and what weakened it, and thus improve, add, make cuts, take risks. I was isolated from the world; no one in my vicinity could make me lose confidence in myself or bother me, and so I had to become original."

Amadeus Mozart

Haydn's prolific originality led him to be acclaimed as one of the most celebrated composers of his time. Sometimes referred to as the "Father of the Symphony," Haydn wrote also a great deal of sacred and secular vocal music, string quartets, piano trios, and orchestral music. His oratorio, *The Creation*, was one of his major works.

When they first met, Haydn was over 50 years old and was already one of the major composers in Europe. Mozart, at 28, was also well known. His opera *The Abduction from the Seraglio* had recently premiered successfully in Vienna. The two became friends and would often get together in informal sessions to play their musical compositions. Mozart referred to the older man as "Papa," which was a gesture of respect and not a slight to his father who was instrumental in his career.

Mozart also dedicated six string quartets, called the *Haydn Quartets*, to Haydn.

The dedication, unusual in an age when dedications were usually given to aristocratic patrons, read:

> A father who had decided to send his sons out into the great world thought it his duty to entrust them to the protection and guidance of a man who was very celebrated at the time, and who happened moreover to be his best friend. In the same way I send my six sons to you. Please then, receive them kindly and be to them a father, guide and friend. I entreat you, however, to be indulgent to those faults which have escaped a father's partial eye, and in spite of them, to continue your generous friendship towards one who so highly appreciates it.

Haydn, duly impressed and appreciative, told Mozart's father: "I tell you, before God and as an honest man, your son is the greatest composer known to me by person and repute. He has taste and what is more the greatest skill in composition."

To friends, Haydn also made two other significant statements:

- "I have often been flattered by my friends with having some genius, but he [Mozart] was much my superior."

- "If only I could impress Mozart's inimitable works on the soul of every friend of music, and the souls of high personages in particular, as deeply, and with the same musical understanding and with the same deep feeling, as I understand and feel them, the nations would vie with each other to possess such a jewel."

Overall, Mozart composed more than 600 musical pieces including symphonies, concertos, string quartets, operas, and chamber music. He was prolific, with his most famous operas including *The Magic Flute*, *Don Giovanni*, and *Cosi Fan Tutte*. But he was often in need of money, perhaps due to inclinations to gamble and a desire for fine clothing. He often borrowed from friends, impressed with his talent. Even Beethoven came to Vienna at one point to study with Mozart.

True to his inspirations, Mozart said: "I pay no attention to anybody's praise or blame. I simply follow my own feelings."

Haydn, meanwhile, received an offer to go to London and conduct his new symphonies. His first visit was in 1791–92 with a repeat stay in 1794–95. Both interludes were quite successful, making Haydn financially secure so he no longer needed a patron.

Mozart tried to dissuade Haydn from going to London, pointing out the discomforts of such a long journey across the continent by coaches. A contemporary biography by Christopher Dies recounted this exchange:

"Papa, you have had no training for the great world, and you speak too few languages."

To which Haydn responded: "Oh, my language of music is understood all over the world."

Mozart, probably overworked in meeting deadlines for commissions he received, died in 1791 at the age of 35. He was survived by his wife Constanze, who unfortunately destroyed some of his sketches and drafts. They had five children but only two made it out of infancy. Informed of Mozart's death while in London, Haydn wrote to a mutual friend, "For some time I was quite beside myself over his death, and could not believe that Providence should so quickly have called away an irreplaceable man into the next world." Haydn had married but the couple didn't have any children.

Haydn wrote to Constanze offering musical instruction to her children, which he later provided. He returned to Vienna in 1795 and continued to create masterful works, with this latter group including his famous *Emperor quartet*. He died in 1809 at the age of 77, not long after an artillery attack by Napoleon's army. He is reported to have said to members of his household, "My children, have no fear, for where Haydn is, no harm can fall."

Joseph Haydn

Some quotes from Mozart:

• Neither a lofty degree of intelligence nor imagination, nor both together, go to the making of genius. Love, love, love — that is the soul of genius.

• The passions, whether violent or not, should never be so expressed as to reach the point of causing disgust; and music, even in situations of the greatest horror, should never be painful to the ear but should flatter and charm and thereby always remain music.

And from Haydn:

• I was cut off from the world. There was no one to confuse or torment me, and I was forced to become original.

• I listened more than I studied. Thereby, little by little, my knowledge and ability were developed.

Chapter 24. Ludwig von Beethoven and His Patrons/Friends

Ludwig van Beethoven

One of the greatest composers in history depended in part on the generosity of patrons, who also became friends, to subsidize his studies and work.

Beethoven was born in Bonn, Germany in 1770, and was taught how to play various instruments at an early age. He wrote his first music at the tender age of 12. He quickly came to the attention of probably his first patron, Count Ferdinand Waldstein, a member of the Teutonic Knights, a formidable military contingent. The Count took Beethoven to Vienna, a major bastion of music in Europe, in 1787. Whether or not he met Wolfgang Amadeo Mozart, whose music he was supposed to emulate, at that time is uncertain. On a second Waldstein-sponsored trip to Vienna after Mozart had died in 1791, Beethoven stayed as a student of Joseph Haydn for around 14 months in 1792–94. In a famous encouragement to his young charge, Waldstein said: "Dear Beethoven! You go to realize a long desired wish. The genius of Mozart is still in mourning and weeps for the death of its disciple. By incessant application, receive Mozart's spirit from Haydn's hands."

Beethoven subsequently dedicated one of his sonatas to Count Waldstein.

The Elector Maximilian Frederick, a major political figure in the mélange of German states and principalities, was another key patron who recognized Beethoven's immense talent and subsidized his studies. Beethoven dedicated sonnets to the Elector as well as to other patrons. He earned income from publication of his music, as well as performances; but he did depend on the generosity of these patrons. The patrons, in return received private performances as well as copies of works they might have commissioned for an exclusive period before they were published for everyone.

Haydn, extolling the praises of his pupil, told the Elector: "Beethoven will in time become one of the greatest musical artists in Europe, and I shall be proud to call myself his teacher."

One of Beethoven's most important patrons was probably Archduke Rudolph, the youngest son of Emperor Leopold II. Rudolph, who rose to be become a Cardinal in the Roman Catholic hierarchy, began to study piano and composition with Beethoven. Their meetings, which brought about a fruitful friendship, continued until 1824. Beethoven dedicated 14 compositions to Rudolph who dedicated one of his compositions to his teacher.

As his fame grew, Beethoven showed less and less tolerance for authority and social rank. He wasn't always prepared to give impromptu performances at soirées, and if he did, he would stop if anyone chatted or showed less than full attention. Rudolph finally, using his royal status, decreed that the customary rules of court etiquette didn't apply to Beethoven.

When Napoleon's imperial sway threatened to consume Europe, Beethoven, disenchanted with the Corsican general, tore Napoleon's name from the title page of his third symphony (the "Heroica") and rededicated the work to yet another patron, Prince Joseph Franz von Lobkowitz.

Starting with his first public performance in 1795 in Vienna, Beethoven went on to a prodigious amount of musical creativity including nine symphonies as well as many piano sonatas and concertos (the *Moonlight Sonata* is probably the most famous), string quartets, chamber music, one opera (*Fidelio*), and various other compositions. A giant of classical music, he widened the scope of instrumental music among his many accomplishments while also serving as a pivotal figure in the transition from 18th century classicism to 19th century romanticism.

Beethoven never married, but he had an eventful love life. In 1799 he taught music to the daughters of a Hungarian countess. He fell in love with Josephine, the youngest daughter, but she married a fellow aristocrat. He still wrote a number of impassioned letters to her after she was single again; but she again married someone on the same social scale, possibly afraid to lose custody of her children if she married a commoner. The famed letter to the *Immortal Beloved*, discovered after Beethoven died, might have been to Josephine; but there are several other distaff candidates as well adding to the speculation that has long existed (and been the subject of movies).

Remarkably, Beethoven composed much of his great musical output when he was struggling with advancing deafness. He began to lose his hearing when he was around 26 and it got progressively worse. He was almost totally deaf by 1814. After a difficult performance in 1811, he never performed in public again. Tradition has it that at the end of the première of his ninth symphony, friends had to turn him around to see the appreciative applause from the audience. Thinking his work had failed, he had started to weep. When Napoleon's forces bombarded Vienna in 1809, Beethoven retreated to the basement of his brother's house and covered his ears with a pillow in fear the noise would destroy what was left of his hearing. It's believed that Beethoven probably had a severe case of tinnitus that produced a ringing in his ears. But he could "hear" the music he composed in his mind.

He tended to start avoiding conversations, later utilizing conversation books during the last decade of his life. His friends could write their comments in these books and he could answer in the book or vocally. Some of the exchanges were quite candid and intimate.

Beethoven had another key friend in Anton Schindler, who served as a secretary of sorts and then became an early biographer. His biography of Beethoven was published in 1840 and was subsequently expanded in two more editions. While Schindler claimed to have been Beethoven's best friend, his reputation for accuracy has been challenged. Schindler apparently inserted some false entries into his collection of Beethoven's conversation books. He also destroyed others that he might have considered too revealing of Beethoven's opinions on contemporary issues and how he perceived himself as an artist. It has been estimated that out of a total of some 400 conversation books, over 250 were destroyed — a great loss.

Beethoven died in 1827; thousands marched in his funeral procession. His music, gloriously, lives on.

Some of Beethoven's quotes:

- A great poet is the most precious jewel of a nation.

- Music is the mediator between spiritual and sensual life.

- Nothing is more intolerable than to have to admit to yourself your errors.

- Beethoven can write music, thank God, but he can do nothing else on earth.

- What you are, you are by accident of birth. What I am, I am by myself. There are and will be a thousand princes but there is only one Beethoven.

- Only the pure in heart can make a good soup.

Chapter 25. Hegel, Holderlin and Schelling

Friedrich Hegel

Three German students of theology became close friends while roommates attending
a seminary for Lutheran pastors in Tubingen in
the latter part of the 18th century. Both Georg
Wilhelm Friedrich Hegel and Friedrich Holderin were born in 1770, with Joseph Schelling
five years later. Each achieved a measure of
fame — Holderlin as a poet, Schelling as a phi-
losopher, and Hegel eclipsing his friends to become a world-wide figure whose
philosophy works have greatly influenced other writers and philosophers.

The trio were in favor of the French Revolution with their motto, "Freedom
and Reason." In their talks they shared many ideas about other subjects as well,
which provided a fulcrum for their later work. Subsequently, their careers and
intellectual lives often intertwined, though the endings of their friendship were
difficult.

At first Holderlin helped Hegel get a position in 1797 as a tutor in a Frankfurt
home with a fine library where the two, and other friends, could get together
and discuss their ideas. But their paths diverged and the last time the two were
together was at Hegel's wedding in 1803, when Holderlin had already been di-

agnosed as mentally ill. Holderin spent the rest of his life in seclusion, without either Hegel or Schelling coming to see him. He died in 1843.

Hegel went to Jena where he resumed his friendship with Schelling, who helped him secure a position as a lecturer with the University of Jena. The two lived together for some time. At this point, though Hegel's junior, Schelling was better known for his philosophical writings and lectures. Schelling was in a running philosophical dispute with J.G. Fichte, another prominent philosopher. Hegel backed his friend Schilling with a book, *The Differences Between Fichte's and Schilling's System of Philosophy*, in 1801. This led, unfortunately, to Hegel sometimes being accused of being a mere follower or acolyte of Schelling rather than as an independent thinker.

Nevertheless, the two as co-editors established a magazine in 1802, the *Critical Journal of Philosophy*, where they published their reviews and essays. The publication lasted until the spring of 1803 when Schelling relocated to Wurzburg.

In 1807 Hegel completed his first major work, the *Phenomenology of the Spirit*, in which he tried to overcome the seeming divisions of philosophy and create a comprehensive approach. He sent a copy of the manuscript to Schelling and asked him to write the foreword. However, as it turned out, Schelling interpreted certain comments in the prologue (which didn't name him) as a barb against his work. He wrote to Hegel asking for an explanation or clarification of his intent. Was it to mock his followers or Schelling himself?

Hegel never replied, and thus their friendship was broken.

In the same year, 1807, Schelling delivered a speech at the Munich Academy of Fine Arts about the relationship between nature and the visual arts. Hegel wrote a negative review, further deepening their split. From that time on they consistently took opposing views and criticized each other's positions in lectures and books. They did meet again by chance in 1829 and managed to disagree again, this time on the tenor and mood of the encounter.

Hegel, who married Marie in 1811, had his two volume *The Science of Logic* published during 1812–1816. In 1816 he became a professor at the University of Heidelberg. Just two years later he relocated to teach at the University of Berlin. He finally rose to become rector of the university in 1829. The first edition of his *Encyclopedia of Philosophical Sciences* came out in 1817; a second edition came out in 1827, and a third in 1830. As a Lutheran, Hegel voiced criticism of Catholic doctrines and its history, but his works were never put on the Vatican's *Index of Forbidden Books*.

Hegel died first, in 1831, from cholera, at the age of 61, while Schelling lived on to 1843; but it was Hegel's philosophy whose system of logic triumphed. His ideas, which led to existentialism, centered somewhat on the concept that reality is the result of a historical process that culminates in an understanding of existence. He called this process "the dialectic" and his philosophy of evolution developing out of conflict is often termed Hegelian Dialectic. Hegel believed there was really just one philosophical system, faced with discordant elements that were still evolving toward a general conclusion. All philosophical approaches were stages worthy of analysis, providing a unity in their differences.

He did note, with an incisive insight, that philosophers are a product of their own times and are not able to surmount this basic limitation.

Philosophies, as Hegel wrote, take on a life of their own. Believers in Hegel's ideas evolved into left and right factions, though he himself wrote on a generic political basis. But Karl Marx used his ideas, to some extent, to develop his materialistic concept of history. Søren Kierkegaard, the Danish philosopher, and Jean-Paul Sartre from France, both had their existential viewpoints spring from Hegel. Many other writers were and still are influenced by Hegel.

Interestingly, Hegel completed his major work on *Phenomenology of the Spirit* on the same day that Napoleon and his army occupied Jena during the Napoleonic Wars. Hegel wrote of the occasion: "It is truly a wonderful sensation to see such an individual concentrated here on a single point, astride a single horse, yet reaching across the world and ruling it."

Many have pondered the ramifications of this sentence. Hegel, it should be noted, lived during a period of major upheavals in Europe. These major transformations included political revolutions in France and the start of the Industrial Revolution, mostly in England. The old social order of Europe was changing, and while Hegel may have started on a more idealistic keel, he became more conservative in his later years.

Some of Hegel's quotes:

- Whatever is reasonable is true, and whatever is true is reasonable.
- America is therefore the land of the future, where, in the ages that lie before us, the burden of the World's History shall reveal itself.
- An idea is always a generalization, and a generalization is a property of thinking. To generalize means to think.
- Education is the art of making man ethical.
- Genuine tragedies in the world are not conflicts between right and wrong. They are conflicts between two rights.
- Governments have never learned anything from history, or acted on principles deducted from it.
- Mere goodness can achieve little against the power of nature.
- Mark this well, you men of action! You are, after all, nothing but unconscious instruments of the men of thought.

Chapter 26. William Wordsworth and Samuel Coleridge

William Wordsworth and Samuel Coleridge were two 19th-century English poets and friends who collaborated in verse and created what has been termed the "Romantic Movement" in English literature. They were born two years apart, Wordsworth in 1770 and Coleridge in 1772. They sought to capture the sense and meaning of common, everyday language and the essence of man's innate connection to nature. The use of more stilted poetic diction, previously the norm, was held in lesser awe.

Their joint burst of creativity, where their minds benefited from each other, led to the publication of *Lyrical Ballads* in 1798. The two poets fed off of each other's encouragement and creativity, and their poems often included references to the other. Both were excited by the French Revolution and were active in radical circles; and then both were dismayed by the lethal excesses that followed the revolution.

Both attended Cambridge but never finished their studies. Perhaps to escape debt, Coleridge even enlisted in a military regiment with the colorful name of Silas Tomkyn Comberbache. As he proved to be a poor horseman, he was relegated to clerical and nursing duties. He was eventually discharged when a contrived plea of insanity was accepted by his commanding officer.

The two poets had first met in 1795 in Bristol where Coleridge was lecturing and they quickly found a kindred soul in each other. But they knew of each other and had already read some of the others poetry. Coleridge was better known and connected, and he recommended Wordsworth's poem, *Salisbury Plain* to a publisher.

William Wordsworth

A brief visit by Coleridge to Wordsworth and his younger sister, Dorothy, led to the two bonding even further. Wordsworth was very close to his sister, who kept a journal that Wordsworth could refer to when writing. The three, in their twenties, got along well together. Subsequently, Coleridge and his wife took a cottage in the English countryside about three miles from the Wordsworth's larger house at Alfixton Park during 1797/98. The trio spent many hours together in the woods and fields, drinking in the bounties of nature. Some of the values stemming from the French Revolution gave a radical impetus to their poetic and worldview. Wordsworth concentrated more on revealing poetic themes concealed in common events and lives while Coleridge dealt more with less mundane and even paranatural subjects to get at the underlying essence of humanity.

Together, they strived to merge differing motifs and methods — visionary ideals versus practical realities. In his definition of poetry, Wordsworth expressed their approach as "the spontaneous overflow of powerful feelings." Coleridge referred once to the trio as "three people but one soul."

Wordsworth was presumably familiar with a project Coleridge and another prominent poet Robert Southey (later to be named a poet laureate) had conceived. Their notion foresaw a utopian community to be called "Pantisociacy" which would be settled with ten other families along the banks of the Susquehanna River in the then wilds of Pennsylvania. The idea died after a short life.

The trio also traveled together for a time, primarily to Germany. Subsequently, they lived in England's Lake District where they, along with Southey, were known as the "Lake Poets." Problems arose as Coleridge, usually sickly, became more and more dependent on opium. Doctors could then prescribe opium which was sometimes dissolved in brandy. Coleridge readily admitted that the inspiration for *Rime of the Ancient Mariner* and another famous poem, *Kubla Khan*, came during a dream after taking opium. Coleridge also took prodigious amounts of laudanum to soothe his feelings of anxiety and depression. Intake of this drug led to the opium addiction. Scholars have suggested that Coleridge might have had bipolar disorder, a condition not known at the time.

Coleridge envisioned an epic poem that would be a masterpiece like Milton's *Paradise Lost*. The poem was projected to capture the essence of man's struggle for knowledge, redemption, and place in the world. However, perhaps recognizing in Wordsworth a superior talent, Coleridge encouraged his friend to undertake the work. Called *The Recluse*, Wordsworth did work on the massive poem but finally abandoned it.

The duo parlayed their poems into *Lyrical Ballads*, which was published anonymously. The opus had 19 poems by Wordsworth and four by Coleridge, but his *Rime of the Ancient Mariner* — a stirring inquiry into human guilt — was the longest poem in the collection. A second edition, some years later, was attributed to Wordsworth. It had 59 poems by Wordsworth and six by Coleridge.

Subsequently, Coleridge grew despondent due to what he felt were his waning creative powers. At the age of 28 he already wrote that when Wordsworth "shewed to him what true Poetry was, he made him know that he himself was no Poet."

Tension grew over Coleridge's growing dependency on opium, and he and Wordsworth went their separate ways to a large extent in 1810. They had an argument over disparaging remarks attributed to Wordsworth, which was patched up but they were never as close as before. They saw each other intermittently at events in London where Coleridge lived, with Wordsworth only coming to the capital occasionally.

Wordsworth, by this time, had married and had children. He kept writing, especially his semi-autobiographical poem, *The Prelude*, which was dedicated to Coleridge. In two other major poems, *Tinturn Abbey* captured the majesty of nature, while *The Ruined Cottage* showed the damage of rural poverty. Coleridge also kept writing, despite his affliction. His *Biografia Literaria*, published in 1817, was a mix of an autobiography and philosophy, and it received favorable criticism.

Wordsworth was named poet laureate in 1843. He thought he was too old and unproductive for the honor but he was convinced to take it by friends and fellow poets. He died in 1850.

Coleridge's lack of stability, which made some think him to be potentially suicidal, led him to move in with Doctor James Gillman. He lived in the physician's house for the last 18 years of his life. He died in 1834, having never received quite the acclaim that came to Wordsworth, though many gave him credit for his poetry as well as his large spate of literary criticism. Some contemporaries did call him "a giant among dwarfs."

Some phrases from Coleridge's *Rime of the Ancient Mariner* have, with some editing by other people, become part of everyday vocabulary to some extent. To illustrate: "Water, water, everywhere; but not a drop to drink anywhere" and an "albatross around one's neck."

Upon hearing of Coleridge's death, Wordsworth extolled his old friend as "the most wonderful man that he had ever known."

In *Christabel*, one of Coleridge's poems, there are opening lines that give a touching glimpse of a friendship that suffered after burning brightly:

> Alas! They had been friends in youth;
> But whispering tongues can poison truth;
> And constancy lives in realms above;
> And life is thorny; and youth is vain;
> And to be wroth with one we love
> Doth work like madness in the brain.

Both poets have been the subject of biographies and many scholarly examinations and deconstructions of their literary output.

Among Coleridge's quotes:

- Only the wise possess ideas; the great part of humanity are possessed by them.

- If you would stand well with a great mind, leave him with a favorable impression of yourself; if with a little mind, leave him with a favorable impression of himself.

Samuel Coleridge

And fromWordsworth:

- The mind that is wise mourns less for what age takes away than what it leaves behind.

- Come forth into the light of things, let nature be your teacher.

- Faith is a passionate intuition.

- Fill your paper with the breathings of your heart.

- Getting and spending, we lay waste our powers.

Chapter 27. John Keats and Charles Brown

John Keats' poetry was perhaps more appreciated after his death than in his lifetime, but that wasn't the fault of his friends, especially Charles Brown.

Keats was born in 1795, eight years after Brown, An English poet in the Romantic era, Keat's poems are noted for their rich and sensual imagery. But he began as a medical student, a career that he finally turned away from (though he retained his textbooks and notes and advised friends on their health problems). But he was consumed by a tremendous desire to be a poet, so much so that his brother George once wrote that Keats feared that if he never became a poet he would do away with himself.

Fortunately, that was not to be the case. His first poem, *O Solitude*, was published in 1816 when he was 21. His first volume of poems soon followed. Keats wrote: "I am certain of nothing but the holiness of the heart's affections and the truth of the imagination. What imagination seizes as beauty must be truth."

These words become the matrix of the famous and concluding lines of *Ode on a Grecian Urn*:

> Beauty is truth, truth beauty.
> That is all you know on Earth
> And all ye need to know

Brown, a writer and author of the comic opera *Narensky*, met Keats in 1817. He was older than Keats and well off financially. The pair became close friends, and were soon off on a walking tour of Scotland, duly described in their letters and in *Walks in the North*.

John Keats

After the death of a brother from consumption (tuberculosis) in 1818, Keats moved into Brown's more spacious home (two semi-detached houses with separate entrances) at Wentworth Place in Hampstead, a London suburb. The duo collaborated on a play, *Otho the Great*, which was printed but not produced until many years later. Many of Keats' odes, including *Ode to a Nightingale*, were written during this time at Brown's home. *Endymion* represents one of Keat's most famous collections of poetry, though contemporary reviews were not particularly good. Lord Byron, a poetic eminence of the period, used a sexual metaphor in his scathing review of Keat's poems.

Shelley, another major English poet who had met Keats in London, was more sympathetic. He even went to the extent of offering to look after him in Italy when Keats was seriously ill. Shelley wrote: "I am anxiously expecting him in Italy where I shall take care to bestow every possible attention on him. I am aware indeed in part that I am nourishing a rival who will far surpass me and this is an additional motive and will be an added pleasure."

Unfortunately, they never did meet again. Ironically, when Shelley drowned later in Italy, a book of Keat's poems was found with his body that washed up ashore.

Keats didn't have much of a love life, but he was much taken by 18-year-old Fanny Brawne. Chances are their relationship was platonic. Among his many letters to her, not all of which have survived, he wrote: "I have two luxuries to brood over in my walks — your loveliness and the hour of my death. O that I could have possession of them both in the same minute."

Concerned over his place in English letters, while he was alive and posthumously, Keats also confided in a letter to Fanny: "If I should die, I have left no immortal work behind me, nothing to make my friends proud of my memory. But I have lov'd the principle of beauty in all things, and if I had had time I would have made myself remembered."

Keats then contracted tuberculosis himself, and Brown took care of him, handling his affairs and lending him money. Keats seemed to recover — he was a young man — but then his health gradually deteriorated again. Following medical advice that another harsh London winter wouldn't be good for him, Keats decamped for Rome in 1820. Intentions were for Brown to accompany Keats but there was a mix-up in ships and Keats went with another friend.

Keats didn't survive Rome either. Tuberculosis caught up to him in 1821 and he died at the young age of 25. He wrote his last letter to Brown in late 1820: " 'Tis the most difficult thing in the world to me to write a letter. I have a habitual feeling of my real life having passed and that I am leading a posthumous existence."

Overall, Keats created three volumes of poetry in his all too short life.

Brown was urged by others to write a biography about Keats, a task he set about in 1829. He wrote: "My motive for writing Keat's life is that he may not continue to be represented as he was not. I am resolved, seeing that Keats is better valued, to write his life."

However, it took to 1836 for a draft to be completed. A hang-up took place as Keats' brother, George, decided not to let Brown use some of Keat's unpublished poems. Finally, George relented and Brown completed a rough draft of *The Life of John Keats* around 1841, a good 20 years after Keats' death. He added a note that his work was "very much a personal memoir based on friendship and not very objective."

Another situation arose which affected the putative biography. Brown had an illegitimate son, Charles "Carlos" Brown. Father and son, 17 at the time, had decided to go seek their fortune in New Zealand where they would settle at New Plymouth. Accordingly, Brown then turned his material over to Richard Moncton Milnes, a well-known poet and patron of the arts. Milnes' own biography, *The Life and Literary Remains of John Keats* — which included over 60 of his poems — was published in 1848. The volume was dedicated to Brown. By this time Brown had himself died in New Zealand in 1842 at the age of 55. The centenary of Keats death provoked some interest in Brown, and his grave in New Zealand was finally found in 1921. A marker was added: "Charles Armitage Brown, mentor of poet John Keats."

Some quotes from Keats:

- A thing of beauty is a joy forever: its loveliness increases; it will never pass into nothingness.

- Do you not see how necessary a world of pains and troubles is to school an intelligence and make it a soul?

- Heard melodies are sweet, but those unheard are sweeter.

- Love is my religion, and I could die for it.

- My imagination is a monastery, and I am its monk.

- I would sooner fail than not be among the greatest.

- Land and sea, weakness and decline, are great separators; but death is the great divorcer forever.

Chapter 28. Washington Irving and Walter Scott

Washington Irving is generally credited with being one of America's first men of letters and the first to have written international best sellers. He owed a debt of gratitude to Walter Scott, a Scottish novelist who had already established himself as a famous writer, penning such famous works as *Ivanhoe*, *Rob Roy*, and *Lady of the Lake*.

The two met in 1815. Irving, who was born in New York City in 1783, had gone to England to try and restore the fortunes of his family hardware trading business at its Liverpool branch. While he had opposed the War of 1812, Irving still enlisted in the American army after English soldiers burned Washington D.C. But business is business, and wartime feelings subsided. Unfortunately for the family, but luckily for literature, his hardware efforts failed. Somewhat adrift, and needing to make a living, he succeeded in meeting and visiting Scott — born in 1771, and 12 years older — at his home in 1817. They became lifelong personal and professional friends.

Scott encouraged Irving, then 35, to write for a living. Irving already had writing credits back in the U.S., primarily as a journalist under a pen name of Jonathan Oldstyle for a newspaper his brother owned. He had also authored a history of New York, published under the playful pseudonym of Diedrich Knickerbocker (this name has been much used since, including by the pro basketball team, the New York Knicks). But Irving was basically unknown in England and Europe.

Washington Irving

Irving took Scott's advice, which turned out well for him. He stayed in Europe for the next 17 years, which led some later critics to label him as an anglophile. Irving wrote *The Sketch Book* which contained 30 tales, many about England, but also with two of the most famous American stories ever written: *Rip Van Winkle* and *The Legend of Sleepy Hollow*. The first part came out in 1819. As Scott used Scottish folk tales as the background for some of his novels, Irving turned to the

Old Dutch period in New York. He used the alias of Geoffrey Crayon, and only turned to his own name much later in his career.

This book was very successful, making Irving among the first American writers to achieve positive criticism in Europe. Besides Scott, Irving won acclaim from such other literary figures as Charles Dickens and Lord Byron. He began a correspondence with Dickens and later hosted the novelist and his wife during Dickens' 1842 tour of the U.S.

There were no international copyright laws at this time, and piracy of works was prevalent. Initially, Irving had the *Sketch Book* published in seven installments in New York and in two volumes in England. Some parts of the book were reprinted in English periodicals without his permission. Consequently, Irving paid to have the first four installments published in London as a single volume. He also turned to Scott, who helped him to make an agreement with a reputable London-based publisher for the remainder of his opus and for future books. From then on he had his books published concurrently in the U.S. and England to protect his copyright.

Later, when he was a much-admired figure in the U.S., Irving lobbied in 1840 to have copyright legislation passed in Congress to protect American writers from copyright infringement. He argued: "We have a young literature springing up and daily unfolding itself with wonderful energy and luxuriance which deserves all its fostering care."

Congress thought otherwise, and the legislation didn't pass. Irving, though, was a source of encouragement to other writers just as Scott had been for him. Among the writers he encouraged were Herman Melville, Nathaniel Hawthorne, Edgar Allan Poe, and Henry Wadsworth Longfellow.

As an important precedent for his fellow writers, Irving managed to secure a 12 per cent royalty for his revised works to be printed by an American publisher.

Irving was a prolific author. He wrote biographies on Christopher Columbus, Oliver Goldsmith, and a five-volume work on George Washington. His historical works include books about New York City and the American West. (Some critics have argued that his historical books included enough fiction to term them as historical fiction.)

Irving is also given credit for helping to make the expression "Gotham" mean New York City, and to put the expression "the almighty dollar" into circulation.

After returning to the U.S. in 1832, Irving continued to write extensively, but in his later years he was entrusted with a diplomatic mission. He served as the U.S. ambassador to Spain, 1842–1846. The experience was disillusioning, judging from this comment: "I am wearied and at times heartsick of the wretched politics of this country. The last ten or twelve years of my life passed among sordid speculators in the U.S. and political adventurers in Spain has shewn me so much of the dark side of human nature that I begin to have painful doubts of my fellow man; and to look back with regret to the comforting period of my literary career when, poor as a rat but rich in dreams, I beheld the world through the medium of my imagination and was apt to believe men as good as I wanted them to be."

The Spanish period of his life led to two other books, *Conquest of Granada* and *Tales of the Alhambra*.

After a long and highly successful career, Irving passed away in 1859 at the age of 76.

***

Walter Scott was born in Edinburgh in 1744. He suffered from lameness due to a childhood bout with polio. He began writing professionally around the age of 25, after being trained as a lawyer. Subsequently, he enjoyed a productive literary career, becoming the first English-language writer to achieve international fame during his lifetime.

Initially, he came to recognition as a poet. His *The Lay of the Last Minstrel*, in 1805, was well received. Lines in this poem, used in *The Man Without A Country*, a short story by Edward Everett Hale, have been memorized by many American students.

> Breathes there a man without a soul
> Who never to himself hath said
> This is my own, my native land
> Whose heart had n'er within him burned
> From wandering on a foreign strand
> As home his footsteps he hath turned?
> If such there breathe, go mark him well
> For him no minstrel raptures swell
> High though his title, proud his name
> Boundless his wealth as wish can claim
> Despite these titles, power and pelf
> The wretch, concentred all in self
> Living, shall forfeit fair renown,
> And doubly dying, shall go down
> To the vile dust from whence he sprung,
> Unwept, unhonored, and unsung. . .

Marmion, in 1810, also had the famous lines:

> Oh, what a tangled web we weave
> When first we practice to deceive

Subsequently, Scott turned to fiction, with *Waverly* his first novel. More novels followed in due course. He kept writing, despite some financial losses, until 1831. Despite failing health he went on a grand tour of Europe, where he was much celebrated. After returning to Scotland, he died in 1832.

Sir Walter Scott

Among Irving's quotes:

- Great minds have purposes, others have wishes.

- There is a healthful hardiness about real dignity that never dreads contact and communion with others, however humble.

- A sharp tongue is the only edge tool that grows keener with constant use.

- Acting provides the fulfillment of never being fulfilled. You're never as good as you'd like to be. So there's always something to hope for.

- Age is a matter of feeling, not years.

- Great minds have purposes; others have wishes.

- I am always as a loss at how much to believe of my stories.

And from Scott:

- He that climbs the tree has won right to the fruit.
- All men who have turned out anything worthwhile have had the chief hand in their own education.
- For success, attitude is equally as important as ability.

CHAPTER 29. LORD BYRON AND PERCY BYSSHE SHELLEY

Lord Byron, born as George Gordon Byron and as a member of nobility, and commoner Percy Bysshe Shelley, were two great English Romantic poets of the early 18th century. Only four years apart in age, they were friends and competitors who both came to early and tragic ends. Both defied the social conventions of their times.

Lord Byron was born in 1788 with a clubfoot, but he made up for his lameness with his good looks and extraordinary talent. He also had a prodigious appetite for sex, usually but not always with women. His wild and adventurous life, and multiple affairs and liaisons with women including a half-sister, led to the term "Byronic" entering the vocabulary.

"The great of object of life is sensation," Byron wrote, and he lived his life accordingly.

Among his early friends at the prestigious Harrow School was John Fitzgibbon, the second Earl of Clare and later the governor of Bombay as well as a member of the House of Lords. Byron claimed to love Fitzgibbon forever and he could seldom hear the word Clare without "a murmur of the heart."

Another lifelong friendship dating from his scholastic days was Francis Hodgson, the provost of Eton at Oxford. Their friendship was well recorded in many letters that were finally sold for a tidy sum.

Byron took little time in establishing a reputation for his verse as well as his amatory exploits. His scandalous affair with Lady Caroline Lamb was the talk of London. She described the youthful Byron as "mad, bad and dangerous to know." He also served in the House of Lords before he was 21, advocating social reform and greater freedom for the individual from the clutches of the government and church. His poem, *Childe Harold's Pilgrimage*, had proved to be quite popular. Byron wrote: "I woke up one morning and found myself famous."

Lord Byron

Finally, no longer feeling welcome in his native England due in large part to his satirical verse and bedroom antics, Byron took his entourage — including a personal physician, John Polidori — to Europe in 1816. He never returned to his homeland.

***

Percy Bysshe Shelley, born in 1792 just four years after Byron, was very much a poetic prodigy and iconoclast as well. But he was less prolific and outrageous in private and personal matters. But he did experience a good deal of turbulence in his love life that finally led him to self-exile in Europe. Byron had already left for more permissive cultures than of less than merry England. Both men were truly unconventional and very much in the idealistic mode. Shelley had actually been expelled from Oxford for co-authoring *The Necessity of Atheism*, an early work pushing for social reform. In his *A Defence of Poetry*, written much later, Shelley declared that poets were the "unacknowledged legislators of the world."

Percy Bysshe Shelley

Their families intertwined in a mélange of twisted relationships that led Shelley, already a well-known poet (though not as much as Byron) to rent a house in Geneva, Switzerland next to where Byron lived. The two fellow "exiles" discussed poetry and politics and sundry other subjects, sometimes horseback riding and occasionally sailing on Lake Geneva. Mutual encouragement led Byron to start his great opus, *Don Juan*, while Shelley embarked on his equally famous *Prometheus Unbound*.

At night the two familial groups would entertain themselves telling stories, often ones involving ghosts. One night while reading aloud from *Tales of the Dead*, a collection of horror tales, Byron suggested they each take a turn at creating their own story involving fantasy. Mary Shelley, Shelley's second wife — with whom he had scandalously run away with when she was just 16, composed *Frankenstein* or *The Modern Prometheus*. Polidori submitted parts of *The Vampyre*, which may have launched a new sub-genre of horror literature. Interestingly, *The Vampyre* was the first vampire story published in English. To Polidori's dismay, and despite Byron's disavowal, it was long believed that Byron wrote the tale. Some people also believed that Byron himself was the model for the Polidori book.

Shelley wrote *A Fragment of A Ghost Story* which he didn't finish, while Byron also abandoned his *Fragment of A Novel*. It has been the influential works of Mary Shelley and Polidori which lasted. The word "Frankenstein" has entered the general vocabulary and is often used in non-horrific contexts and no end of movies.

In 1822 Shelley paid for an English editor, Leigh Hunt, to come to Venice where they, along with Byron, would create a journal to be called *The Liberal*. They would write for the periodical themselves, espousing liberal viewpoints. The magazine, unfortunately, didn't come to fruition.

Meanwhile, the friendship of Byron and Shelley rested precariously on competition in their creative lives. Byron was the brighter light but Shelley was right behind him in recognition of his poetic prowess. They respected each other's talent and recognized they were literary rivals. Shelley also wasn't particularly sympathetic to Byron's pursuit of frequent and often tawdry escapades which included bargaining with parents about the availability of their daughters. He spent a good deal of money on his revels that led to health problems. Polidori kept a diary of his decade with Byron, including his wild flings, which was subsequently published (with some salacious parts deleted).

In July 1822 Shelley decided to go on a nautical jaunt on the Bay of Spezia in Italian waters. His schooner, custom built for him in Genoa, had been named *Don Juan*, without his permission, by a friend in honor of Byron's epic poem. Shelley changed the name to "Ariel" from Shakespeare's play, *The Tempest*. But Byron made sure the name Don Juan was painted on the mainsail. Among other non-nautical differences Byron and Shelley didn't always agree on the virtues and values of Shakespeare's plays. In a great tragedy, the boat sank in a storm with all aboard drowned. Shelley's body finally washed ashore at Viareggio, badly decomposed. Byron reputedly couldn't stand the cremation scene and withdrew. He also turned down the bequest to him in Shelley's will.

Shelley wasn't yet thirty and the world probably lost many more memorable poems. As it was, Shelley's radical non-violence stance is believed to have influenced both Henry David Thoreau and Mahatma Gandhi.

Byron, less disposed to non-violence, was a strong champion of the Greek drive for independence from the Ottoman Empire. He contributed money for their cause and also wrote *Hellas* in 1821 to highlight and advance the Greek struggle. Seeking action to support his words, Byron decided to join the Greek forces facing the Turks at Missolonghi. He armed a brig at his expense and set sail for Greece. While he died from malaria in 1824 before any combat (being bled by doctors didn't help his chances for recovery), he still became a national hero in Greece. The Greeks eventually did succeed in breaking loose from the Ottomans. Byron received a 36-gun salute, one for each year of his life. His tragic premature death, like that of Shelley, again deprived the world of more masterful poems.

* * *

Among Lord Byron's quotes:

- Always laugh when you can. It is cheap medicine.

- Poetry is the lava of the imagination whose eruption prevents an earthquake.

- The great art of life is sensation, to find that we exist, even in pain.

And from Shelley:

- War is the statesman's game, the priest's delight, the lawyer's jest, and the hired assassin's trade.

- If winter comes, can spring be far behind?

CHAPTER 30. FRANZ SCHUBERT & FRIENDS

No less a personage than Ludwig von Beethoven, whom Schubert had met and greatly admired, said at Schubert's passing: "Truly the spark of genius resides in this Schubert."

Indeed, although devoted friends did their best to bring greater recognition of Franz Schubert's musical genius, his achievements were better noted after his death in 1827. Even some of his best friends weren't fully aware of everything that Schubert wrote.

Schubert was admired by many for his accomplishments during his short life — he died at the age of 31 — and mourned as they thought of what might have been, had he lived longer. Schubert, one of the last of classical composers as European culture evolved into the Romantic Movement, was prodigious in his musical productivity. He established the German "lied" or song as a new art form. Overall, he wrote more than 600 songs among many other musical works.

Schubert was born in Vienna in 1797 and received extensive musical training as a child. Friends, recognizing his talent, brought him to the attention of Antonio Salieri, then the reigning musician in Vienna. Schubert studied with Salieri for several years.

Friends also took it upon themselves to send a batch of Schubert's songs in 1816 — when Schubert was only 19 — to Wolfgang Goethe, the great German writer. Nothing, though, came of this effort. Throughout his sadly short life Schubert earned income mostly from teaching music, fees from publishers, the help of his close friends, and some aristocratic patronage.

Franz Schubert

One of Schubert's greatest friends and collaborators was Johann Vogl, his senior by 20 years. Vogl was a well-known baritone singer and composer. When Schubert first heard Vogl sing in 1813, he became determined to have him sing some of his songs. In the following year, he is said to have sold some of his schoolbooks to afford a ticket to a Vogl performance. The two finally met in 1817, and Vogl was equally impressed with Schubert's songs. Thus began an epic merging of talents that was quite successful.

Vogl helped Schubert get more recognition within the Viennese music circles, and the two even went on a holiday together in 1819 to the Austrian countryside. Moreover, Vogl continued to sing Schubert's songs after his death, including a complete performance of *Winterreise* on the 12th anniversary of Schubert's death. Schubert's version of the famed *Ave Maria* religious song was often performed as well.

At one point Schubert roomed around the 1814 period at the home of a friend, Franz von Schrober, who was a poet. Schubert wound up writing over 40 songs and two of his operas (which weren't successful) based on Schrober's lyrical poems. Schrober wrote the libretto in 1821 for Schubert's opera *Alfonso and Estrella*. Schubert wrote of this period: "I compose every morning, and when one piece is done, I begin another."

Schubert was also close friends with the Huttenbrenner brothers, Anselm, a composer, and Josef, who was also a musician.

Schubert sent his *Unfinished Symphony* to Anselm around 1823. Subsequently, another friend, Johann Herbeck, a composer, visited Anselm. Impressed by the work as far as it was done, he took it with him to Vienna where he conducted it for the first time in 1825. Herbeck played his own *Requiem in C Minor* at Schubert's funeral.

Musical scholars have puzzled for years over why Schubert didn't finish this symphony, but it's believed that he contracted syphilis in 1822. At that time, those diagnosed with syphilis were treated with mercury, and some patients are believed to have ultimately died from mercury poisoning rather than syphilis. This may have been Schubert's fate.

But in happier days, during the early 1820s, Schubert enjoyed the company of a close knit group of friends in Vienna who spent evenings together playing and listening to music, often his own. These soirees were later termed "Schubertiaden." Friends nicknamed Schubert, who was somewhat short in height, as "schwammer" or "little mushroom."

Unfortunately, in the aftermath of the French Revolution and the political disarray after the Napoleonic Wars, the Austrian police were suspicious of groups meeting like this and the bunch were arrested. Only one was really punished, while Schubert and the others were just reprimanded.

Schubert's only public concert came during the 1820s, and its success allowing him to purchase a piano. But the ravages of syphilis (or mercury) finally tore him down and he died in 1828 at the young age of 31. At his request, he was buried next to Beethoven, his contemporary. He may not have had much interaction with Beethoven, but he had been a torchbearer at his funeral procession just a year earlier in 1827. Ironically, the bodies of Schubert and Beethoven were both exhumed in 1863 for scientific studies.

Quotes by Schubert:

- A man endures misfortune without complaint.

- Happy is a man who finds a true friend, and far happier is he who finds that true friend in his wife.

- The world resembles a stage on which every man is playing a part.

- I try to decorate my imagination as much as I can.

- Easy mind, light heart. A mind that is too easy hides a heart that is too heavy.

- Approval or blame will follow in the world to come.

- Secretly, in my heart of hearts, I still hope to be able to make something of myself, but who can do anything after Beethoven?

Chapter 31. Alexandre Dumas and Auguste Macquet

Alexandre Dumas, a 19th century French writer, had a prodigious ability to churn out novels and plays. He read a great deal and was not averse to borrowing ideas and themes from other periods and sources and then transforming them into major works of thrilling adventure that have enthralled French and world-wide readers. His books have been translated into many languages and made into many movies.

During this great output Dumas was ably assisted by a collaborator, Auguste Macquet, a writer in his own right. While there were other editorial assistants, it was Macquet who was the primary contributor.

Dumas, who was born in 1802, was 11 years older than Macquet (born in 1813).

The two met in 1838 when Dumas was already famous. Initially, Dumas wrote plays that were quite successful. Later, he turned to novels. Given a play, *Soir de Carneval* by Macquet, Dumas rewrote it and produced the play under the new name of *Bathilde*. This play was also successful, and led to a fruitful collaboration of writing historical novels. Overall, Macquet collaborated with Dumas on 18 novels including *The Three Musketeers, The Count of Monte Cristo, Twenty Years Later, and The Queen's Necklace.*

Generally, Macquet would assist in outlining the plot and characters with Dumas adding dialogue and details and producing the final version. The novels were mostly serialized as newspapers of the day wanted serial novels. Macquet's name, however, didn't appear on any title pages, presumably because Dumas had a marquee name that would help sell newspapers. Macquet, apparently, didn't object to this arrangement as he received handsome fees in return. Some criticism was leveled at the Dumas-Maquet "novel factory" but the collaboration created a series of popular works.

Alexandre Dumas, Père

But circumstances changed later on and Macquet felt he wasn't being treated well enough. He finally sued for recognition of his co-authorship in the novels written in collaboration with Dumas. An 1858 judgment gave him 25 per cent of authors' rights for 18 co-written novels but denied him any proprietary rights. Dumas, of course, was displeased and accused his erstwhile collaborator of filching from his just income. Eventually they reconciled — to some extent.

Auguste Macquet

Macquet died, relatively well off, in 1888. Dumas, who had risen from genteel poverty to a position of fame, passed away in more inelegant circumstances, supported to some extent by his illegitimate son of the same name who had also become a successful author. Dumas also had a considerable appetite for women. Besides being married he had several mistresses and fathered several illegitimate children. The father is known as Alexandre Dumas, Pere and the son as Alexandre Dumas, fils.

While Dumas made a good deal of money, he also spent a lot in a reckless fashion and accumulated debts. He was overly generous to mistresses and acquaintances. In 1851, King Louis-Philippe (formerly the Duke of Orleans for whom he had worked as a scribe after coming to Paris) was overthrown. To elude his creditors, and the unsettling political situation, Dumas fled to Brussels in Belgium. For a number of years he also traveled through Europe and North Africa while turning out travel books. In 1853 he came back to Paris and started a newspaper *Le Mousquetaire*, covering art and literature as well as his *Mémoires* (a type of essay). This publication lasted until 1857. Undaunted, he founded a weekly paper, *Monte-Cristo*, which perished after about three years.

Dumas was so immersed in multiple writing ventures that he even used different colored pages for what he was writing. Yellow was for plays and blue for novels. He often left punctuation, not his strong suit, for secretaries to insert.

In 1858 he went to Russia, where his books were quite popular. French was the second language in the Russian court and aristocratic circles. For several years afterwards he was involved in the Italian unification. Finally, he returned to Paris and kept writing. His books were still popular but he, himself, was less of a celebrity during his latter days.

His mixed-race background was often a problem (his father had some Afro-Caribbean blood lines), but Dumas was equal to the situation. He responded to one man who insulted him: "My father was a mulatto, my grandfather was a Negro, and my great-grandfather was a monkey. You see, sir, my family starts where yours ends."

When Dumas died in 1870, at the age of 68, the writer George Sand (actually a woman, Lucile Dudevant, who used a man's name) commented: "He was the genius of life; he has not felt death."

In 2002 Dumas' body was exhumed from where it was buried and reburied in a lavish funeral ceremony next to other French luminaries in the mausoleum at the Pantheon of Paris. His new coffin was flanked by four guards in the costumes of the renowned musketeers, Athos, Aramis, Porthos, and D'Artagnan, made famous in his novel, *The Three Musketeers*. The then president of France, Jacques Chirac, said in the televised ceremony that the shame of racism that had been used against Dumas had been removed.

***

Among Dumas' quotes:

- All generalizations are dangerous, even this one.

- Rogues are preferable to imbeciles because they sometimes take a rest.

- Business! It's quite simple. It's other people's money.

Chapter 32. Felix Mendelssohn and Ignaz Moscheles

Felix Mendelssohn, a child prodigy, was the pupil and Ignaz Moscheles, a well-known composer in his own right, was the teacher.

But Moscheles quickly recognized when he met the young Mendelssohn in 1824 that his student was special. He commented: "Felix, a boy of 15, is a phenomenon. What are all prodigies compared to him? He is already a mature artist."

After giving his initial "lesson," Moscheles wrote: "This afternoon I gave Felix Mendelssohn his first lesson without losing sight for a moment of the fact that I was sitting next to a master and not a pupil."

Felix Mendelssohn

Mendelssohn's musical talents were quickly recognized, with his mother giving him piano lessons at the age of six. Records indicated he participated in his first joint concert at the age of nine, and wrote his first symphony for a full orchestra at the age of 15.

What began as a student-teacher relationship evolved into a lifetime of friendship that extended beyond Mendelssohn's premature death in 1847 at the age of 38. Both men of music were born in the German states, Moscheles in 1794 and Mendelssohn in 1807.

Mendelssohn had an unusual childhood in a cultured and well-to-do family. He was born into the Jewish faith, but his father gave up Judaism — possibly to save his children from the prevalent anti-Semitism of the period. Mendelssohn wasn't circumcised as was (and is) the custom for Jewish boys. He was raised as a Christian, finally being baptized into the Lutheran denomination in 1816, a development that still didn't stop him from facing anti-Semitism as an adult. The family took an appendage to its name, now being Mendelssohn-Bartholdy. But his original name is how he was basically known then and certainly in history.

Ignaz Moscheles

Moscheles, also born into the Jewish faith and also musically talented, still had a less dramatic upbringing. He was already well established, both as a composer and teacher, when he met Mendelssohn.

In 1826, when he was just 17, he wrote the famous overture to Shakespeare's *A Midsummer Night's Dream.*

Moscheles, who had excellent connections from appearances in London, set up Mendelssohn to conduct at the Royal Harmonic Society in the English capital in 1829. His appearance was a huge success and he soon was giving comparable performances at other European capitals and cities. The duo sometimes performed together. A favorite work was Bach's concert for multiple keyboard instruments.

Mendelssohn, who became fluent in English, went often to England, where he was quite popular. He played for Queen Victoria and her husband/consort, Prince Albert, with the royal couple sometimes singing duets to the accompaniment of his music.

Mendelssohn had already received acclaim in some quarters for helping with others to revive Bach's music. Bach had died in 1750. He arranged and conducted a performance in Berlin of Bach's *Saint Matthew Passion.* In bringing sacred music back into attention, Mendelssohn displayed his tendency to a conservative approach during a period when romanticism was in vogue. He wasn't very much in tune with such other more "romantic" contemporaries as Franz Liszt and Hector Berlioz. Moscheler had the same taste in music, another reason the two bonded so well.

After the Berlin performance Mendelssohn, cognizant of the irony, wrote: "To think that it took an actor and a Jew's son to revive the greatest Christian music for the world."

Mendelssohn went on to write symphonies such as the Italian and Scottish symphonies, oratorios, overtures, piano and chamber music. In 1843 he composed the "Wedding March," which is one of the most recognizable and utilized musical pieces ever created.

When Mendelssohn established a Conservatory in Leipzig in 1843, he brought in Moscheles as the head of the department for playing and composition. Under the arrangement Moscheles was given ample time to write and conduct his own music. The Conservatory helped make Leipzig the musical capital of the soon-to-emerge German state. In effect, the Conservatory as well as his musical creations became a legacy to Mendelssohn and the musical traditions he favored.

Moscheles was determined to maintain the Conservatory along the musical lines that both he and Mendelssohn espoused, and he spent the rest of his life doing so. He also defended his friend and former pupil from attacks by other composers, most notably the composer Richard Wagner — considered anti-Semitic — who penned a nasty treatise, *Jewry In Music*, attacking Mendelssohn and other Jewish composers of the period.

Considerable correspondence between the pair is held at the University of Leeds in England. Moscheles described his friend's last days in his diary. Mendelssohn, subject to fits of temper and stress from overwork, finally succumbed in 1847 at the early age of 38. One report, a bit fanciful, has it that Mendelssohn was lying on his deathbed, surrounded by a doctor, Moscheles, and other family members and friends when a marching band passed by his house. As a servant had left the front door open, the music could be clearly heard. Mendelssohn supposedly rose suddenly in bed as if ready to conduct but then sank back and died.

In a letter, not far from his final days, Mendelssohn wrote about death as a place "where it is to be hoped there is still music, but no more sorrow and partings."

Moscheles, who lived on to die in 1870 at the age of 76, was one of the pallbearers at Mendelssohn's funeral.

Quotes from Mendelssohn:

- The essence of the beautiful is unity in variety.

- Though everything else may appear shallow and repulsive, even the smallest task in music is so absorbing, and carries us so far away from town, country, earth, and all worldly things, that it is truly a blessed gift of God.

- If you really feel for what is beautiful, if it truly gladdens you, then your mind becomes enlarged rather than narrowed.

- People often complain that music is too ambiguous, that what they should think when they hear it is so unclear, where as everyone understands words. With me, it is exactly the opposite, and not only with regard to an entire speech but also with individual words.

Chapter 33. Susan Anthony and Elizabeth Stanton

Susan Anthony and Elizabeth Stanton were pioneers in the first feminist movement in the United States. Close in age — Anthony was born in 1820 and Stanton in 1815 — they believed that American social progress would be limited until women were granted equal rights to men. Their joint efforts finally led to the 19th amendment to the Constitution that gave women the right to vote.

Susan Anthony

The pair also fought for women to have equal pay for the same work as men, to keep their children in case of divorce, and the right to control their own property and have a measure of financial independence. While the two didn't always agree — Stanton was considered more radical — they were lifelong friends. Their talents also blended with Stanton saying: "I am the better writer, she the better critic."

They both kept journals, and were prolific letter writers. As an indication of their extensive travels, an entry in Anthony's diary during 1871 cited over 170 lectures and some 13,000 miles of travel. Anthony's efforts even included wearing the famed "bloomer" of the period — loose trousers that came to the knees under a full skirt — as a sartorial symbol of protest against the more restrictive garments worn by women. She also supported the anti-slavery movement from 1856 to the outbreak of the Civil War.

Both women participated in the "Daughters of Temperance," a movement to lessen the substantial amount of male drunkenness that impacted wives and families. They met in 1851 at a Daughter of Temperance meeting, which called for suffrage for women, and quickly bonded. Earlier, in 1848, Stanton had been responsible for the "Declaration of Sentiments" which came out as part of an initial convention about women's rights held at Seneca Falls, N.Y. In a parallel to the Declaration of Independence, the document declared: "We hold these truths to be self-evident: that all men and women are created equal...." The document was signed by 68 women and 32 men.

The pair helped to publish *The Revolution*, a New York-based liberal weekly editorializing for equal pay for women and other causes. The masthead read: "Men Their Rights and Nothing More — Women Their Rights and Nothing Less." Anthony also helped organize the "New York Working Women's Association."

A major protest arose in 1872 when Anthony demanded that women be given the same civil and political rights as Black males had received in the 14th and 15th amendments. She led a group of women to the election booths in Rochester, New York, as a test of the right of women to vote. She was arrested but was out soon and went on a lecture tour around the country. In March 1873, she again tried to vote in municipal elections, and this time she was convicted of violating the election laws. She was fined $100 but without any imprisonment, as the judge didn't want to create more publicity over the case. However, she refused to pay the fine, arguing that the laws were unconstitutional and that the basic rights of Americans were for "we, the people, not we, the white male citizens." She vowed: "I shall never pay a dollar of your unjust penalty." And she never did. No action was ever taken against her by the government to collect this sum.

Anthony never married, though Stanton did and had several children, the last when she was 43. At the 1860 women's rights convention, there was considerable opposition to their changing the divorce laws to help women. One man, who did oppose slavery, argued: "You are not married. You have no business to be discussing marriage."

Seldom at a loss for words, Anthony parried: "Well, you are not a slave. Suppose you quit lecturing on slavery."

The Civil War held up the women's rights movement. Stanton thought the role of Northern women in the war effort would help the cause but Anthony didn't agree; much later, in her biography, she admitted that Anthony had been right.

While their approaches to problems and issues didn't always mesh, their friendship endured. Stanton once wrote: "Our friendship is of too long standing and has too deep roots to be easily shattered. Nothing that Susan could say or could break my friendship with her; and I know nothing could uproot her affection for me."

After the war, Anthony and Stanton tried to have the new 14th amendment enlarged to cover the rights of women. Anthony even moved to Washington D.C. to lobby for the cause but without much success; but some states, on their own, did pass legislation extending women's rights. One of her parting comments in a speech as president of the National American Woman Suffrage Association in the nation's capital was "Failure is impossible." These words bring to mind the more famous latter-day space exploration axiom: "Failure is not an option."

Elizabeth Stanton

When she was already 80, in 1895, Stanton wrote, against Anthony's advice, *The Woman's Bible*, which discussed Biblical passages that related to women. Subsequent criticism even labeled Stanton as a heretic. Stanton dedicated her 1898 autobiography, *Eighty*

Years & More, to Anthony: "To Susan B. Anthony, my steadfast friend for half a century."

After Stanton died, Anthony declared: "I am too crushed to say much, but if she had outlived me she would have found fine words with which to express our friendship. I can't say it in words. She always said she wished to outlive me that she might pay her tribute to me to the world, for she knew I couldn't pay my tribute to her."

After long and productive lives that didn't extend to seeing the full success of their major platform, Stanton died in 1902 and Anthony in 1906. As the 20th century progressed, Anthony's reputation surpassed that of Stanton as the founder of the women's rights movement. But they were both giants in this struggle. Neither lived to see the 19th amendment (sometimes referred to as the Susan B. Anthony amendment) give women the right to vote in 1920. The U.S. issued a silver dollar bearing her image in 1979 marking the first coin to depict a woman in American history.

***

Among Anthony's quotes:

- It was we, the people, not we, the white male citizens, but we, the whole people who formed the Union. Men, their rights, and nothing more; women, their rights, and nothing less.

- The older I get, the greater power I seem to have to help the world. I am like a snowball — the further I am rolled, the more I gain.

- No man is good enough to govern any woman without her consent.

And from Stanton:

- Truth is the only safeguard to stand on.

- Self-development is a higher duty than self-sacrifice.

- That only a few, under any circumstances, protest against the injustice of long-established laws and customs, does not disprove the fact of the oppressions, while the satisfaction of the many, if real only proves their apathy and deeper degradation.

Chapter 34. Nathaniel Hawthorne and Herman Melville

A chance meeting of two American writers at a picnic in 1850 led to a friendship that in turn helped lead to creation of a literary masterpiece.

The two writers were Nathaniel Hawthorne and Herman Melville. Both are considered major American writers now, though that wasn't true of Melville in his lifetime. Hawthorne, 46 at this point, was 15 years older than Melville. Hawthorne was born in 1804 and Melville in 1819. The two conversed at a picnic at Stockbridge, Massachusetts while taking shelter during a rain storm and got on well together. Both had already been published, but Hawthorne was much more of a literary figure. At one point Melville declared to Hawthorne that "All fame is patronage."

Hawthorne wrote to a friend about the meeting: "I liked Melville so much that I have asked him to spend a few days with me."

This would become the first of a series of visits, enhanced by a stream of correspondence. Getting together to discuss their literary ideas and projects was easy as the two New Englanders lived nearby in Massachusetts in the Berkshire Hills area.

Melville wrote to Hawthorne at one point: "Since you have been here I have been building some shanties of houses (connected with the old one), and likewise some shanties of chapters and essays. I have been ploughing and sowing and raising and printing and praying."

Melville was well into finishing *Moby Dick*, whose original title was *The Whale*. He had promised it to his London publisher (some books at this time were first published in London and then in the U.S.) by autumn 1850. Hawthorne had already had his novel, *The Scarlet Letter*, published in 1850 to considerable acclaim.

Herman Melville

Melville, in his mid-twenties, had already made a name for himself with his book *Typee*, about his adventures in the South Seas. This book was followed up by similar exotic experiences recounted in *Oomoo* and *White Jacket*. Even before they met Hawthorne had praised *Typee* in a review. Sometime around their meeting, Melville had positively reviewed *Mosses From an Old Manse*, a work by Hawthorne.

Greatly influenced by the senior writer, and by the allegorical elements of *The Scarlet Letter*, Melville went back to work on his book and enriched it with far deeper allegorical meaning than the initial adventure-oriented story. Inspired by Hawthorne, Melville apparently wrote with a kind of frenzy (no doubt conscious of his deadline with his English publisher) and once shouted, "Give me Vesuvius' crater for an inkstand!"

Finally, the retitled *Moby Dick* came out, first in England in October 1851 and then a year later in the United States. It didn't do that well in either country. Less than 3,000 copies of the initial printing were sold in the U.S. and Melville didn't earn much money. Melville, in an act of gratitude, dedicated *Moby Dick* to Hawthorne. He wrote: "In token of my admiration for his genius, this book is inscribed to Nathaniel Hawthorne."

Melville, in fact, was in need of more financial solvency. Hawthorne attempted to line up a paying position for him with a local Customs Office through his friendship with President Franklin Pierce; but nothing materialized and the failure may have rankled with both of them. Reports of the time had less than complimentary mentions of Melville's mental health during this period.

In 1852 Melville suggested that Hawthorne utilize a true story of a New England woman who had taken in and then married a shipwrecked sailor. The tentative title was *The Story of Agatha*. Not too enthusiastically, Hawthorne took a stab at the story but then turned it back to Melville to use. Melville agreed to work on the story himself, but it isn't known if he ever did. By this time, Hawthorne had already had another major work published, *The House of the Seven Gables*.

Their active friendship tapered off and lasted a little more than two years. Melville only saw Hawthorne again once, when he stopped off in Liverpool on a trip to Europe in 1856. Hawthorne, through the auspices of President Pierce, was installed at this time in the English city as the American consul. They spent a couple of days together, presumably catching up on their lives and literary careers.

Hawthorne wrote in his journal: "Herman Melville came to see me at the consulate, looking much as he used to do (a little paler, and perhaps a little sadder) in a rough outside coat, and with his characteristic gravity and reserve of humor. We soon found ourselves on pretty much our former terms of sociability and confidence. Melville has not been well of late, and no doubt has suffered from too constant a literary occupation, pursued without too much success...."

Nathaniel Hawthorne

The two never corresponded again, but Melville did continue to read and comment on Hawthorne's works. In his later years Melville concentrated more on writing poetry. A character in Melville's 1876 epic poem, *Clarel: A Pilgrimage To The Holy Land*, is believed to be partly based on Hawthorne. A part of his 1891 poem, *Timoleon*, may also spring from Melville's thoughts about his companion of earlier years. *Billy Budd*, a tragic story of a seaman and one of Melville's greatest works, was written several years before his death.

Hawthorne died in 1864, Melville in 1891. Both literary giants, especially in American literature, live on through their books.

***

Among Hawthorne's quotes:

- What other dungeon is so dark as one's own heart! What jailor so inexorable as one's self?

- No man, for any considerable period, can wear one face to himself and another to the multitude, without finally getting bewildered as to which may be true.

And from Melville:

- Life's a voyage that's homeward bound.

- A man thinks that by mouthing hard words he understands hard things.

- Of all the preposterous assumptions of humanity over humanity, nothing exceeds most of the criticisms made on the habits of the poor by the well-housed, well-warmed, and well-fed.

CHAPTER 35. PRESIDENT FRANKLIN PIERCE AND NATHANIEL
HAWTHORNE

Franklin Pierce and Nathaniel Hawthorne were born in the same year, 1804. School classmates at Bowdoin College in Maine, and fellow New Englanders, they visited and corresponded with each other over the years in a lifelong friendship.

However, they disagreed on opposition to slavery and the anti-abolitionist cause. Hawthorne was against slavery; and while Pierce didn't favor slavery he was against the abolitionists and what he considered their dangerously divisive tactics. But their different policy on this major issue of the day didn't stop Hawthorne, by then a famous novelist (*The Scarlet Letter* and *House of the Seven Gables* had already been published) from writing a campaign biography of Pierce when he was nominated, rather unexpectedly, to run as the presidential nominee of the Democratic Party in 1852. Pierce, a dark horse, was surprised at his nomination; and his wife, Jane, was said to have fainted.

Hawthorne's fairly brief biography helped Pierce win the election handily, defeating General Winfield Scott from the Whig Party (which was the last time this party, fading from the political scene, ran a candidate). Ironically, General Scott had been Pierce's commanding officer in the Mexican-American War when Pierce had been a Brigadier General. Pierce, the 14th president at the age of 48, became the youngest man ever to attain the office until Ulysses S. Grant in 1868 at the age of 46. (Both were eclipsed in the next century by John F. Kennedy at the age of 42.) He has been the only president thus far from the state of New Hampshire.

Franklin Pierce

Hawthorne's campaign biography, *The Life of Franklin Pierce*, was complimentary. It described Pierce as a statesman and soldier who believed slavery should be allowed to vanish in due course rather than be arbitrarily dissolved. Pierce was called "a man of peaceful pursuits." No mention was made of Pierce's much-rumored bouts with alcohol.

Not everyone agreed with Hawthorne's positive descriptions. Famed newspaper editor Horace Mann, who was instrumental in creating the Republican Party, quipped: "If he makes out Pierce to be a great man or a brave man, it will be the greatest work of fiction he ever wrote."

Hawthorne was rewarded in 1853 — the spoils system was very much in vogue — by President Pierce naming him as the U.S. consul in Liverpool, England. This was considered a well-paying foreign service position and second only to the American Embassy in London. The end of Pierce's administration brought the finish to Hawthorne's post, and he went on to tour Europe, even giving up his clean-shaven appearance to grow a mustache in Italy.

Pierce's private life had a notable sadness, as none of his three children survived from childhood and none saw him become president. In a horrible accident near Andover, Massachusetts, en route to his inauguration in Washington D.C. his remaining son, Benjamin, was crushed to death at the age of 11. He and Jane weren't badly hurt; but it affected their lives greatly. Jane, who didn't care for life in the capital, was depressed and was subsequently characterized as "the shadow in the White House."

Pierce, who had a very troubled four years in office (some claimed he was the worst president the country ever had), became the first president in American political history to be denied renomination by his own party. James Buchanan, considered less controversial, was nominated and won the 1856 presidential election. Pierce was asked by some friends to take another stab at the presidency in 1860 and as late as 1864, but he declined each time.

Pierce was loathed by many in the North and called a "doughface" — a Northerner with Southern sympathies. In his inaugural address, Pierce affirmed the constitutionality of slavery and the Fugitive Slave Law (which sought to return escaping slaves to their owners). Two key issues in his administration both went against Pierce who tried to preserve calm and business prosperity against all the forces leading the nation to the Civil War. The Missouri Compromise was overturned by the 1854 Kansas–Nebraska Act which brought about fierce debate about the expansion of slavery in the west. And then the Ostend Manifesto, which called for the U.S. to buy Cuba from Spain — or take the island by force if the offer was refused — was leaked. Observers in the North thought this was a move to add territory serving Southern interests.

During the Civil War, Pierce's reputation was further damaged when his correspondence with Jefferson Davis, the president of the Confederacy, was discovered. Davis had been Secretary of War during Pierce's administration, after having campaigned for him in the South in the 1852 presidential election. The two men, a former president of the U.S. and the future president of the Confederacy, became friends. They saw eye to eye on the key issues of the times, especially preserving peace between the North and South. Copies of their correspondence were leaked after the Battle of Vicksburg when Union soldiers captured Davis' plantation.

In a January 1860 letter Pierce wrote Davis: "Without discussing the question of right, or abstract power to secede, I have never believed that actual disruption of the Union can occur without bloodshed; and if, through the madness of Northern Abolitionists, that dire calamity must come, the fighting will not be along Mason and Dixon's lines merely. It will be within our own borders, in our own streets, between the two classes of citizens to whom I have referred."

Harriet Beecher Stowe of *Uncle Tom's Cabin* fame promptly called Pierce an "arch traitor."

Out of office, Pierce and his wife went on a trip to Europe and met again with Hawthorne in Rome where Hawthorne and his family had moved after his stint in Liverpool ended. Hawthorne was greatly worried about the health of his teenage daughter, Una, who had contracted malaria. Pierce consoled Hawthorne on walks around Rome while Una recovered — though her doctor said she wouldn't survive. Hawthorne wrote of this period: "Never having had any trouble before, I did not know what comfort there might be in the manly sympathy of a friend, but Pierce has undergone so great a sorrow of his own, and has so large and kindly a heart, and is so tender and strong that he really did us good, and I shall love him better for the recollection of those dark days."

Subsequently, Hawthorne returned to the U.S. in 1860 and came out with *The Marble Faun*, his first book in seven years. He admitted to friends that he had aged, describing himself as "wrinkled with time and troubles." He did go to meet Abraham Lincoln in the White House as well as other notables, writing about his perceptions in an essay, *Chiefly About War Matters* in 1862. Despite the objections of his publisher and friends, he dedicated his 1863 book, *Our Old Home* — collected memories of England — to Pierce. Many still felt that Pierce, as president, had been too much a friend of the South.

Though in failing health, Hawthorne still insisted on going on a trip with Pierce to the White Mountains in his native New Hampshire. Hawthorne died in his sleep in May 1864, with Pierce having the sad duty of sending a telegram to Hawthorne's wife.

Pierce proclaimed that Hawthorne was the greatest writer yet to come from the United States. Generously, he subsequently paid tuition for Hawthorne's son at Harvard.

Pierce survived for another five years, dying from cirrhosis of the liver in 1869. He maintained his opinions, which included opposing Lincoln's Emancipation Proclamation. He wrote of himself, "Some men are so constituted that they do not incline to bend before a storm." In his will, Pierce gave bequests to the children of Hawthorne.

Comments from Pierce:

- Frequently the more trifling the subject, the more animated and protracted the discussion.

- With the Union my best and dearest earthly hopes are entwined.

- A Republic without parties is a complete anomaly. The histories of all popular governments show how absurd is the idea of their attempting to exist without parties.

- The dangers of a concentration of all power in the general government of a confederacy so vast as ours are too obvious to be disregarded.

CHAPTER 36. FLORENCE NIGHTINGALE AND SIDNEY HERBERT

Florence Nightingale

Florence Nightingale met, probably by design, Sidney Herbert, a prominent English politician, on his honeymoon, in Rome. She was committed to helping the sick. He was interested in works of charity and hospital reform. Their mutual interests led to a lifetime friendship. It also led to vastly improved medical treatment of battle wounds and helped make nursing a respectable and eminently useful profession. Quite outspoken, Nightingale also supplied opinions and advice to Herbert in his political career.

Herbert, who became secretary of war in the English cabinet, reacted to the chilling reports about the treatment of casualties in the 1854–56 Crimean War by sending Nightingale — eager for the assignment — with 38 Nightingale-trained and privately-paid nurses to the Selimiye Barracks in Istanbul (where there is a Nightingale museum today). This was a controversial and highly significant move, it being the first time women nurses were used in wartime conditions.

Nightingale was born in 1820 with her first name coming from Florence, the city of her birth. Her parents were quite wealthy. They were also opposed to her choice of career, feeling the rightful role for women was as wives and mothers. Nightingale disagreed, making it clear she felt a calling for something else. She soon began training and working as a nurse at a London clinic. In 1853, assisted by Herbert's contacts and influence, she assumed the post of superintendent at the Institute for the Care of Sick Gentlewomen in London. Despite his disapproval, her father provided an annual income of about $65,000 that gave her financial independence. Though she had some suitors, she never married.

Sidney Herbert

At Scutari, Nightingale found conditions were worse than had been reported to London. Doctors and male orderlies were overworked. Vital medicines were in short supply or simply not available. Even linen for bandages was lacking. Hygiene was deplorable, with rats and fleas having a feast. Fatal infections were commonplace with many more soldiers dying from such diseases as typhoid, typhus, cholera, and dysentery than from battle wounds. Sewers were defective, with a cesspool under the barracks. Ventilation was poor. Processing of food for patients was inefficient and not terribly clean.

Contagious diseases were poorly understood and the germ theory had not yet changed medical care and prevention.

Official/military indifference to the welfare of the common soldiers, who were too often considered as cannon fodder, added to the plethora of problems. One British general opined that ambulances were for those who weren't brave and resolute. Preparations by the British army for care and treatment of the wounded was deplorable. In a new era of wartime reportage, searing details about this military/health fiasco came to the attention of an increasingly disturbed Parliament as well as an aroused public. Accountability for the cause of the military health problems, as well as means to improve care, became a growing issue — with Nightingale in the forefront of the debates.

Nightingale fought doctors and ranking officers, seeking improvements as well as an extension of the range of her authority, which was limited. She also convinced London to set up and send a Sanitary Commission to the Crimea, which led to considerable improvement and a lowering of the death rate. She also used some of her own money to buy medical supplies. As a result of her efforts, she received a good deal of fame, with the soldiers hailing her as a saint and angel. The reaction of the Army hierarchy might have been different, but she had Herbert on her side. Her nickname as "The Lady With A Lamp" emanated from a phrase in a London newspaper report, which later got more circulation in Longfellow's 1857 poem, *Santa Filomena*. The iconic image, which greatly helped boost the public's respect for the nursing field, showed Nightingale making her nighttime rounds at the wards in Scutari. Actually, a candle inside a folded paper shade served as her illumination.

After the war's end, Nightingale returned to England as a heroine. She even was received by Queen Victoria and her husband/consort, Prince Albert, who formed a royal commission to investigate wartime medical conditions. This was a study that wasn't particularly favored by some in the medical field, especially those who had mismanaged things at Scutari. She worked hard with commission members including Herbert and collected useful findings and statistical evidence. Statistics, Nightingale wrote, "is the most important science in the world."

Unfortunately, Herbert's health wore down. However, Nightingale tended to dismiss his declining health and pushed him to keep working when doctors advised him to take it easy. She was dismayed when her friend and collaborator of many years died of kidney disease at the relatively early age of 51.

Though her health was also shaken by the Crimean years, Nightingale was able to continue her life's work. She lobbied to reduce deaths in the army even during peacetime by improving sanitary conditions and care at hospitals and to standardize the reporting of deaths at hospitals. A Nightingale Fund for the training of nurses was established, and received quite a few generous donations. Herbert, whom she had nicknamed "The Cid" (a reference to the Spanish hero who conquered the Moors in Spain), had served as honorary secretary of the fund. She also created the Nightingale Training School in 1860, which is now part of King's College in London.

In 1859 her *Notes On Nursing* came out, becoming the first book of its kind to be published. The material became part of the curriculum at the school. She wrote: "Every day sanitary knowledge, or the knowledge of nursing, or in other words, of how to put the constitution in such a state as that it will have no disease, or that it can recover from disease, takes a higher place. It is recognized as the knowledge which every one ought to have — distinct from medical knowledge, which only a professor can have."

More caustically, she also wrote: "No man, not even a doctor, ever gives any other definition of what a nurse should be than this — 'devoted and obedient.' This definition would do just as well for a porter. It might even do for a horse."

Despite the impact of her own writings, Nightingale opined: "I think one's feelings waste themselves in words; they ought all to be distilled into actions which bring results."

Nightingale is also considered somewhat of a pioneer in medical tourism, as she wrote in her letters about spas in the Ottoman Empire, which extended into Southern Europe, that people could visit. With her usual diligence she covered facilities and diets, among other aspects.

Famed throughout the world, Nightingale was contacted by the Union government during the Civil War on how to better organize field medical units. Not unexpectedly, matching her Crimean experience, her advice met with some official resistance but improvements were made to Union campsites. In the 1870s Nightingale taught Linda Richards, and enabled her to return to the United States as "America's First Trained Nurse."

After a long and fruitful life, Nightingale died in her sleep in 1910 at the age of 90. She had written of herself: "I have lived a more public life than ever queen or actress did."

The feelings of British soldiers is captured in this stanza from a popular Crimean War ballad:

> On a dark and lonely night on Crimea's dread shores
> There'd been bloodshed and strife on the morning before;
> The dead and the dying lay bleeding around,

Some crying for help — there was none to be found
Now God in His mercy He pitied their cries,
And the soldiers so cheerful in the morning do rise

Refrain:

So forward my lads, may your hearts never fail
You are cheered by the presence of a sweet Nightingale.

CHAPTER 37. CHARLES BAUDELAIRE AND EDOUARD MANET

It isn't often that a poet can shock a nation. But Charles Baudelaire did just that with his prose poem, *The Flowers of Evil*, that colorfully and incisively depicted the rigors and realities of a much changing Paris in the 1850s as the city struggled with the impact of industrialization. Sex and death, as well as corruption, were broad themes. Baudelaire even coined the term "modisme" to characterize the epochal changes he saw while frequenting taverns and quite a few prostitutes. His sorties led to a highly influential literary work, many debts, and syphilis.

This was a period when Paris was experiencing seminal changes in its layout and architecture, most of it by the design of Baron Georges-Eugène Haussmann. New buildings came up to lodge the growing middle class, with open boulevards replacing narrow streets and alleys. New bridges were built, a new sewer system installed, and streets were better illuminated. Baudelaire could hail the new while mourning the past, and questioning the balance.

This 1857 collection of 100 prose-poems, which initiated a new form of poetic expression, also brought condemnation from the authorities. Only around 1300 copies of the work were printed. Baudelaire was accused of being a drug addict, dissolute, depraved, blasphemous, and a few other endearments. Perhaps based on a line from one poem — "It is the devil that pulls the strings that moves us" — he was also accused of Satanism. Baudelaire was fined 100 francs, a sum later reduced to 50 francs. He was also forced to take out six of the more disturbing poems, which were put back in a subsequent edition. This 1861 edition has an opening poem that castigated readers for their original hypocrisy. It only took around 100 years for this verdict to be reversed by governmental edict in 1949 with the six suppressed poems restored to France's literary life.

Charles Baudelaire

Paul Poulet-Malassis — who was born in 1825 — was actually imprisoned for printing Baudelaire's book on the grounds of offending public morals. Malassis, a lifelong friend of Baudelaire, was more concerned with literary than financial values and tended to support writers he liked. He was willing to help Baudelaire, who generally was short of money. Baudelaire's book was beautifully bound, on fine paper, but suffered from a lack of advertising and exposure. At the prompting of Baudelaire, Poulet-Malassis opened an expensively decorated bookstore in the center of Paris that became more of a lounge for writers, including Baudelaire, than a commercial outlet. The store soon failed, and Malassis went bankrupt. He fled to Brussels, Belgium, to escape creditors, and continued to publish, with some works he printed considered pornographic. He was sentenced in absentia for a year's imprisonment for conspiring to send obscene material into France.

Malassis and Baudelaire spent a great deal of time together in the Belgian capital, where Baudelaire had gone to deliver a series of lectures. Loyal to Baudelaire to the end, Malassis died in 1878.

Baudelaire, who was born in 1821 to a well-to-do family, was unapologetic about any of his jabbings at society. He wrote about marriage: "Unable to suppress love, the Church wanted at least to disinfect it, and created marriage." On the artist, he opined: "The more a man cultivates the arts, the less randy he becomes. Only the brute is good at coupling, and copulation is the lyricism of the masses. To copulate is to enter into another — and the artist never emerges from himself."

Though he received a law degree in 1839, Baudelaire was more interested in non-legal subjects and work. He received a sizeable inheritance at the age of 21, which he managed to squander through spending lavishly on clothing and like pursuits, which gave him the reputation of being a dandy as well as impecunious. Baudelaire, though, had a somewhat different view of dandyism, seeing it more as a dignified elevation of one's personality. He also drank, and smoked opium. Consistently through his life, and to the consternation of his mother, he was short of money. Finally, his mother had a legal arrangement constructed which effectively made him a legal minor and cut him off from family assets. He was given a monthly allowance, which still didn't prevent him from asking his mother for money and scrounging off friends.

Baudelaire, living large and self-destructively in the Latin Quarter, continued the same errant lifestyle. As his opus became a byword for immorality, Baudelaire wrote to his mother: "You know that I have always considered that literature, and the arts, pursue an aim independent of morality. Beauty of conception and style is enough for me."

Baudelaire busied himself with writing more poems, essays, articles, art and music reviews, etc. His *Le Spleen de* Paris, prose poems realistically describing the changing face and contemporary character of the French capital, continued his dissent from more traditional poetry. The collection was published posthumously in 1869. Baudelaire had already assessed his own work previously, writing: "These are the flowers of evil again, but with more freedom, much more detail, and much more mockery."

Having learned English as a child, he became fascinated with the macabre works of Edgar Allan Poe, who he felt was a kindred spirit. His much admired translations of Poe's stories into French, starting around 1846 and lasting until 1865, received considerable praise.

Baulelaire was also an early champion of the works of painter Eugene Delacroix and composer Richard Wagner. He felt both were ahead of the times in their bold works suggesting pre-Impressionism and operatic romanticism. Of Delacroix he wrote: "Delacroix was passionately in love with passion, but coldly determined to express passion as clearly as possible."

He also became a close friend with Edouard Manet, another painter who had yet to achieve much fame but who was finally credited with an innovative transition from the realistic to Impressionist school of painting. Manet, like Baudelaire, was considered somewhat of a dandy as he was often seen with a cane, silk top hat, and leather gloves.

Baudelaire would often accompany Manet — born in 1832 and 11 years younger — on his outings through Parisian parks and gardens to sketch. He was also the subject of a painting by Manet that featured the writer, Emile Zola. Manet, like some other friends, also lent Baudelaire money. When Baudelaire went to Brussels to deliver a series of lectures (which failed to produce more income), Manet attended to his affairs in Paris. In addition, at Baudelaire's request, Manet sought to find him a literary agent in Paris.

Baudelaire, not one to shrink from criticism, encouraged Manet to withstand criticism much as he had. He opined: "Manet has great talent, a talent which will stand the test of time. But he has a weak character. He seems to be crushed and stunned by shock."

Manet, however, survived quite nicely. His painting, *Le Dejeuner sur l'Herbe* (The Luncheon On The Grass), showing a nude woman relaxing with a pair of fully-dressed males in a picnic setting, created a scandalous stir in an 1863 exhibit of paintings. The prestigious Salon, whose jury selected paintings for an annual exhibit in Paris, had already rejected this painting from its annual showing of new works. Many people considered Manet's innovative and daring painting an affront to public morality, while others claimed it struck a blow for the freedom of artists. Nudes traditionally were displayed in a formal setting and by themselves, for the most part. The nude in this painting seemed very natural, staring with a bemused glance at viewers as if a bit surprised by their attention. Another famous painting of a nude, *Olympia*, also was a departure from the ways nudes had been represented in paintings.

Edouard Manet

Overall, Manet's paintings sought the natural beauty of everyday things, and many people felt they could be subjects of Baudelaire's poems — or vice versa. The two artists were believed to have considerable influence on the other.

Meanwhile, syphilis caught up to Baudelaire. He had a stroke in 1866, and he died in 1867 at the age of 51 after spending his final days in a semi-paralyzed state. Manet and his wife were occasional visitors, with Mrs. Manet playing passages from Wagner on the piano.

Many of Baudelaire's works were published posthumously. His mother, who survived him by four years, paid his debts. She also noted, with some satisfaction: "I see that my son, for all his faults, has his place in literature."

Manet also fell a victim to syphilis, dying shortly after one of his gangrenous legs was amputated, in 1883, at the age of 51.

***

Some quotes from Baudelaire:

- I consider it useless and tedious to represent what exists because nothing that exists satisfies me. Nature is ugly, and I prefer the monsters of my fancy to what is positively trivial.

- It is by universal misunderstanding that all agree. For if, by ill luck, people understood each other, they would never agree.

- Curiosity has to be considered the starting point of genius.

And from Manet:

- There is only one true thing: instantly paint what you see. When you've got it, you've got it. When you haven't, you begin again. All the rest is humbug.

- There are no lines in nature, only areas of color, one against another.

- No one can be a painter unless he cares for painting above all else.

- It's not enough to know your craft. You have to have feeling. Science is all very well, but for us imagination is worth far more.

- Color is a matter of taste and of sensitivity.

Chapter 38. David Henry Thoreau and Ralph Waldo Emerson

Encouraged and enabled by Ralph Waldo Emerson, his friend and mentor, David Henry Thoreau become one of the seminal writers of the 19th century and an inspiration for other writers and leaders including Mahatma Gandhi and Martin Luther King. Much of his work provided underpinnings as well for ecology and environmental issues in later years. Thoreau was also one of the first American supporters of Darwin's controversial theories on evolution that were much disputed in those days (and still are in some quarters).

David Henry Thoreau

Emerson's fame as a writer and lecturer grew, starting with his 1836 work, *Nature*. His many lecture series were much attended. Among the many subjects he discussed: *Philosophy of History, Human Culture, Conduct of Life, Topics of Modern Times*, and *Natural History of the Intellect*. The *Concord Hymn*, about this famous battle in the American Revolution, is one of his most noted poems. Many of his lectures, essays, and prose works were published. Emerson is acknowledged as one of the strongest influences in the development of American intellectual culture.

Thoreau, most famous for his book, *On Waldon Pond*, and essay on *Civil Disobedience*, was born in 1817 in Concord, Massachusetts. At Harvard University he met Emerson, who was 14 years his senior. Emerson took an interest in Thoreau and encouraged him to submit essays and poems to a new quarterly periodical,

Dial, which he was involved with. Emerson, who was born in 1803, was a champion of the U.S. establishing literary and cultural independence from Europe. He urged American writers to develop more of a distinctly American flavor to their works.

Ralph Waldo Emerson

Emerson also asked Thoreau, "Do you keep a journal?" This simple question led Thoreau to initiate a journal in 1837 that eventually contained many profound observations among some two million words.

Thoreau was also a believer in transcendentalism, a philosophy espoused by Emerson and other writers of the day, which opined that one achieves insight into nature and the world more by personal intuition than religious dogma. *Know thyself*, was the Emersonian dictum. One could find the source of the divinity in themselves. Both men were very much in the anti-slavery camp.

As their connection deepened Thoreau moved into Emerson's home for a three-year period, 1841-1844, where he had multiple responsibilities of tutoring Emerson's children as well as being his editorial assistant. He also threw in some house repair and gardening work. In addition, he had access to all the books in Emerson's well-stocked library. Subsequently, he worked for some periods in his family's pencil factory.

Eager to concentrate on his writing, Thoreau was granted the right to build a small house for himself by Waldon Pond on 14 acres of land Emerson had purchased. His intention was to conduct a two year experiment in living as simply as possible. However, the site — though pristine — was only a couple of miles from Emerson's home. When Thoreau wrote his famous book, describing his thoughts on his experience, he condensed it to one year's worth of observations.

Thoreau was approached by the tax collector for some delinquent tax payments. He didn't pay and was promptly jailed, though for just a day as his family paid up. The experience led to Thoreau's angry work on the causes and possible reasons for civil disobedience.

Thoreau wrote another book, *A Week On The Concord & Merrimack Rivers*, which was a description of nature in this area which he had shared with a now dead brother. The book, also an elegy to his brother, was self-published at Emerson's suggestion under the auspices of Emerson's publisher when Thoreau couldn't find a publisher. He printed 1000 copies but sold less than 300.

After leaving Waldon Pond in 1847 Thoreau moved back, at Emerson's request, into his house to help Emerson's wife, Lidian, while he was on an extended trip through Europe. Emerson was a world-famous figure by this time. But next year Thoreau moved back into his family's home where he stayed for the rest of his life. Occupied with work in the family business while trying to pay off his debts, he also found time to revise and edit his manuscripts.

Thoreau also had the misfortune of contracting tuberculosis in 1835. He suffered sporadically from the disease which finally caught up to him in 1862 when he died at the relatively young age of 44. His relatives were surprised by his tranquility over his coming death. His Aunt Louisa is said to have asked in his last days if he had made his peace with God. Thoreau's response was: "I did not know we had ever quarreled." His actual last words were "Now comes some good sailing."

Emerson, who called Thoreau his best friend, delivered the eulogy at Thoreau's funeral. He said of Thoreau: "He had a beautiful soul."

Among Thoreau's many quotes:

- Beware of enterprises that require new clothes.

- Any fool can make a rule, and any fool can mind it.

- Men have become the tools of their tools.

- It is never too late to give up your prejudices.

- It is as hard to see one's self as to look backwards without turning around.

- My friend is one who takes me for what I am.

- Happiness is like a butterfly; the more you chase it, the more it will elude you, but if you turn your attention to other things, it will come and sit softly on your shoulder.

- If a man does not keep pace with his companions, perhaps it is because he hears a different drummer. Let him step to the music which he hears, however measured or far away.

And some from Emerson:

- Democracy becomes a government of bullies tempered by editors.

- Let not a man guard his dignity, but let his dignity guard him.

- A friend is one before whom I may think out loud.

- Jealousy is ignorance; imitation, suicide.

- Nothing can bring you peace but yourself. Nothing can bring you peace but the triumph of principles.

- A foolish consistency is the hobgoblin of little minds.

- Make the most of yourself. That's all there is of you.

- Men are better than their theology.

Guiseppe Verdi

Guiseppe Verdi and Angelo Mariani, two stalwarts of the Italian operatic scene in the 19th century, worked well together until a rupture in 1869. Verdi transformed the scope and nature of opera with several masterpieces including *Aida* (*an Ethiopian slave in Egypt*), *La Traviata* (*The Fallen Woman*), *Rigoletto*, *Il Trovatore* (*The Troubador, Don Carlos,* and *La Forza del Destino.* Mariani conducted several of these operas, including world premieres. Among the most famous parts of Verdi's operas, played worldwide, are *La Donna e Mobile* from *Rigoletto*, the drinking song from *La Traviata*, and the *Grand March* from *Aida*.

Verdi, born in a village in northern Italy in 1813, showed early talent that was quickly recognized. After studies in Milan, he launched a successful career. Italian opera at the time was characterized by arias coming in loosely conceived scenes. Verdi pioneered, and very successfully, in writing operas that had scenes that were more tightly connected and told a stronger story in operatic terms. He also expanded the expressive power of an operatic chorus. In doing so, he created music that made him famous and wealthy. Some of his fees for his works broke records.

Angelo Mariani

But success might not have come, after his first wife died tragically at the age of 26. Their two children had already died in infancy. His depression was lifted by the enthusiastic reception of an 1842 performance of *Nabucco*, which had the rousing chorus of downtrodden Hebrew slaves (*Va pensiero*) that many Italians believed was in essence a cry for Italian independence. In an autobiographical sketch of 1879, Verdi said the reaction to the chorus inspired him to write music again. By the 1850s, he was the most renowned opera composer in Europe.

A fervent nationalist, and much in favor of Italian unification which took place during this period, Verdi often had to contend with official censorship of his operas. Eventually, his fame led into political spheres and he finally became a senator in the national parliament after Italy did become independent.

Verdi and Angelo Mariani met around 1853. Mariani, who was born in 1821, had already made a name for himself as a conductor. The two become friends. In 1857 Mariani conducted the premiere of Verdi's *Aroldo*, a reworking of his earlier opera called *Stiffelio*. Next, Mariani conducted the Italian premiere of Verdi's *Don Carlos* in 1867.

Problems arose in late 1868. Verdi was planning a collaboration of 13 composers in a requiem honoring the death that year of fellow composer Antonio Rossini. Each composer wrote his own section, but the musical project fell through before it could take place. Verdi blamed Mariani, who he said had been unenthusiastic and less than fully committed. Their friendship was never the same after that, though Mariani wrote several letters trying to heal the rift and expressing admiration for Verdi.

Complicating the matter was the tangled nature of their respective love lives.

Mariani had a mistress, the soprano Teresa Stolz, to whom he became engaged. Stolz was a favorite of Verdi. She had sung in several of his operas, and there was speculation that he had an affair with her, though this was never proven. Around 1871, Stolz changed her mind about marrying Mariani, and it was understood — more or less — that Verdi and his new wife, Giuseppina Strapponi, encouraged the break-up.

After Verdi's wife died in 1897, Stolz became the companion of Verdi for the last few years of his life. She died in 1902, a year after Verdi passed away in 1901.

Despite their differences, Verdi still valued the skills of Mariani as a conductor and asked him to conduct the world premiere of *Aida* in Cairo in 1871. Verdi had been commissioned to write an opera commemorating the opening of the Suez Canal in Egypt. However, Mariani — suffering from the early impact of cancer that killed him two years later at the age of 52 — declined on the basis that he was too ill to travel.

Stolz also declined to travel to Cairo, though the lead role in *Aida* was written for her. Nor did Verdi attend the premiere of his own opera. Subsequently, Stolz did sing in the European premiere of *Aida* in 1872.

Verdi was active in writing music even as a senior. Two of his later operas were *Otello* written in 1886, and *Falstaff* written in 1890 when he was in his seventies.

Interestingly, Verdi and Richard Wagner — who never met — were quite critical of each other's musical direction. Verdi commented about Wagner: "He invariably chooses, unnecessarily, the untrodden path, attempting to fly where a rational person would walk with better results."

More tersely, Wagner said after hearing Verdi's *Requiem Mass*: "It would be better to say nothing."

But a great deal was said in 1901, by over 25,000 mourners in the funeral procession for Verdi, who was hailed as a great Italian hero.

Two quotes from Verdi:

- I adore art ...when I am alone with my notes, my heart pounds and the tears stream from my eyes, and my emotion and my joy are too much to bear.

- You may have the universe if I may have Italy.

Chapter 40. Karl Marx and Friedrich Engels

Working with independent socio-economic ideas that often meshed (though not always), Karl Marx and Friedrich Engels — two tremendously influential 19th century writers — had a pivotal effect on history.

Karl Marx

Born two years apart to well-to-do families in a still not united Germany — Marx in 1818 and Engels in 1820 — both men showed early tendencies to criticize the existing social order and to favor revolutionary ideas. To counter these inclinations, Engel's father dispatched him to Manchester, England, to work as an office clerk in a cotton-spinning factory he partially owned. The policy backfired as young Engels was dismayed by the horrific working conditions and general squalor of the laborers. His experiences led to an 1845 book, *The Condition of the Working Class in England.*

Marx, meanwhile, had become editor of a German-language newspaper in Berlin in 1841 which gave him an outlet for his emerging theories on class oppression and how the ordinary worker was exploited by the powerful and rich for their own benefit. Engel sent Marx a series of articles from Manchester, excerpted from his book.

Friedrich Engels

Displeased by Prussian censorship, Marx lamented: "Our newspaper has to be presented to the police to be sniffed at, and if the police smell anything un-Christian or un-Prussian, the newspaper is not allowed to appear." Hardly a supporter of organized religion, Marx later called religion "the opiate of the people."

He also lambasted "the dictatorship of the bourgeoisie," predicting that their control of society would inevitably lead to tensions causing self-destruction and the rise of socialism. Later, this belief metastasized into a conviction that socialism, or the workers' democracy, would eventually evolve into a classless communistic society. This "progress," both Marx and Engels contended, needed revolutionary activity to get the process going.

The newspaper was shut down in 1843, and Marx departed for Paris where he launched another German-language newspaper with a partner. Engels sent the paper another article, *Outline of a Critique of Political Economy* in 1843.

Intending to return to Germany, Engels stopped off in Paris in 1844, where he met Marx at the Café de la Régence. The two soon discovered that their ideas were very much in harmony and this accord began a lifelong friendship and collaboration. They agreed, in essence, that the workers of the world would become the instrument of an epochal and inevitable revolution in history.

Later that year, Engels went to Germany and fought in the Revolution of 1848, which gave him some background for his future commentaries on the role of industry and the manufacture of arms. Marx tended to focus more on the political nature of warfare. Engels displayed great prescience in predicting that future wars would be total wars. These conflicts, he averred, would be more dominated by technology and dependent on a strong industrial base. In an 1848 letter he said: "No war is any longer possible for Prussia-Germany except a world war, and a war of an extension and violence hitherto undreamt of."

Despairing finally of his exile in continental Europe, which included Paris and Brussels, Marx and family relocated to London where they lived in considerable poverty. He managed to spend a great deal of time in the reading room of the British Museum where he accumulated a tremendous range of notes on labor, wages, industrialization, agriculture, foreign trade, and related topics. Engels returned to Manchester in 1864 in a well-paid executive role that enabled him to subsidize Marx, whose growing family was generally in need of money.

They both worked to organize German workers into a cohesive party, joining the underground German Communist League. They essentially agreed, as Engels put it, that the workers were: "A class which bears all the disadvantages of the social order without enjoying its advantages. Who can demand that such a class respect the social order?"

Subsequently, Marx and Engels were authorized by this group to draft a basic manifesto explaining the basic principles of communism. This manifesto started with the statement: "The history of all hitherto existing society is the history of class struggles." It ended with the famous words: "Let the ruling classes tremble at a Communist revolution. The proletariat have nothing to lose but their chains. They have a world to win. Workers of all countries, unite!"

Both men continued to write, with Engels providing ideas, editing and translating. A master linguist, and fluent in quite a few languages, Engels was described as able "to stutter in 20 languages." Methodical and precise, he was given the family nickname of "The General."

In this fashion, Marx produced the first volume of his seminal work, *Capital*, making use of all his notes taken from his research at the British Museum. In one of his later works, he came out with another famous quote: "From each according to his ability, to each according to his need."

Marx was in failing health for the last year or so of his life. He died in 1883, still stateless. His estate was mostly his notebooks and letters, which came under Engels' control. Engels edited Marx's papers to turn out the second and third volumes of the massive work. Some of the material probably reflects Engel's viewpoints as well as those of Marx.

In a eulogy at his funeral, Engels said: "On the 14th of March, at a quarter to three in the afternoon, the greatest living thinker ceased to think. An immeasurable loss has been sustained both by the militant proletariat of Europe and America, and by historical science, in the death of this man. The gap that has been left by the departure of this mighty spirit will soon enough make itself felt."

Engels, in contrast perhaps to his sober economic theories, enjoyed life — women, good food, fine wine, and intelligent company. One wag said he was a "great beheader of champagne bottles."

Still writing, and espousing his joint theories developed with Marx, Engels passed away in 1895.

***

Comments from Marx include:

- The writer may very well serve a movement of history as its mouthpiece, but he cannot of course create it.
- Capital is dead labor, which, vampire-like, lives only by sucking living labor, and lives the more, the more labor it sucks.
- History repeats itself, first as tragedy, second as farce.

Among Engels' sayings:

- An ounce of action is worth a ton of theory.
- The state is nothing but an instrument of oppression of one class by another — no less so in a democratic republic than in a monarchy.

CHAPTER 41. GUSTAVE FLAUBERT, GEORGE SAND, AND MAXIME DU CAMP

Gustave Flaubert

Gustave Flaubert, a very influential 19th century French writer, was as painstaking an author who ever wrote. He could spend an inordinate amount of time looking for the exact word or phrase. This dedication to his craft accounted for why it took so long for him to finish his novels. *Madame Bovary*, his most famous work, took five years to complete. *Salammbo* came out in 1862 after four years of effort, and a *Sentimental Education* — his last complete novel — was published in 1869 after seven years of fine-tuning to achieve his desired lean and precise style.

Always polishing his work, and never settling for a word that didn't seem precise enough, Flaubert wrote to a fellow author that he spent his time "trying to write harmonious sentences, avoiding assonances." His search for the right word, which could mean taking a week to finish a page, earned him the sobriquet from some observers as a "martyr of style."

Flaubert, who was born in 1821, started writing as a child. He showed considerable ability that might have accounted for him abandoning the study of law to become a writer. He also experienced seizures which might have been epilepsy. As a young man he had a romance with Louise Colet, a poetess, that had an epistolary element. Flaubert, through his life, was a much more prolific letter writer than he was as a writer of fiction; some of his correspondence has been collected into several publications. When this relationship soured he seemed to lose interest in achieving a meaningful relationship. This didn't mean, however, that he wasn't interested in women. He consorted frequently with prostitutes and wasn't at all abashed by candidly writing about his experiences, again choosing the appropriate words. Terming his preference in women as "the bitter poetry of prostitution," he also wrote: "It may be a perverted taste, but I love prostitution, and for itself, too, quite apart from its carnal aspects."

In a telling quote, he wrote: "What I crave is a woman beautiful and ardent and whorish through and through."

But writing — he read his works to friends — consumed a good deal of his time. He commented once: "Ah, what vices I'd have if I didn't write."

Flaubert paid a heavy price for his sexual excesses as he suffered from venereal disease for most of his life, with the disease becoming progressively worse.

Maxime Du Camp

Flaubert also enjoyed travel. He went on a walking tour of Brittany in 1846 with his lifetime friend, Maxime Du Camp. He met Du Camp, who was a year older, in 1843. They quickly bonded, to the extent that they exchanged rings of friendship. They wrote about their domestic trampings, and the experience was so pleasant they took off on an extended foreign trip to the Middle East in 1849/50, visiting Egypt and Greece among other countries. Flaubert, as was his habit, wrote candidly of his impressions and experiences, amatory and otherwise. As he was already a bit stout, guides had to help him navigate ascension of a pyramid. The travel books that Du Camp, an early amateur photographer, wrote were among the first to be illustrated with photos.

Flaubert also used Du Camp, and Louis Bouilhet, another literary confidant and editor, as sounding boards for his writings. Writer George Sand (pen name of Lucile Dudevant, the lover of Frederik Chopin), who was much his senior, took an interest in his writings. After Flaubert's mother died — he never married and lived for years with his mother — Sand was almost like a mother substitute as well as a literary companion. To Sand, he wrote after his mother's death, "I'd like to have you here at Croisset, to have you sleeping near me, in my mother's room." Russian novelist Ivan Turgenev was another encouraging friend.

The friendship of Du Camp and Flaubert cooled, primarily over remarks made by Du Camp who wanted Flaubert to live in Paris while Flaubert preferred his country retreat at Croisset, a town near Paris. Eventually they reconciled.

After returning from the Middle East, Flaubert began work on *Madame Bovary*. The novel was put out in serial form in 1856 and promptly brought down the wrath of the government censors on the grounds that the book was immoral in showing the sexual nature of the novel's tragic heroine. Both Flaubert and the publisher were sued by the French government. Fortunately, both were acquitted in 1857, with the novel coming out in a print version to a favorable reception. Not everyone, however, was receptive to the novel's new and thoroughly realistic and unsparing depiction of provincial French life. The novel did represent a literary break through, influencing many other writers and helping to usher in a more honest and less sentimental brand of authorship.

Flaubert used the same style in *Sentimental Education*, writing to Sand about part of the basis of the book: "I was cowardly in my youth. I was afraid of life."

Flaubert continued to write, churning out novellas and a drama which didn't do much to add to his literary stature. He spent a good deal of the rest of his life working on *Bouvard et Pecuchet*, an unfinished satire on men trying to acquire knowledge against the limits of their own capability. The book depicts the adventures of two Parisian clerks who search in vain for knowledge. Flaubert thought it would be his masterpiece. The book was published posthumously in 1881 with critics disagreeing over its literary value.

Despite his disabilities, Flaubert still vented his satirical spirit with his amusing *Dictionnaire des idées reçues* (dictionary of received ideas). Some examples:

- *Debauchery* — Source of all ailments suffered by elderly bachelors.

- *Baldness* — Always premature, caused by youthful indiscretions or the gestation of great thoughts.

- *Hemorrhoids* — Comes from sitting on stone benches and on hot stoves. Do not attempt to treat them.

- *Mercury* (which was used in various forms to treat syphilis; Flaubert took his in syrup) — Finishes off the patient along with the disease.

The dictionary, which might have been intended as an appendix for *Bouvard et Pecuchet*, was published posthumously in 1911–13.

As his condition worsened, Flaubert complained to Du Camp of his aches and pains: "Venus is no doubt partly to blame, but I think it's mainly because of our ultra nervous temperaments."

In his later years Flaubert lived in genteel poverty. He was called the "hermit of Croisset." Suffering from poor health, he died in 1880 at the age of 58. Du Camp outlived his friend, dying in 1894.

George Sand

Some of Flaubert's maxims are memorable.

- Be regular and orderly in your life like a bourgeois, so that you may be violent and original in your work.

- To be stupid, selfish, and have good health are three requirements for happiness, though if stupidity is lacking, all is lost.

- The whole dream of democracy is to raise the proletarian to the level of stupidity attained by the bourgeois.

- Language is a cracked kettle on which we beat out tunes for bears to dance, while all the time we long to move the stars to pity.

And from George Sand:

- Life resembles a novel more often than novels resemble life.

- Admiration and familiarity are strangers.

- Charity degrades those who receive it and hardens those who dispense it.

- Don't walk in front of me. I may not follow. Don't walk behind me. I may not lead.

- There is only one happiness in life, to love and be loved.

- The artist's vocation is to send light into the human heart.

CHAPTER 42. PAUL CÉZANNE AND EMILE ZOLA

At a provincial French school in the 1850s, three boys were such good friends they were termed "the three inseparables." They often swam together on the River Arc among other joint activities, and each had specific career goals. Two of them became famous figures, Paul Cézanne as a painter, and Emile Zola as a writer. The third boy, Baptistin Baille, became a professor of optics and acoustics.

Cézanne, who was born in 1839, just a year before Zola, studied law for a while at the University of Aix at his father's behest; but he also took drawing lessons. Finally, encouraged by Zola who had already left for Paris to pursue his career, Cézanne made a break too and went to the French capital. The two exchanged correspondence through the years, with the early letters often recounting their experiences with women. One of his early paintings was a portrait of Zola with another friend from Aix-en-Province, Paul Alexis, entitled *Paul Alexis Reading to Emile Zola.*

His initial paintings weren't particularly well received by the Salon of Paris, an organization that greatly helped determine which painters got ahead by exhibiting their work at annual exhibits. Zola provided support, sometimes written, but it wasn't enough. This was the era when painters, experimenting with techniques labeled as the "impressionist" movement, were criticized if not ridiculed by traditionalists. But then Cézanne veered off into concentrating on the shape and structure of objects rather than the impressionistic drive to capture the impact of light on things. In so doing, Cézanne, as a post-impressionist, served as a bridge between late 19th century impressionism and the cubism that emerged in the early 20th century. Both Picasso and Matisse acknowledged this factor, terming Cézanne "the father of us all."

Paul Cezanne

Cézanne was helped when his father, a well-to-do banker who had reconciled himself to his son's choice of career, gave him a sizeable inheritance that eased financial concerns. It wasn't until late in life that Cézanne's paintings sold well.

Emile Zola

Meanwhile, Zola was making himself known through articles and then with novels including an ambitious series of "Rougon-Macquart" books about one family during the entire Second Empire — the imperial regime of Napoleon III from 1852–1870. One of the initial novels was *Therese Racquin*, which was both hailed for its realism and damned as semi-pornographic. He became a significant writer in the literary school of naturalism. He wrote of these collective novels: "I want to portray, at the outset of a century of liberty and truth, a family that cannot restrain itself in its rush to possess all the good things that progress is making available and is derailed by its own momentum, the fatal convulsions that accompany the birth of a new world." Other much noted and much read novels included *Germinal,* about poor labor conditions for miners, and *Nana,* which excoriated the *demi-mondaines* of Paris for their decadent influence on men and their families. Ironically, Zola was attacked himself for decadence. Controversy doubtless helped his book sales as his reputation grew. Zola regularly sent copies of his books to Cézanne as they maintained correspondence.

Cézanne, starting around 1872, began a fruitful association with Camille Pissaro, an older painter whose work was realistic, including countryside scenes and people at work in ordinary settings. Nine years apart in age (Pissaro was born in 1830), Cézanne considered Pissaro his mentor. He wrote that Pissaro "was like a father to me. A man to consult and a little like the good Lord." In a later exhibition catalog, Cézanne even listed himself as "Paul Cézanne, pupil of Pissaro."

Cézanne closely observed nature and its forms but he combined this method with some elements of classical composition. Many critics consider him to be one of the foremost landscape painters in the history of art. He wrote: "I want to make of Impressionism something solid and lasting like the art in the museums." A devout Catholic, Cézanne also penned: "When I judge art, I take my painting and put it next to a God-made object like a tree or flower. If it clashes, it is not art."

Unlike Zola, who thrived in Paris and an urban location, Cézanne much preferred a less hectic lifestyle which he found in his native Aix and Provence in the south of France.

Problems arose between the two when Zola came out with his novel, *L'Oeuvre* (The Work), which depicted the experiences of an impressionist painter. Cézanne believed that he was the model for this character. Some contemporaries thought the character was a composite of painters, not just Cézanne. Zola was, after all, friends with other painters, most notably Edouarde Manet, whose work he regularly praised. Regardless, Cézanne took exception and a friendship dating back to childhood was broken. They never spoke again.

Cézanne eventually inherited a house in Aix and built a new studio. Difficulties arose, ironically involving Cézanne and Zola, when they were no longer friends. This situation emerged during the Dreyfus Affair which divided France into two camps with strong emotions flaring. Captain Dreyfus, who was Jewish, was falsely accused of giving military secrets to the Germans. He was convicted and sent to prison in the dread Devil's Island off the coast of French Guiana in South America. Subsequently, when evidence materialized showing that it was another officer who was guilty, many in France thought the honor of the French Army was more important than a French Jew wrongly imprisoned. Captain Dreyfus was finally pardoned — but not found innocent until much later.

In 1898, Zola — risking his career — wrote a famous open letter to the French president with the famous "J'accuse" headline. The front-page newspaper article (300,000 copies sold the first morning with many burned by Army supporters) electrified France and created worldwide interest in the case that had plummeted France into a serious public division. Zola pummeled the French establishment — government, army, and church — for anti-Semitism and willful obstruction of justice. Ironically, Zola had displayed considerable anti-Semitism earlier, such as in his novel *L'Argent* (Money) about the French stock market. This novel was the 18th in the Rougon-Macquart series.

Zola was convicted of criminal libel, forcing him to flee to London. But soon he was allowed to return to France and in time to see the government fall. He wrote, before passing away in 1902, that: "The truth is on the march, and nothing shall stop it."

However, during this highly charged period, the people of Aix connected Cézanne with Zola, showing where they stood on the matter. Cézanne was trying to auction some paintings, once owned by Zola, which were called by locals "the art dear to Zola." Messages were left by Cézanne's house suggesting that he leave the town "he was dishonoring." Cézanne stayed, only to get caught in a thunderstorm in 1906 and die of pneumonia at the age of 67.

Zola perished earlier, in 1902, at the age of 62, in his home from carbon monoxide poisoning, stemming from a closed vent in a coal stove in his bedroom. Questions over whether his death was an accident or not arose, given the number of death threats he had received over the Dreyfus affair. The police report ruled that an accident had occurred.

***

Among Zola's quotes:

- There are two men inside the artist, the poet and the craftsman. One is born a poet. One becomes a craftsman.

- The artist is nothing without the gift, but the gift is nothing without work.

- I am an artist. I am here to live out loud.

And from Cézanne:

- We live in a rainbow of chaos. Right now a moment is fleeting by! Capture its reality in paint! To do that we must become that moment, make ourselves a sensitive recording plate. Give the image of what we actually see, forgetting everything that has been seen before our time.

- There must not be a single link loose, not a crevice through which the emotion, the light, the truth, can escape.

- With an apple I will astonish Paris.

Chapter 43. Auguste Renoir and Claude Monet

Auguste Renoir and Claude Monet, two pioneering stalwarts of the mid-19th century French art scene, collaborated on the birth of the Impressionistic style of painting which in turn helped usher in the modern world of art. They were contemporaries, with Monet born in 1840 and Renoir a year later.

Pierre Auguste Renoir

Young painters at this time were often given permission to copy the Old Masters whose paintings hung in the Louvre Museum. The jury of the Paris Salon decided which works would be shown at its annual exhibition, and its preference was more for works that showed a classical style. Selection of one's paintings was a great honor and a significant spur to success.

Renoir and especially Monet experimented with a fresh new style of painting in the open air as opposed to in a studio. Monet had learned to paint in the open air in Le Havre (though he was born in Paris). Instead of copying the Old Masters, he copied nature, in a fashion. Some of Renoir's early "instruction" came when he was apprenticed to a porcelain factory and painted plates. Money was tight, and Renoir often lacked money to buy paint.

Monet and Renoir met in Paris in 1862 while studying at the College of Fine Arts in Paris. Neither was particularly receptive to the more traditional instruction of their teachers. Monet much preferred painting in natural outdoor light than in the light offered by a studio. Subsequently, they worked side by side at La Grenouille, a bathing place along the Seine River. They realized that shadows aren't necessarily the more somber black and shades of black but are affected by other colors in the immediate surroundings. Moreover, the color of an object can be changed by the light in which one sees it. Appearances can vary momentarily, daily or seasonally. Their styles, brighter and more vivid than the prevailing motifs, were quite similar; however, they diverged later with Monet continuing his landscape paintings and Renoir returning to a more conservative approach in some of his works.

Renoir, at one point, declared: "I've been 40 years in discovering that the queen of all colors is black."

Claude Monet

In 1873, Renoir went to stay with Monet at a town near Paris where they continued to paint in the open air. They also worked together the following summer in 1874.

To gain exposure for his works, and those by other painters not favored by the Salon jury, Monet and Renoir participated in a separate exhibit in 1874. One of Monet's paintings, *Impression: Sunrise*, a Le Havre port scene, drew a good deal of attention. Not all commentary was favorable. Some criticism charged that the painters were only interested in their own reactions and impressions. One critic coined the style after the name of the painting as *Impressionism*. The exhibition, while drawing crowds, did little for the painters' pocketbooks. The cash-needy artists then held a public auction in which Renoir managed to sell 20 paintings for a total of 225 francs, which wasn't much. Some works went for as little as a painful 50 francs.

One comment from Renoir was: "One morning one of us had run out of black, and that was the birth of impressionism."

As far as Monet, Renoir told his son, Jean, that his friend was an inspiration.

However, approval and appreciation grew as they produced more paintings depicting scenes of everyday life in vibrant colors and a sort of natural intimacy. Eventually, their paintings were accepted and exhibited by the influential Paris

Salon. Acclaim might have come even sooner if it weren't for the Franco--Prussian War in 1870–71 and the resultant civic and political discord.

Monet is generally considered to be one of the greatest landscape painters in the history of art. Paul Cézanne, another famous and contemporary French painter, said: "Monet is the most prodigious eye since there have been painters."

In a telling comment Monet wrote: "Color is my day-long obsession, joy, and torment. To such an extent indeed that one day, finding myself at the deathbed of a woman who had been and still was very dear to me, I caught myself in the act of focusing on her temples and automatically analyzing the succession of appropriately graded colors which death was imposing on her motionless face."

The woman actually was Camille, his first wife.

Many of Renoir's paintings were more oriented to figures — especially women — and to everyday social life situations than to landscapes. During the latter part of his career he became more conservative in his artistic outlook.

Their paintings have eventually sold for millions. Renoir, himself, produced about 6,000 paintings during 60 years of work. Monet produced over 2,000 paintings.

In response to the marketplace, Monet wrote one dealer: "I know my value, and I am more demanding for myself than anyone else can be. But one must see things from a commercial point of view."

Each retired to keep working at their homes. Renoir's retreat at Giverny, near Paris, is probably more famous. Visitors come just to see the lovely gardens. He kept working in his later years, despite having arthritis. Sometimes an assistant would tie a brush in his crippled hand. His *Water Lilies* paintings, painted in the open air in his garden during the 1906–26 period, are among the most famous works during this period of his life. One of his lily paintings sold in 1998 for the tidy sum of $39 million.

Both Renoir and Monet lived to a ripe old age. Renoir died in 1919 and Monet in 1926.

Quotes from Monet:

- It is a tragedy that we live in a world where physical courage is so common and more moral courage is so rare.

- Everyone discusses my art and pretends to understand as if it were necessary to understand, when it is simply necessary to love.

- I am following Nature without being able to grasp her.

- Color is my day-long obsession, joy and torment.

- One must know how to seize the moment of the landscape on the very instant, for that moment will never return.

And from Renoir:

- An artist, under pain of oblivion, must have confidence in himself, and listen only to his real master: nature.

- The pain passes, but the beauty remains.

Chapter 44. Friedrich Nietzsche and Richard Wagner

Friendship can take drastic turns between admiration and disapproval, as shown by the relationship between Friedrich Nietzsche and Richard Wagner.

Ironically, the two 19th century titans — Nietzsche in philosophy and Wagner in music — had themes of their works misappropriated to some extent in 20th century Nazi Germany. Both have had, and continue to have, enormous influence in the world at large. Wagner affected the music of language and his operas — especially the four-opera *Ringcycle* (*The Ring of the Nibelung*) — are performed regularly, most notably at Bayreuth, a site in Germany set aside for production of his works. Wagner is also noted for having written both the music and libretto for all of his works. Two of his best-known operatic extracts are *Ride of the Valkyries* from *Die Walkure* and the *Wedding March* from *Lohengrin*. His *Tristan and Isolde* helped usher in modern music. *Tannhauser* is another famous and often produced opera. *Parsifal* was his last opera. In later years, Wagner referred to his operas as "music dramas."

Nietzsche's philosophical works, most notably *Thus Spoke Zarathustra* and *Beyond Good and Evil*, have affected the thoughts of countless readers, writers, and other philosophers.

Both men were born in Germany, which became a unified nation during their lifetimes. Wagner, the elder, was born in 1803; and Nietzsche much later in 1844. Each achieved some measure of fame by the time of their first meeting in 1868 in Leipzig. Nietzsche was 24 and a rising scholar at this time and Wagner, at 55, a famous and acclaimed composer. They soon discovered that they both admired Wagner's musical genius; Wagner was not one to deny his talent. In addition, they appreciated the philosophy of Arthur Schopenhauer, a fellow German, who argued that music was highest among the arts for expressing the sheer natural state of the human will.

Friedrich Nietzsche

Nietzsche joined the inner circle around Wagner at Tribschen near Lucerne in Switzerland and later at Bayreuth. He became a frequent houseguest. He termed his friendship with Wagner in those days as "the greatest achievement of his life." Nietzsche lauded Wagner's musical achievements in his first book, *The Birth of Tragedy*, that came out in 1872 when he was 27. Nietzsche, a professor of classical philology, argued that Wagner's expressive music was bringing about a rebirth of European culture.

Nietzsche understood Wagner's dictum that "Joy is not in things. It is in us."

However, Nietzsche also found, to his chagrin, that when he wasn't able to honor invitations to the Wagner enclave, his absence was seen as a betrayal. He was also asked to attend to some errands, such as arranging shipment of some special clothes for Wagner. Up to the task, Nietzsche dryly observed: "He who loves his god should decorate him."

But with the advance of time, Nietzsche increasingly broke loose from the domineering personality of Wagner and asserted his own brand of philosophy. He admired Wagner as a person and for his extraordinary musical ability but took exception to some of his philosophical views, which he felt were decadent. Nietzsche opposed most religions (Buddhism may have been an exception) as meaningless — rendering the famous statement that "God is dead." In discussing most theological beliefs, especially faith-based ones, he raised the question: "Can one believe that such things are still believed in?" He took a dim view of the use theologians had made with the teachings of Christ. Comparing Buddhism and Christianity, he wrote: "Buddhism makes no promises but keeps them. Christianity promises everything but keeps nothing." Christianity, he opined, robbed mankind of its strength and self-reliance with its emphasis on guilt and sinfulness.

Nietzsche's viewpoint was also colored by the growing acceptance of Darwin's theories on evolution, which he shared to some extent. He took exception, however, with the "survival of the fittest" dictum, arguing that even so-called less fit figures in history have still dominated their eras. Nietzsche was also prophetic in writing: "The time for petty politics is past: the very next century will bring with it the struggle for mastery over the whole earth."

Nietzsche didn't particularly agree with Wagner's anti-Semitic diatribes in his essay *Jewry In Music*. Wagner was critical of such Jewish composers as Felix Mendelssohn and Giacomo Meyerbeer for allegedly confusing the public about different styles of music — especially Romanticism versus more conservative and classical music. In effect, he accused German composers who were Jewish of weakening German music.

Ironically, Nietzsche turned the tables on Wagner, criticizing his erstwhile friend, whom he had looked up to, for similarly confusing the public with overly heavy and serious works. Whereas Wagner claimed the Jewish composers he lambasted were saturated by their religion, Nietzsche asserted that Wagner was similarly corrupted by Christian theology. Despite this criticism, Nietzsche still appreciated some of Wagner's music for its sheer power in expressing the suffering of the human condition.

Nietzsche also repudiated the Romantic surge in music, applying this criticism to Wagner's music which he had originally championed. Life, to Nietzsche, lacked basic value; hence, the need for mankind to develop a new value, that of self-mastery and "the will to power" which led to the so-called "superman" label subsequently attached to his theme. In effect, Nietzsche questioned any doctrine that sapped human energies, which meant opposing many that were socially and culturally accepted and established.

The two strong-minded men were still in contact. Wagner, heavily involved in details over his productions, wrote Nietzsche in 1875: "I'm not a pure businessman. In other words, I've become a theatre impresario. I feel dizzy, not just sometimes, but every day." At his Bayreuth bastion, Wagner came up with a couple of innovations. He placed the orchestra in a pit the audience couldn't see, and darkened the auditorium during performances.

Richard Wagner

Soon the split between the duo became even more drastic, a change in 1876 that Wagner never forgave. Nietzsche wrote some tracts that openly opposed some of Wagner's viewpoints. He felt that Wagner was pandering to all the limiting pieties of Christianity but that there was some value in providing the new German nation with music that heightened the ideal of the nation. First came *Human—All Too Human* in 1878, *The Wagner Case* and *Nietzsche Versus Wagner*, both in 1888. His *Twilight of the Idols*, during this same period, also mocked Wagner's opera *The Twilight of the Gods*.

Wagner, in return, put out some unflattering references to Nietzsche.

Wagner's autobiography, *My Life*, came out in 1880. He passed away in 1888 at the age of 69. His wife, Cosima (the daughter of fellow composer Franz Lizst and 24 years younger than Wagner) kept the Bayreuth Festival going. It's still popular today.

Nietzsche, who had been ill for much of his adulthood due to a problematic nervous system, became mentally ill around 1889 and spent the remaining years of life being cared for by his family. He died in 1900 at the age of 56. Neither man ever saw how their work and themes were misappropriated by the Nazis.

***

Among Nietzsche's quotes:

- Be careful when you fight monsters lest you become one.

- When you stare into the abyss, the abyss stares back.

- Man is the cruelest animal.

- Madness is the result not of uncertainty but of certainty.

- It is hard enough to remember my opinions, without also remembering my reasons for them.

- No price is too high to pay for the privilege of owning yourself.

- The visionary lies to himself; the liar only to others.

And from Wagner:

- I have long been convinced that my artistic ideal stands or falls with Germany. Only the Germany that we love and desire can help us achieve that ideal.

- I hate this fast growing tendency to chain men to machines in big factories and deprive them of all joy in their efforts. This plan will lead to cheap men and cheap products.

- Even if I know I shall never change the masses, never transform anything permanent, all I ask is that the good things also have their place, their refuge.

- I write music with an exclamation point.

- Imagination creates reality.

- Never look at the trombones; it only encourages them.

Chapter 45. Peter Ilyich Tchaikovsky and Nadezhda von Meck

Without the annual princely stipend and the moral support he received in his extraordinary epistolary relationship with his wealthy patroness, Nadezhda von Meck, Peter Ilyich Tchaikovsky might have given in to his more destructive traits and not created some immortal music.

They were nine years apart in age; von Meck — born in 1831 — was the senior. Tchaikovsky was born in 1840.

For 13 years von Meck helped Tchaikovsky financially, which allowed him to focus on his music and such works as the opera *Peter Onegin*, the *1812 Overture*, the *Sleeping Beauty* and *Swan Lake* ballets, the *Violin Concerto*, and several symphonies including the much played 5th *Symphony and* the 6th *Symphony* or *Pathetique*. Tchaikovsky dedicated his 4th *Symphony* to von Meck.

After a start in the civil service area, Tchaikovsky realized that music was his future. He began his formal training in 1862 at the St. Petersburg Conservatoire, which was the initial academy of this type in Russia. He soon became a star pupil at the school, and was brought to the attention of von Meck, a music lover and one with the financial resources to help outstanding musical prospects.

But there was a fascinating condition she set to their relationship, which developed into a strong friendship: they were never to meet. Tchaikovsky was once a guest at her estate. But the house and grounds were so spacious they arranged never to be anywhere at the same time, though once they briefly passed without recognizing each other when she was in a carriage and he was walking. Initially, von Meck — impressed with Tchaikovsky's talent — commissioned him to compose some pieces for violin and piano which could be played at her estate. Realizing that she was a potential patron, he quickly agreed. Subsequently, he took on other commissions from her for musical pieces.

Peter Ilyich Tchaikovsky

Overall, they exchanged over 1,200 letters between 1877–1890, sharing intimate aspects of their lives. Their letters were often long, quite flowery in language, and filled with sincere and highly personal revelations about their opinions and observations, musical and otherwise. Both felt that they shared a strong degree of shyness. Much of Tchaikovsky's personal and professional life was covered in revealing detail by the composer, and von Meck often bolstered Tchaikovsky's flagging spirits over poor reviews of his works and other problems.

Meanwhile, Tchaikovsky received a grant of 6,000 rubles a year, which was a great deal of money in those days. The subject of money could be delicate, judging from one comment in his letters to her: "In my relations with you there is the ticklish circumstance that every time we write to one another, money appears on the scene." He often felt compelled to ask her for extra amounts to handle debts and other financial circumstances.

Tchaikovsky was subject to his nerves and depression. Critics didn't always like his compositions, and von Meck was quick to shore up his moods.

One of Tchaikovsky's greatest problems came from his being a homosexual, which was taboo in Russia. He tried to keep his amatory inclination a secret, and it isn't certain whether von Meck knew or not; chances were that she did, either with her own research or through gossip by some of her children (who weren't overjoyed at her generosity which decreased their inheritance).

To gain respectability, satisfy his father who wanted him wed, and to ward off revelations about his secret proclivities, Tchaikovsky married a 28-year-old former student, Antonina Milyukova, in 1876 when he was 36. He was much taken by her avowal of love for him, which began with a letter. Their marriage was a disaster and they separated after a month but never divorced. Financial negotiations to settle matters with her, and to perhaps help Tchaikovsky conceal his double life, were difficult. Many years later his "wife" was committed to an insane asylum.

Hardly surprised or disappointed at his marital woes, and as one who didn't believe much in marriage, von Meck wrote: "You may think, my dear Pyotr Ilyich, that I am a great admirer of marriage, but in order that you not be mistaken in anything referring to myself, I shall tell you that I am, on the contrary, an irreconcilable enemy of marriage. Yet when I discuss another person's situation, I consider it necessary to do so from his point of view."

Nadezhda von Meck

Tchaikovsky responded: "You are quite right, Nadezhda Filaretovna, to suppose that I am of a disposition sympathetic to your own unusual spiritual feelings, which I understand completely."

It should be noted that von Meck and her engineer husband Karl, who made the family's fortune in railway construction, had 18 children, with 12 surviving. She was married when she was 16. She spurred her husband to quit his government job and concentrate on rail construction on his own. Subsequently, while her husband spearheaded rail expansion in Russia, she became the family's business manager and did quite well in the role.

Her feelings for Tchaikovsky were clearly warm but platonic. They did eventually exchange photographs of themselves at her request. But not meeting each other in person supposedly kept a somewhat exalted image of Tchaikovsky alive as her "beloved friend."

Another problem arose when von Meck's son Nikolai married Tchaikovsky's niece, Anna. Though von Meck and Tchaikovsky had worked as matchmakers, the marriage didn't prosper. Tchaikovsky came to the wedding; von Meck, who severely limited contact with her progeny, didn't.

In 1890, von Meck sent Tchaikovsky 6,000 rubles by messenger and not by mail, and not in her usual monthly installments. She also informed him that this was the last stipend as there had been a reversal in her financial situation. But by this juncture Tchaikovsky had become a well-known composer and was less in need of her money. He had received a generous pension from Tsar Alexander III. Still, he was disturbed. He wrote to her to at least keep their friendship going, but never received a response. At this time von Meck was in ill health, suffering from tuberculosis, and writing was difficult; and it was too awkward to dictate her feelings to someone else.

Von Meck asked Tchaikovsky to destroy all their correspondence, and she believed he had followed her instructions. However, Tchaikovsky chose to save them.

Tchaikovsky died first, at the age of 53 in 1893, possibly from cholera which was raging in Russia at this time. A huge public funeral was held for him. Depressed by his death, and her own health problems, von Meck passed away just two months later.

One revealing quote from Tchaikovsky:

- The notion that someday people will try to probe into the private world of my thoughts and feelings is very sad and unpleasant.

Chapter 46. Andrew Carnegie and Thomas Scott

The mentoring of young Andrew Carnegie by his boss, Thomas Scott, led to a great business and industrial success — and many philanthropic gifts to society.

Scott was born in 1823. He was 12 years older than Carnegie, who was born in 1835 in Scotland. Scott was general superintendent of the Pennsylvania Railroad — one of the largest businesses in the U.S. — in 1853, when Carnegie was hired as a telegraph operator at $40 a week. Trains were running in both directions on a single track and effective communications was imperative. Scott took interest in guiding aspiring railroad men in whom he saw potential. As Carnegie, hard-working and intelligent, passed this test, Scott instructed him in the rudiments of railroad management including cost control. Carnegie learned fast and well, and all this knowledge was instrumental in his later astounding business success. He worked for Scott, also as a personal assistant, for over six years.

Subsequently, Carnegie rose quickly through the ranks to become superintendent of the Pittsburgh division in 1859 at the age of twenty-four. He instituted some new policies including around-the-clock telegraph service that allowed trains to operate on a 24-hour basis.

Scott also helped Carnegie learn about the world of financial investments, while providing some seed money. Taking advantage of insider trading, Scott was involved in sleeping cars and oil interests among other areas of investment. Thriftily reinvesting his returns, Carnegie slowly accumulated enough capital to strike out on in a new direction in 1868, albeit with some partners, including Scott. Foreseeing that industrialization would require more use of steel, he began purchasing firms involved in steel production and then consolidating them

into the Carnegie Steel Company. A millionaire at an early age, Carnegie operated with the motto: "Watch costs and the profits take care of themselves."

Andrew Carnegie

On paper Carnegie favored the rights of workers to create unions, a policy
many other so-called "Captains of Industry" didn't go along with. But in the
bloody Homestead Strike of 1892 at the Carnegie Steel Mill (in Homestead,
Pennsylvania), Carnegie sided with management, which employed Pinkerton
armed guards as strike-breakers. Ten persons were killed and more wounded
in the ensuing violence. He later claimed that he was out of the loop in busting
the union, as he was out of the country; but the deadly incident tarnished his
reputation.

Thomas Scott

Meanwhile, with the advent of the Civil War, Scott was appointed Assistant Secretary of War by President Lincoln. In turn, Scott appointed Carnegie as superintendent of the military railways and the North's telegraph lines in the East. Their combined effort in creating efficient rail and telegraph links helped the North defeat the Confederacy and keep the country united. Scott was also quite influential in convincing Lincoln to travel secretly when he went anywhere by train to prevent assassination attempts.

Scott went on to become president of the Pennsylvania Railroad in 1871/72. He had a stroke in 1878 and died in 1881. Carnegie went on to become one of the richest men in the world, especially after he sold his company to J.P. Morgan, in 1901, to the tune of around $485 million.

"The man who dies rich dies disgraced."

This is one of the maxims of Carnegie, who lived up to his own point by giving away a good deal of his fortune in his last years. Before he passed away in 1919 at the age of 84, he had settled about $350 million to various causes and charities including the creation of more than 2,500 libraries around the English-speaking world. Overall, he donated about 90 per cent of his wealth to cultural, scientific and educational institutions for the "improvement of mankind."

However, he still believed in people making their own way, as he had done, from his less than wealthy roots in Scotland. Having risen from rags to riches, he remarked: "The richest heritage a young man can have is to be born into poverty." On the other hand, unlike many other moguls, he believed that in "taxing estates heavily at death, the state marks the condemnation of the selfish millionaire's unworthy life."

The Palace of Peace in The Hague, the Netherlands, was funded by Carnegie. The institution, which had its grand opening in 1913, evolved into the World Court. He also played a key financial hand in establishment of the Carnegie Institute of Technology in Pittsburgh in 1900.

An anti-imperialist and a member of the Anti-Imperialist League which sprang up after the Spanish–American War in 1898, Carnegie even offered the Philippines $20 million to buy their independence; this sum was the same the U.S. was going to pay Spain to purchase the islands.

Even before the advent of World War I, Carnegie advocated the formation of a world organization like the League of Nations. Though he was a pacifist to some extent, his company — profits being profits — still made armor plate for the U.S. navy and other navies.

While evolving into a great philanthropist as well as industrialist, Carnegie was labeled by many as one of the robber barons who emerged in the rapid industrialization of the U.S. in the latter part of the 19th century. His beneficence in his later years has to be reconciled with dubious business practices and harsh labor conditions in his factories.

When he was nearly 80, Carnegie commented on his life: "When I go for a trial for the things done on Earth, I think I'll get a 'Not guilty' verdict through my efforts to make the Earth a little better than I found it."

He wrote several books. *Round the World* collected his impressions garnered by a lengthy overseas trip in 1878. His perspective on many aspects of business came in *Gospel of Wealth* that was published in 1889.

Carnegie died in 1919 at his Massachusetts estate. He and his wife, Louise, also had a summer home in Scotland.

Some of his other quotes:

- It is more difficult to give money away intelligently than it is to earn it in the first place.

- It is the mind that makes the body rich.

- Take care of your pennies and the pounds will take care of themselves.

- You can't push anyone up a ladder unless he is willing to climb a little.

CHAPTER 47. SIR ARTHUR SULLIVAN AND W.S. GILBERT

Both Arthur Sullivan and W.S. Gilbert, two well-born Englishmen, had separate independent and successful careers in the music and theater worlds of late 19th century England. Their collaboration together in the light classical opera field gave the world popular operettas that are still performed everywhere.

Among the 14 shows that they devised during the 1871–1896 period, with Sullivan providing the music and Gilbert the text, are such famous favorites as *The Pirates of Penzance, H.M.S. Pinafore*, and *The Mikado*. Some lyrics have entered the English language, such as: *What, never? Well, hardly ever* and *Let the punishment fit the crime.*

The pair, with different personalities and views of their work, didn't always see eye to eye. Both were noted luminaries when they began collaborating. Gilbert was recognized as a poet, artist, and playwright. Sulllivan was famed as a conductor as well as for symphonic music. Gilbert was said to be more irreverent and confrontational with Sullivan less ready to handle conflict. Sullivan, who was knighted for his achievements by Queen Victoria in 1883, sometimes disdained the lightness of his operettas created with Gilbert and longed to do more serious music. In a sense, they both felt burdened with the awareness of their creative energies being yoked to the other's persona.

But for most of their remarkable time working together, they produced work that has withstood the passage of time. They were six years apart in age — Gilbert was born in 1836 and Sullivan in 1842.

Sullivan and Gilbert, mostly through the auspices of others, joined forces in 1871 with a light opera *Thespis*. Subsequently, they went their own way. Both were prolific. Sullivan, overall, composed some 23 operas, 13 major orchestral pieces, various choral works, and some hymns and songs including *Onward, Christian Soldiers*. Gilbert had plays and other works produced and published.

Arthur Sullivan

Gilbert also assisted Sullivan with his choral piece, *The Mayor of Antioch*, in 1880. In return, Sullivan gave Gilbert an engraved silver cup with the inscription: *W.S. Gilbert from his friend Arthur Sullivan.*

W.S. Gilbert

Along came Richard D'Oyly Carte, a producer, who commissioned them in 1875 to write a one act piece, *Trial by Jury*, which became a considerable hit to everyone's pleasant surprise.

The duo then starting working together steadily, with their shows produced at the Savoy Theatre (with their works sometimes referred to as Savoy operas). *HMS Pinafore* followed in 1878 and clearly established their fame. Other shows quickly followed: *Pirates of Penzance* in 1879, *Iolanthe* in 1882, *The Mikado* in 1885, *Yeoman of the Guard* in 1888, and *The Gondoliers* in 1889.

Trouble arose in 1890 over a charge to Gilbert and Sullivan, as partners, over the cost of new carpeting for the theater. Gilbert thought the cost should be borne by D'Oyly Carte; but Sullivan took Carte's side. Gilbert sued, and won the case. But acrimony poisoned the relationship. Sullivan, at one point, wrote that he was "physically and mentally ill over this wretched business. I have not yet got over the shock of seeing our names coupled in hostile antagonism over a few miserable pounds."

Gilbert, on his part, made this scathing comment to Carte: "I left him with the remark that it was a mistake to kick down the ladder by which he had risen."

It didn't look too likely that they would work together again. Sullivan wrote to Carte: "It's impossible for me to do another piece of the character of those already written by Gilbert and myself."

But they tried, though Sullivan vetoed an idea for a comic opera that Gilbert proposed. The impasse was resolved with a new idea by Gilbert which led to the resounding success of *The Mikado*.

Still, Sullivan, longing to write more serious music, wrote, "I have lost the liking for writing comic opera and entertain very grave doubts as to my power of doing it."

Sullivan was proved wrong when they created *The Gondoliers* in 1889. Unfortunately, this show turned out to be the last of their significant successes.

With the help of others Carte managed to reunite the pair. Sullivan's only grand opera, *Ivanhoe*, produced in 1891, had not been a roaring success. Nor had collaborating with another person in comic operas been anything like the success he had with Gilbert. They combined talents again and came out with *Utopia Unlimited* in 1893. But then another disagreement surfaced, this time over the talent of Nancy McIntosh, the leading lady. Sullivan took the position that he would never write another opera featuring her, while Gilbert was just as adamant that she appear in his next work. The difficulty subsided when the lady announced her retirement. Gilbert and Sullivan then wrote *The Grand Duke* but this show didn't do well in 1898.

After failure of this show, their collaboration ended. Sullivan, who never married (he did have serious affairs) died in 1900 at the age of 58. In 1904 Gilbert wrote: "Savoy opera was snuffed out by the deplorable death of my distinguished collaborator, Sir Arthur Sullivan. When that event occurred, I saw no one with whom I felt I could work with satisfaction and success and I discontinued to write libretti."

Gilbert, however, went on to write more plays and other works. While he married, the couple didn't have any children. He passed away in 1911 at the age of 75 from a heart attack while trying to save a drowning girl. The inscription on his memorial on the Thames Embankment in London reads: *His foe was Folly, and his Weapon Wit.*

***

Among Gilbert's quotes:

- No one can have a higher opinion of him than I have, and I think he's a dirty little beast.

- When everyone is somebody, then no one's anybody.

- Things are seldom what they seem; skim milk masquerades as cream.

Chapter 48. Wyatt Earp & Doc Holliday

Wyatt Earp and John Henry "Doc" Holliday are extraordinarily famous in western lore and legend due to in great measure to their part in the famous "Gun Fight at the O.K. Corral" in Tombstone in the Arizona Territory in October 1881. Subsequently, many books, movies and television shows have depicted this legendary shoot-out. Fact and fiction overlap, and the latter usually wins as far as popular entertainment.

In the case of Doc Holliday there is considerable confusion over the extent of his misdeeds; but there is no confusion over his strong friendship with Earp. He was born in Georgia in 1851 and was three years younger than Earp, who was born in 1848. As a historical oddity he was also, through a relative's marriage, a distant cousin to Margaret Mitchell who later wrote *Gone With The Wind*. He graduated from dental school in 1872 and set up practice only to be diagnosed with tuberculosis which was called "consumption" in those days. Feeling he hadn't long to live he set out west hoping a warmer and dryer climate would prolong his life.

While still working part time as a dentist, he soon switched to gambling. He also worked as a faro dealer which he saw as a lucrative sideline. As carrying arms was commonplace he also became dexterous with guns. He first met Wyatt Earp in Fort Giffin, Texas. The two were very different personalities. Doc was impulsive, given to quick action; Earp was more in control of his emotions. But they still befriended each other, with the relationship cemented in 1878 in Dodge City, Kansas when Doc helped defend Earp in a saloon fracas. Earp credited Doc with saving his life in another barroom brawl.

Earp, and his brothers, migrated to Tombstone, Arizona which was in the midst of a silver mining boom. They purchased an interest in a mine and some water rights and got involved in the town's politics. Friction arose with a cowboy group including the Clanton and McLaury families. Being called a cowboy at that time had a different meaning than today. Cowboys were little more than outlaws in some eyes, with legitimate cowboys often termed cattle herders and ranchers.

Wyatt Earp

Doc was invited to join the Earps and he soon came there. Dodge City perhaps had grown too civilized for his taste. He lived, possibly with his common-law wife, Big Nose Kate, in a boarding house that was close to the O.K. Corral.

Earp, now a lawman in town, had his brothers and Doc deputized. They confronted five of the Clantons and McLaurys in a 30-second gunfight that has gone down in history. Who shot first has never been proven one way or another and never will be now. But three of the "cowboys" were dead after an exchange of around 30 shots at close range. The only one who wasn't killed or wounded was Earp, with Doc just grazed by a bullet. In a subsequent trial, Earp and others were exonerated.

However, the gunfight hardly settled matters. The vendetta went on for several more months with Virgil Earp ambushed and seriously maimed. Morgan, another brother, was killed. Earp, along with Doc and others, hunted down and killed everyone they thought responsible. Warrants were issued in various jurisdictions.

Doc and Earp then split up, with Doc going to Denver. But he was arrested there on an Arizona warrant. Now Earp came to the rescue of his companion. He contacted Bat Masterson, another famous lawman, who was an old friend. Masterson succeeded in getting the Colorado governor to refuse the warrant on some pretext. Doc was freed, but his health had suffered considerably. The high altitude in Denver, gave him shortness of breath; and he was dependent on alcohol as well as laudanum, a popular opiate and pain-killer, to ease the growing impact of tuberculosis. He died in 1887, and true to his life, there is uncertainty over a detail on his final days.

In one account he was lying in bed with his boots off, which he found ironic for a gunman. (rather than dying with his boots on — in other words, in a fight). Supposedly he said, "Damn, this is funny."

Earp had actually seen Doc a bit earlier, and seeing the end was near for his friend, said: "Isn't it strange that if not for you, I wouldn't be alive today. Yet you must go first."

Doc Holliday at the age of twenty

Doc was asked once in a newspaper interview if his conscience ever troubled him. He was credited, accurately or otherwise, with killing various men over the years. Doc's answer was: "I coughed that up with my lungs years ago."

Later, Earp, who lived on to more adventures and business ventures until passing away in 1929 at the ripe old age of 81, wrote in a newspaper article.

Doc was a dentist, not a lawman or an assassin, who necessity had made a gambler. He was a gentleman whom disease had made a frontier vagabond; a philosopher whose life had made him a caustic wit; a long, lean, ash-blond fellow nearly dead with consumption, and at the same time the most skillful gambler and the nerviest, speediest, deadliest man with a six-gun that I ever knew.

A related quote from Earp:

• Fast is fine, but accuracy is everything.

Chapter 49. Butch Cassidy and the Sundance Kid

Details of the demise of Butch Cassidy and the Sundance Kid, two of the most famous Old West outlaws, may be uncertain; but the legends that have sprung up about them, abetted by the famed movie using their names with Paul Newman playing Cassidy and Robert Redford the Sundance Kid, are very much in vogue. Together, the pair — as part of the "Wild Bunch" — carried out what is probably the longest number of successful bank and train robberies in U.S. history.

Only a year apart in age, Robert LeRoy Parker, alias Butch Cassidy, was born in Utah in 1866, and Henry Alonzo Longabaugh in Pennsylvania in 1867.

Parker fell in with a horse thief by the name of Martin Cassidy, whose last name he assumed later on in his own crime career. They were working as cowhands at the same ranch. One of Cassidy's assorted jobs, before turning to crime, was as a butcher, which is how he got the nickname of Butch. Longabaugh, who came west at the age of 15, began his life in crime in 1887 when he made off with a horse and a gun from a ranch where he was working in Sundance, Wyoming. Captured and convicted, he spent 18 months in prison, where he adopted the name of the Sundance Kid.

But the Sundance Kid was suspected of more misdeeds after release, though he did work as a ranch hand. Finally, considered fast with a gun, he joined the Wild Bunch in the late 1890s. Their saga in crime, glamorized somewhat by cinematic depictions, suggests that they attempted to be non-violent in their robberies. They tended to employ intimidation more as a tactic and to shoot at the horses of posse members pursuing them rather than at the men. Cassidy once claimed that he had never killed a man, meaning within the U.S., as his record was reportedly a good bit more lethal in South America where he and the Sundance Kid eventually fled.

However, it is known that other members of the Wild Bunch did kill several people.

Butch Cassidy

Sundance Kid and Etta Place

The outlaws often retreated to a famous site called the "Hole-In-The-Wall," a curious geological formation near Kaycee, Wyoming, that afforded good cover from all directions and served as a very effective hideout. After a robbery, they would split the loot and then go off in several directions until reassembling at a designated place later on. Meanwhile, the Union Pacific Railroad hired the

Pinkerton National Detective Agency to hunt down, capture, or kill the outlaws. "Wanted Dead Or Alive" posters sprang up with a $30,000 reward offered. Some posters had a photo of the famed pair, one they had foolishly taken between robberies and which was quickly employed by the Pinkerton detectives. Cassidy also liked to perform acrobatic feats on a bicycle to entertain the "ladies" at one bordello where they stayed, and this lark might have attracted attention as well.

The Pinkerton group was persistent and professional, and the ranks of the bunch diminished. Feeling that sticking around had become too dangerous, the pair — along with the Sundance Kid's consort, Etta Place (whose real name might have been Ann Bassett), departed for New York City. They took a ship to Buenos Aires, Argentina. With money accumulated from their robberies, they attempted to go straight, buying a 15,000 acre ranch near the Andes Mountains in Argentina. But after several years they sold their property, in around 1906. They might have been spotted by a visiting American.

Subsequently, they relapsed into another crime spree in Argentina and across the mountains in Chile. Etta, however, tired of being on the run and the Sundance Kid, under the alias of George Maxwell, escorted her back to the U.S. in 1907.

The Sundance Kid returned to South America and the pair made another stab at peaceful pursuits. They worked for a silver mine in the mountainous area of southern Bolivia, with the ironic responsibility of guarding the company's payroll.

In November 1908, two bandits, said to be American by locals, robbed a courier bearing the payroll money of the Aramayo Silver Mine. These robbers, taking the mine mule with them, went to stay in a boarding house in the nearby village of San Vicente. The owner of the boarding house, a miner himself, was suspicious about the two. He recognized a mule as belonging to a friend, a muleteer who transported payroll. He contacted authorities. A Bolivian army unit was stationed nearby and soon the boarding house was surrounded. After a shootout, the authorities entered the house and found two men dead. Theories include one that the Sundance Kid was mortally wounded and was put out of misery by Cassidy, who then shot himself. Neither man, it's believed, wanted to be taken alive. The Bolivians couldn't identify either man. They were buried in unmarked graves. Their remains have never been found despite assorted efforts to determine, through DNA, precisely who is buried in various plots. Interestingly, the Pinkerton detectives were hardly convinced the two were really dead, continuing their search for several years.

More theories have arisen that both men somehow eluded capture and successfully went on to live out their lives elsewhere, possibly in the United States. Chances are their fate will never be known factually. But their legend lives on.

CHAPTER 50. G.K. CHESTERTON, GEORGE BERNARD SHAW, AND HILLAIRE BELLOC

Gilbert Keith Chesterton, generally known as G.K. Chesterton, was considered one of the major men of letters straddling the English literary scene during the first third of the 20th century. He exchanged witticisms with George Bernard Shaw, criticized H.G. Wells, and agreed with Hilaire Belloc.

Chesterton was born in 1874 and rose to become a prolific writer including newspaper columns, plays, detective novels (the famed Father Brown mysteries), short stories, essays, etc. He was also a social critic and Catholic enthusiast. Overall, he turned out around 80 books during a long and illustrious career.

Chesterton, at six feet and four inches in height and nearly 300 pounds in weight, was noted for his girth as well as his opinions. His attire, featuring a cape and crumpled hat, also become trademarks of his persona. In a famous anecdote during World War I, a woman asked Chesterton why he was "not at the front." He replied, "If you go around to the side, you will see that I am."

Chesterton was also famous for not always knowing exactly where he was. In one noted incident, he sent a telegram to his wife, Frances: "Am at Market Harborough. Where ought I to be?"

His witty and ironic comments led to him to sometimes being called "the prince of paradox." He had a way of inverting popular sayings. For example: "Thieves respect property. They merely wish the property to become their property that they more properly respect it."

George Bernard Shaw, no slouch at witticisms and a "friendly enemy" of Chesterton when it came to ideas, political, religious and otherwise, said of his rival, "He was a man of genius." The two men, while often disagreeing, were friends who respected each other's intellect.

G.K. Chesterton

George Bernard Shaw

Once Chesterton told a much thinner Shaw: "To look at you, anyone would think a famine had struck." Not at all at a loss for a comeback, Shaw retorted: "To look at you, anyone would think you have caused it."

On a more serious note, Chesterton and Shaw often debated on the path of society. Chesterton opined: "The whole modern world has divided itself into Conservatives and Progressives. The business of Progressives is to go on making mistakes. The business of the Conservatives is to prevent the mistakes from being corrected."

In *Heretics*, one of his books, Chesterton criticized Shaw: "After belaboring a great many people for a great many years for being unprogressive, Mr. Shaw has discovered, with characteristic sense, that it is very doubtful whether any existing human being with two legs can be progressive at all."

Chesterton was also not too partial to Oscar Wilde, another literary luminary of the period. "Oscar Wilde said that suns were not valued because we could not pay for sunsets. But Oscar Wilde was wrong; we can pay for sunset. We can pay for them by not being Oscar Wilde."

One of Chesterton's great friends was Hillaire Belloc, a poet and essayist, whom he first met in 1901. Their opinions mirrored each other so much that

Shaw coined the name "Chesterbelloc," which lasted for some time. Chesterton, who converted to Catholicism in 1922, and fellow Catholic Belloc, were both critical of socialism as well as capitalism. They favored a third economic theory called "distributism." This viewpoint, following Catholic teachings, held that property ownership is a basic right and should be spread around and not left with the state or well-heeled private interests like corporations. Neither was a great fan of Jews, and made their anti-Semitic views known.

Belloc also supported the notion of the "white man's burden" in civilizing less advanced areas of the world. The factors of colonialism and use of advanced technology, such as using the new Maxim machine gun to mow down natives, was a lesser consideration. One of Belloc's ditties was:

> Whatever happens, we have got
> The Maxim gun, and they have not

On the subject of capitalism, Chesterton wrote: "Too much capitalism does not mean too many capitalists, but too few capitalists."

Chesterton's anti-Jewish perspective supported the historic expulsion of Jews from England in the Middle Ages. While he did favor creation of a Jewish homeland, this option was preferred as a means to finding a separate place for Jews because he believed that they didn't sufficiently assimilate in the various European nations — and not because they deserved one. On the other hand, he did quickly oppose Hitler, as early as 1932.

Chesterton passed away in 1936 at the age of 62, having contributed a vast amount of intelligent commentary to the world at large. His autobiography was published posthumously shortly after he died in 1936. Belloc passed away in 1953 at the age of 74, while Shaw lived on to die at 90 in 1950.

***

Among Chesterton's many quotes:

- Don't ever take a fence down until you know the reason it was put up.

- Fallacies do not cease to become fallacies because they become fashions.

- It's not bigotry to be certain we are right; but it is bigotry to be unable to imagine how we might possibly have gone wrong.

- The thing I hate about an argument is that it always interrupts a discussion.

- An adventure is only an inconvenience rightly considered. An inconvenience is only an adventure wrongly considered.

- If there was no God, there would be no atheists.

- Some people when married gain each other. Some only lose themselves.

Hillaire Belloc

And from Shaw:

- A fashion is nothing but an induced epidemic.

- England and America are two countries separated by a common language.

- If all economists were laid end to end, they would not reach a conclusion.

- I often quote myself. It adds spice to my conversation.

- Gambling promises the poor what property performs for the rich — something for nothing.

- Americans adore me and will go on adoring me until I say something nice about them.

Quotes from Belloc:

- From quiet homes and first beginnings out to the undiscovered ends, there's nothing worth the wear of winning but laughter and the love of friends.

- All men have an instinct for combat — at least all healthy men.

- Any subject can be made interesting, and therefore any subject can be made boring.

- Every major question in history is a religious question. It has more effect on molding life than nationalism or a common language

Chapter 51. Helen Keller and Anne Sullivan

What began as a teacher-student relationship between Helen Keller and Anne Sullivan blossomed into a friendship that lasted for decades. Their lives together have been the subject of many books, movies and plays, and most notably the film, *The Miracle* Worker. It was none other than Mark Twain who coined this superlative to describe the efforts of Anne Sullivan.

Anne's remarkable teaching of Helen Keller led her to become the first deaf and blind person to earn a Bachelor of Arts degree. She then went on to a prodigious career as an advocate for the disabled, an activist for various causes including socialism, and as a lecturer and author.

Helen Keller was born in Alabama in 1880 as a normal baby. But at 19 months an illness left her deaf and blind. Her family's search for help led them to the Perkins Institute for the Blind in Boston. Anne Sullivan, who was born in 1866 in Massachusetts, was a former student there herself. Twenty at this time, and visually impaired with a viral eye condition, she was still recommended to be a teacher to Helen. She had been a prize pupil and class valedictorian at the 1886 graduation.

Helen Keller

Anne arrived at Helen's home in Tuscumba, Alabama, in 1887 when Helen was already seven years old. Initially, instruction was difficult. Anne spelled words in Helen's hand, but Helen didn't understand that virtually everything, objects and ideas, had a word to express it. The breakthrough came when Helen finally made the connection between the motions Anne was making in one of her hands and well water splashing over the other hand. Now Helen was eager to learn the names of everything else in her world.

This moment, of course, has been captured many times in artistic depictions.

Keller later wrote: "Before my teacher came to me. I did not know that I am. I was a phantom living in a no-world."

In 1888, Helen and Anne traveled to the Perkins School in Boston. Subsequently, they moved to New York in 1894 to attend the Wright-Humason School for the Deaf. In 1900 Helen was admitted to Radcliffe College. Several industrialists, including Andrew Carnegie, helped subsidize the costs of her college education. Helen also became friends with other luminaries like Alexander Graham Bell and Mark Twain.

Anne attended classes with Helen, communicating lecture notes on her hand and reading texts to her, despite her own poor eyesight. Helen graduated in 1904.

Eventually, Helen learned to speak, read Braille, learn sign language, etc. Through the many years that followed, Helen was prolific in her activities, giving speeches and lectures, writing books, and serving as a wonderful role model for other disabled people.

Anne Sullivan

Anne was her steady companion. Romance came into Anne's life when John Macy, a Harvard instructor 14 years her junior, proposed. Afraid of jeopardizing her relationship with Helen, Anne was reluctant, but she finally married Macy in 1905 when she was 39. The trio lived together for some time, with Macy helping out with editorial work; but Anne's devotion to Helen — she was her constant eyes and ears — put a considerable strain on the marriage. The couple separated in 1914, though they never divorced.

Meanwhile, Helen was extremely busy. She and Anne traveled worldwide raising funds for the blind and disabled. She wrote: "The public must learn that the blind man is neither a genius, nor a freak, and nor an idiot. He has a mind that can be educated, a hand which can be trained, ambitions which it is right for him to strive to realize, and it is the duty of the public to help him make the best of himself so that he can win light through work."

Helen founded the Helen Keller International Organization to conduct re-search in combating the causes and consequences of blindness and malnutrition. She also helped establish the American Civil Liberties Union (ACLU) in 1920. Besides being a suffragette and supporter of birth control, Helen was a pacifist, opposed to war, and a proponent of workers' right. She also joined the Socialist Party as well as the Industrial Workers of the World, nicknamed the "Wobblies."

In 1911, she wrote, as part of a larger statement: "The few own the many be-cause they possess the means of livelihood of all. The country is governed for the richest, for the corporations, the bankers, the land speculators and for the exploitation of labor."

Helen had 12 books published as well as many articles. Among her works are her autobiography, *The Story of My Life*, which both Anne and her husband helped in writing. Other books include *The World I Live In* and *Out of the Dark*. Helen also starred as herself in a 1919 film, *Deliverance*.

Helen was a celebrity and as such met many other celebrities of the day, in-cluding Charlie Chaplin and other Hollywood personalities. She shook hands with every president from Grover Cleveland to Lyndon Johnson. Dog-lovers may not realize that Helen was responsible for introducing Akitas, the Japanese dog, to the United States. She visited Japan several times and liked the Akitas. The Japanese government duly gave her an Akita, named Kenzan-go, as a gift.

On the other hand, the FBI maintained a file on her due to her political stanc-es. But there weren't any unpleasantries released about her, probably due to her great standing with the public.

Among many honors, including statues, buildings and streets named after her, Helen received the Presidential Medal of Freedom in 1964. The following year she was elected to the National Women's Hall of Fame. Temple University gave both Keller and Sullivan honorary degrees of Doctor of Humane Letters.

Anne collected many of her thoughts in an autobiography, *Foolish Thoughts of a Foolish Woman*, which included this comment: "I still think there is not much to life, except to learn all one can about it, and the only way to learn it is to experi-ence much — to love, to hate, to flounder, to enjoy and to suffer."

Anne, meanwhile, continued to have problems with her eyes and finally her right eye was removed in 1929. She became completely blind in 1935 and died in 1936 at the age of 70. Helen, who was then 56, is said to have been holding her hand.

After many years of accomplishments made despite her disabilities, Helen suffered a stroke in 1961 and died in her sleep in 1968 at the age of nearly 88. She is still much remembered as a cardinal example of human drive, persistence, and character.

***

Among Keller's quotes:

- The highest result of education is tolerance.

- Security is mostly a superstition. It does not exist in nature. Life is either a daring adventure or nothing.

- One can never consent to creep when one feels an impulse to soar.

- Although the world is full of suffering, it is also full of the overcoming of it.

- Many persons have the wrong idea of what constitutes true happiness. It is not attained through self-gratification but through fidelity to a worthy purpose.

- Self-pity is our worst enemy and if we yield to it, we can never do anything good in the world.

- I do not want the peace that passeth understanding. I want the understanding that bringeth peace.

And from Sullivan:

- Every renaissance comes to the world with a cry, the cry of the human spirit to be free.

- If all people knew what was good for them and acted accordingly, this world would be a different world, though not nearly so interesting.

Chapter 52. Maurice Ravel and Claude Debussy

Maurice Ravel and Claude Debussy were great early 20th century avant-garde French musicians whose works and lives mingled in friendship, mutual admiration, and rivalry. They both provided impetus for the transition from the late Romantic period of artistic creation of the 19th century into a modern movement advancing in the early years of the new century.

Maurice Ravel

Debussy, born in 1862, was 13 years older than Ravel, who was born in 1875.

The two, each having received a good deal of musical training after showing early talent, met in the 1890s in Paris. Both were impressed with the musical works each had achieved. They were both as well imbued with the values of impressionism, which was much in vogue. They were members of the *Société des Apaches*, a group of innovative artists who worked and created against the established traditions in their respective spheres. The group would meet regularly until World War I broke out. In 1900 Debussy invited Ravel to his home, where they mulled over the musical scene while playing each other's works including piano and chamber music, sonatas, and so forth. Both were creative and proficient. They also attended the same musical events and their works were sometimes on the same bill. Ravel was also a strong supporter of Debussy's controversial opera, *Pelleas and Melissande*, which was based on the play by Maurice Maeterlinck. Many in the musical world thought this opera, which had its premiere in 1902, represented a major change in operatic traditions.

Claude Debussy

As with his previous *Afternoon With A Faun*, which premiered in 1894, Debussy believed in composing music that expressed the deeper layers of life's experiences rather than simply adhering to more traditional methods. In 1885, when only 23, Debussy wrote: "I don't think I'll ever be able to cast my music in a rigid mould. I would always rather deal with something where the passage of events is to some extent subordinated to a thorough and extended portrayal of human feelings."

While they appreciated each other in ability and achievements, their personalities did differ. The public, however, tended to see them as similar. Ravel was said to be more attentive to form and Debussy to be more spontaneous. On this score, Ravel wrote that Debussy's "genius was obviously one of great individuality, creating its own laws, constantly in evolution, expressing itself freely, yet always faithful to French tradition. For Debussy, the musician and the man, I have profound admiration, but by nature I am different."

Eventually, camps formed championing the words of each composer. Disputes arose over who influenced whom, the precise chronology of their compositions, and even the issue of plagiarism. The latter imbroglio arose over Debussy's *Mother Goose* suite and Ravel's *Histoires Naturelles*, which had satirical verse about animals.

Public commentary ultimately brought about a growing distance between the duo. At one point Ravel said, "It's probably better, after all, for us to be on frigid terms for illogical reasons."

One of Ravel's great friends was Ricardo Vines, a Catalan pianist and another Apache. A month apart in age, they had been friends since the age of 13, with their roots both in the Basque region of France close to Spain. Vines had a significant influence on Ravel's Spanish music including the *Rhapsody Espagnole that* was premiered in 1907. Earlier, Vines had premiered Ravel's *Menuet Antique, Jeux d'euau, Pavan for Une Infante Defunte, Miroirs*, and then *Gaspart deo la Nuit* in 1909. Ravel dedicated the second movement of *Miroirs* to Vines.

Interestingly, Ravel didn't actually visit Spain until 1911.

Both Ravel and Vines were bachelors. Vines kept a 10-year diary of their work and times. Discussing his love life, Ravel once said, "The only love affair I have ever had was with music." Debussy, on the other hand, was married twice and had a very turbulent love life.

Debussy had been awarded the prestigious Prix de Rome, a scholarship at the French Academy in Rome, by the French Conservatory. His *Preludes* and *Nocturnes*, and the famed *Claire de Lune* from the *Suite Bergamesque*, had already established him in the musical limelight. *La Mer*, a symphonic tone poem, also received plaudits.

However, despite being favored to win, Ravel didn't get the Prix de Rome in 1905. A scandal, called the "Ravel Affair," arose, with the implication that the head of the French Conservatory favored one of his students for this plum. The upshot was that the head of the Conservatory was forced out of office, but Ravel still didn't go to Rome. Instead, he concentrated on what has been termed his Spanish period.

Debussy was diagnosed with rectal cancer in 1909 and suffered one of the first — if not the first — colostomy operations in 1916. He survived until 1918, dying during a German bombardment of Paris during World War I.

Ravel lived on for many years. He wanted to be an aviator in World War I but wound up being a truck driver during the famed Verdun battle that halted the German offensive threatening capture of Paris. As a bit of interesting trivia, the French unit he served in is believed to have fought against a German group that included Adolph Hitler.

One of his greatest post-war works, the *Bolero*, was nonetheless considered trivial by Ravel. Originally called *Fandango*, the 1928 piece has a mesmerizing and deliberate repetition. It was termed by Ravel as "an experiment in a very special and limited direction" and as a "piece for orchestra without music." He was quite surprised by its popular success. The piece has often been used as background music in film and television, including the movie *Ten*.

Ravel was seriously injured in a 1932 taxi accident which affected his mental state. He agreed to experimental brain surgery which he didn't recover from. He died in 1937. His long time friend, Vines, was said to have lost too much in gambling and died in poverty in 1943.

***

Among Debussy's quotes:

- Music is the space between the notes.

- There is no theory. You have only to listen. Pleasure is the law. I love music passionately. And because I love it, I try to free it from barren traditions that stifle it. It must never be shut in and become an academic art.

- Extreme complication is contrary to art.

- How much has to be explored and discarded before reaching the naked flesh of feeling.

- Works of art make rules; rules do not make works of art.

And from Ravel:

- Unlike politics, in art I'm a nationalist. I know that I am above all a French composer: I further declare myself a classicist.

- Art is a beautiful lie.

CHAPTER 53. JAMES JOYCE AND ITALO SVEVO

James Joyce, who was born in 1882, is widely considered one of the foremost writers in the English language during the 20th century. He disdained traditional plots, and experimented with stream of consciousness, assorted epiphanies, and reveries. His use of language was extraordinary.

But his books aren't particularly easy to read. The last one, *Finnegan's Wake* — on which he labored for 17 long years before it came out in 1939 — is probably more discussed in academic circles than read by everyday readers. His masterpiece, *Ulysses* — which graphically details the Dublin-based events in the life of one man– only took seven years to complete. The novel has parallels of Homer's *Odyssey* transferred to a Dublin setting. While his novels and short stories are primarily about Dublin, he spent a good deal of his life living mostly in Zurich, Trieste, and Paris. He never returned to the city of his birth after 1912.

During his initial stay in Trieste, when it was part of the Austro-Hungarian Empire, he taught English at the Berlitz School. Later, after considerable penury and much borrowing from friends, he finally secured a financial patron in later years. He received a monthly allowance that eased his money concerns. During his Trieste period two friends had a seminal influence on his writing.

Ettore Schmitz, born in 1861 in Trieste and better known by his pseudonym of Italo Svevo, was a student who became a close friend of Joyce after their meeting in 1907. Svevo, a businessman trained in banking, served as a sounding board for Joyce's ideas and was a model for Leopold Bloom, the major character in *Ulysses*. Svevo who was born in the Jewish faith but became a Catholic, was an important source of information about Judaism as the Bloom character was Jewish.

James Joyce

Svevo, an author in his own right and some 20 years older than Joyce, wrote a now classic novel, *Zeno's Conscience*, which was initially self-published in 1923. Greatly interested in the theories of Freud, Svevo's narrative used the memoirs of a man urged by his psychoanalyst to unburden himself by writing a book. However, the novel didn't receive much attention and probably wouldn't have been much read if not for Joyce.

Italo Svevo

Since becoming friends Joyce had read an earlier novel by Svevo, *Senilita (As A Man Grows Older)*, which had also not gotten very far. First, he had *Zeno's Conscience* translated into French from its original Italian, and then managed through his contacts to get the novel published in Paris. As it turned out, the Parisian critics liked the book. Impressed, the Italian critics then took note. Subsequently, bolstered by this critical acclaim, the book has gone on to considerable fame.

Svevo became involved in the movement to have Trieste, a polyglot city, become part of Italy after World War I ended with defeat of the Central Powers which included the Austro-Hungarian Empire. Better known, now, as a writer, he came out with a second edition of *Senilita* nearly 30 years after the first one. He also wrote several plays. Finally an Italian by nationality, Svevo passed away in 1928 at the age of 67.

Frank Budgen, an English painter just a year younger than Joyce, was another Trieste friend. They spent hours together including discussions about the structure and other elements of *Ulysses* and *Portrait of the Artist As A Young Man*. The latter book started literary life as a lengthy work called *Stephan Hero*, which Joyce termed "a work in progress."

Joyce had already had *Dubliners*, a collection of short stories, published in 1914 after a bitter series of problems where would-be publishers feared prosecution for publishing his ultra-realistic portrayals of Dublin life. Initially refusing to rewrite offending portions (including a less than flattering reference about King Edward VII, the reigning English monarch), Joyce finally succumbed to some extent. *Portrait of the Artist As A Young Man* came soon after in 1916, and then *Ulysses* in 1922. He also wrote three books of poetry and various other articles and writings while still experiencing some difficulties with authorities. *Ulysses* was greatly controversial with obscenity cited as a major reason. Initially banned in the U.S. and Great Britain, it was finally published in both countries; a U.S. judge allowed that the novel wasn't "dirt for dirt's sake."

Though he lived away from Dublin for a considerable part of his life, Joyce knew the city's streets and alleys well. He wrote: "For myself, I always write about Dublin, because if I can get to the heart of Dublin I can get to the heart of all the cities of the world. In the particular is contained the universal."

Joyce also declared that "Mistakes are the ports of discovery."

Early in his life Joyce rejected his initial Catholic faith and upbringing. He wrote: "My mind rejects the whole present order and Christianity-home, the recognized virtues, classes of life, and religious doctrines. Six years ago I left the

Catholic church, hating it most fervently. I found it impossible for me to remain in it on account of the impulses of my nature. I made secret war upon it when I was a student and declined to accept the positions it offered me. By doing this I made myself a beggar but I retained my pride. Now I make open war upon it by what I write and say and do."

Joyce left Dublin with his girlfriend, Nora, for the continent when both were in their early twenties. They had two children as well as a troubled relationship. They finally married in 1931. Unfortunately, she burned many of his searingly intimate letters when they fled from Paris in 1940. His eyesight got progressively worse despite several operations. He was nearly blind when he died after his last eye operation in 1941.

The Catholic Church suggested a mass but his wife declined, saying, "I couldn't do that to him."

Some quotes from Joyce:

- I fear those big words which make us so unhappy.

- A man's errors are his portals into discovery.

- Men are governed by uses of intellect and women by curves of emotion.

- Irresponsibility is part of the pleasure of all art; it is the part the schools cannot recognize.

- Better pass boldly into that other world, in the full glory of some passion, than fade and wither dismally with age.

- Ireland is the old sow that eats her farrow.

- My mouth is filled with decayed teeth and my soul of decayed ambitions.

And from Svevo:

- He (Joyce) is twice a rebel, against England and against Ireland. He hates England and would like to transform Ireland.

- I know that when Joyce has written a page of prose he thinks that he has paralleled some page of music that he delights in.

Chapter 54. Igor Stravinski and Robert Craft

Igor Stravinski was already a world-wide celebrity, much lauded for his epochal music accomplishments which influenced so many other composers, when he met Robert Craft in 1948. Craft, who was much younger — he was born in 1923 while Stravinski dated back to 1882 — was himself a noted composer and musicologist. From that point on Craft became a member of the Stravinski household, living first in Los Angeles and then in New York. He and Stravinski then collaborated in both musical and non-musical subjects and occasions.

Craft and Stravinski also worked together on a number of books including *Conversations with Igor Stravinski*, *Expositions and Developments*, *Dialogues and A Diary*, *Themes and Episodes*, and *Retrospectives and Conclusions*. These books encompass conversations, diary material, interviews, essays and opinions of Stravinski. However, many observers believe Craft's viewpoints are abundantly present. Craft, it should be noted, also served as a translator for his friend. Craft also edited *Stravinski: Selected Conversations* which came out in three volumes.

Stravinski in 1903

Stravinski had indeed much to say, musically and otherwise. He was born near St. Petersburg, in Russia, but later lived in Paris and Switzerland. Giving up the law career his father wanted for him, Stravinski turned to studying and composing music. He made a name for himself with *Fireworks* in 1908, the *Firebird Ballet* in

1910, and *Petruska* in 1911. He came to the attention of Sergei Diaghilev, founder of the Ballets Russes. This was a famed artistic troupe which helped launch the careers of several famous choreographers and dancers. Stravinski became the principal composer for the Ballets Russes.

It was, however, the premiere of *The Rite of Spring* in Paris in 1913 that made Stravinski quite famous — or notorious in some musical circles. His composition, breaking with musical tradition in some ways, created an actual riot in the theater. His innovative tonal language and exuberant orchestration ushered in a new era of modernism in music.

Stravinski kept composing, and he became a French citizen in 1934. He provided music for projects with many other creative notables such as Pablo Picasso, Jean Cocteau, and Andre Gide.

A believer in monarchy, Stravinsky disliked the Bolsheviks who took over Russia in 1917. He finally — at the suggestion of Craft, it's believed — made a trip back to his native country after World War II. In his writings, Stravinski lamented, "The greatest single crisis of my life as a composer was the loss of Russia, and its language, not only of music but of words."

After Benito Mussolini came to power in Italy, Stravinski said of Il Duce: "I don't believe that anyone venerates Mussolini more than I. He is the savior of Italy and — let us hope — Europe." He also made it known to the Nazis in Germany that he followed the Russian Orthodox religion, lest there be any confusion over his religious persuasion. Religious motifs, as well as Russian folk tales, were part of the inspiration for his music. He said: "Music praises God. Music is well or better able to praise Him than the building of a church with all its decorations. It is the church's greatest ornament."

But when World War II broke out, Stravinski and his family relocated to the U.S., finally settling in Los Angeles where he became involved with providing scores for some films. He also planted beets, a popular Russian food, in his garden, for use in making borscht. As far as the film studios, he termed them as "separate principalities." After attending some Hollywood parties, which he said were boring, he and his wife were said to resort to reading classic novels at home, by Dostoevski and Tolstoy, to restore their faith in human beings. However, Stravinski did become friends with some celebrities such as Danny Kaye and Edgar G. Robinson.

His *Symphony in C*, one of his major works, was completed in the U.S. and received its first performance in Chicago in 1940.

Concerned over the turbulent world situation, and where an essentially non-political artist could work, he once asked a friend if a revolution was imminent or possible in the United States. When told it was feasible, he mused, "But where will I go?"

Nonetheless, he became an American citizen in 1945 and kept writing other compositions. In 1969 the family moved to New York, where Stravinski died in 1971 at the age of 88. Among many honors he was given, a two-cent stamp with his likeness created by the U.S. Postal Service.

Robert Craft

Craft continued his career in music into his eighties, continuing to work on Stravinski-related matters and his own music and recordings. His books also include: *Stravinski: Glimpses of A Life* in 1992, and *Stravinski: Chronicles Of A Friendship* in 1994. *An Improbable Life: Memoirs* came out in 2002. Among other distinctions he was awarded the International Prix du Disque at the Cannes Music Festival in 2002.

***

In a playful mood perhaps, Stravinski was quoted as saying: "My music is best understood by children and animals."

Other quotes:

- I haven't understood a bar of music in my life, but I have felt it.
- In order to create there must be a dynamic force, and what force is more potent than love?
- I have learned through my life as a composer chiefly through my mistakes and pursuits of false assumptions, not by exposure to founts of wisdom and knowledge.

Chapter 55. Gertrude Stein and Alice B. Toklas

Gertrude Stein, doyenne of artists in Paris before and after World War I, was an American writer, poet, art collector, and critic. Her salon was much visited, and her opinion much sought and valued by artists such as Pablo Picasso and Henri Matisse and writers like Ernest Hemingway, Sherwood Anderson, Thornton Wilder, and Ezra Pound. She was an early supporter of cubism as a new wave in the art world.

Stein, a woman of independent means, was born in 1874. She relocated to Paris in 1903 and lived in Europe, mostly the French capital, for the rest of her life. She and her brother, Leo, opened a successful art gallery on Rue de Fleurus. Matisse and Picasso, whose works were in her gallery, were also part of her social circle which osmosed into Saturday evening get-togethers at her four-room, two-story apartment (which had an attached atelier). As Stein explained: "Matisse brought people, everybody brought somebody, and they came at any time and it began to be a nuisance and it was in this way that Saturday evenings began."

Gertrude Stein

Picasso, who was twenty-four to her thirty-one when they first met, also painted a famous portrait of his hostess.

In 1907, Stein had met Alice B. Toklas, who was born in 1877 and was just four years older than her.

Toklas was a well-to-do and single American woman. The two quickly bonded and were together the rest of Stein's life, with Toklas as her lover, confidant, secretary, cook, and co-hostess.

Then, in 1914, there was a disagreement of sorts about Leo and his wife, and Stein's brother subsequently moved to Settignano, Italy. Their art works were divided. The gallery didn't go on, and World War I also stopped the evening salons. The pair — Stein and Toklas — were finally convinced to aid the French war effort by driving supplies to hospitals.

The two were so close that Stein used her friend's name in her book, *The Autobiography of Alice B. Toklas*, which was really the story of her own life. The book, which was published in 1933, became her most famous book. With a large printing of the book in 1933, Stein and Toklas went on an extended tour of the U.S. Stein's first well-received book was *Three Lives* which — along with *The Making of America* and *Tender Bottoms* — came out before the advent of World War I.

After the conflict ended, the salon started again and the walls of her apartment were covered with avant-garde paintings. Many artists and writers, including American expatriates, again sampled Stein's self-assured comments and criticisms of their assorted artistic efforts. Hemingway even asked Stein to be the godmother of his newborn son; however, they later became bitter enemies. While Stein is often given credit for coining the expression of "Lost Generation," it's quite possible others might have been individually or collectively responsible. Stein, however, came out with some other memorable quotes including "A rose is a rose is a rose is a rose," and "There's no there there" (in referring to Oakland, her childhood home).

Stein's politics tended to be right wing. She was opposed to President Roosevelt and his "New Deal," favored General Francisco Franco's takeover of Spain, and endorsed the Vichy regime that collaborated with Germany during World War II. While she and Toklas were both Jewish, they escaped any problems with the conquering Germans due to a combination of Stein's fame and her friendship with a key Vichy official. They did billet German soldiers at their rural French home in the Vichy-controlled part of France. She favored Marshall Pétain, leader of the Vichy government, even translating some of his speeches into English.

Among her many other writings are *Paris, France*, in 1940 and *Wars I Have Seen*, in 1945. An opera, *Four Saints In Three Acts*, was performed in 1934. Some of her short stories, with lesbian themes, were published after her death in 1946. Stein's final words, which may or may not be genuine, centered around her asking Toklas, "What is the answer?"

Not receiving a reply, Stein then asked, "Well, in that case, what is the question?"

Alice B. Toklas (photo by Carl Van Vechten)

Meanwhile, Alice Toklas published her own 1954 literary memoir, *Alice B. Toklas Cookbook*, which combined reminisces with recipes. In 1963, her real autobiography, *What Is Remembered*, came out. The book comes to an end with Stein's demise. Stein's heirs reportedly made off with some of Stein's valuable art works despite them being willed to Toklas. She died in 1967 at the age of 89 and was buried next to Stein in the Père Lachaise Cemetery in Paris. Her name and dates of birth and death were engraved on the back of Stein's headstone.

***

Among many of Stein's quotes:

- We are always the same age inside.

- Everybody gets so much information all day long that they lose their common sense.

- Anything scares me, anything scares anyone but really after all considering how dangerous everything is nothing is really very frightening.

And from Toklas:

- This has been a most wonderful night. Gertrude has said things tonight it will take her 10 years to understand.

- What is sauce for the goose may be sauce for the gander but not necessarily sauce for the chicken, the duck, the turkey, or the guinea hen.

Chapter 56. Theodore Roosevelt & Joseph Bucklin Bishop

Having a combination top-flight journalist, press agent, political counselor and general loyalist on your side is the mark of having a great friend. On the other hand, having the trust and confidence of a major political personality who became president is also a valuable friendship.

This was the case between Theodore Roosevelt and Joseph Bucklin Bishop, as their careers merged. Roosevelt was the junior figure only in age. He was born in 1858, with Bishop born in 1847.

Roosevelt and Bishop forged a lengthy relationship that began when Roosevelt was Commissioner of Police in New York City in 1895 and Bishop was a major reporter for the *New York Evening Post*. Both men were fighters against corruption and their mutual target was Tammany Hall, the political outfit that had undue civic influence over the city government. Their friendship, marked by many meetings and letters over the years, lasted until Roosevelt died in 1919 at the age of 60. There were hundreds of letters between them during the 1897–1918 period. Bishop, who was 12 years older than Roosevelt, lived on until 1932.

Theodore Roosevelt

Roosevelt aspired to higher office. He was determined to pursue progressive policies including an end to the patronage system; and he needed a top-tier journalist he could count on for newspaper articles supporting him. Bishop also served as a sounding board for Roosevelt's ideas as well as his own. In Roosevelt, Bishop found a kindred and very quotable personality, despite their different backgrounds. Roosevelt was very much a patrician from a distinguished family and Bishop was the son of a New England farmer

Fortified by a Harvard education, the two were always responsive to each other. While they didn't always agree, their viewpoints often meshed well. Roosevelt, it should be noted, was a writer himself. While still at Harvard he had begun a history of the U.S. Navy during the War of 1812 with England. The book was published in 1882 as *The Naval War of 1812*.

Bishop, during his long career, wrote several books, including some about Roosevelt. His *Letters to Roosevelt's Children*, with the missives provided to him by an ailing Roosevelt, was published in 1919 just after Roosevelt died. The book went on to become a best seller, earning Bishop enough in royalties for a worldwide trip. Roosevelt also selected Bishop as his official biographer, and his two-volume *Theodore Roosevelt & His Time: Shown In His Own Letters* was published in 1920.

Roosevelt's political star was bright. He was elected as a New York State assemblyman in 1881 at the tender age of 23, becoming the youngest man to ever serve in that body. Subsequently, he authored more bills than anyone else at the time. In 1889, he was appointed a civil service commissioner in Washington D.C. which led to becoming New York's police commissioner in 1895. His swift rise went on with appointment as assistant secretary of the Navy in 1896.

The Spanish–American War of 1898, which he supported with both words and deeds, gave him a considerable and well-chronicled boost in stature. He resigned from the Navy to take a commission as a Lt. Colonel in a voluntary cavalry regiment, nicknamed the *Rough Riders*. During the combat, he is credited with leading a successful charge up San Juan Hill in Cuba against well-entrenched Spanish forces.

His fame secured, Roosevelt was elected governor of New York in 1898. He then became the Republican vice presidential candidate in the 1900 election. William McKinley, as president, and Roosevelt were duly elected; but then tragedy struck with the president assassinated. Roosevelt became president at the early age of 42.

Bishop, during this meteoric ascendancy, was omnipresent to write about Roosevelt. He sent him clips of articles from time to time, while offering advice and strategy on various key issues. Roosevelt was very aware of the power of the press and was keen to gain public approval of his policies and actions. One of his key accomplishments was ending a prolonged and bitter 163-day coal strike and getting the workers more pay for fewer hours as well.

As part of his ongoing progressive movement Roosevelt championed anti-trust legislation. He sought to limit the power of large corporations and end excessive railroad company economic domination of the economy. The Pure Food and Drug Act and Meat Inspection Act were also major accomplishments, though not everyone in some industries agreed. He worked to create a workmen's compensation law and an eight-hour workday. Not all of his policies went into effect, but he certainly served notice on big business with creation of the Commerce and Labor department.

Roosevelt was also a conservationist, spurred somewhat by his experiences living in and visiting the west. He was a cattle rancher for a while in the *Badlands* of the Dakotas. A lover of nature and the outdoors, he created a network of national parks.

Building of the Panama Canal was one of the achievements Roosevelt is most noted for. As Panama was part of Colombia at the time Roosevelt managed to foment a 1903 "revolution" or coup giving Panama independence and the right — in this tidy geopolitical rearrangement — to lease territory to the U.S. for the canal construction. The Panama Canal, which many years later was returned to Panamanian sovereignty, has been a major economic and military feature in America's rise to world leadership.

Roosevelt visited Panama in 1906, becoming the first president to leave American soil while in office.

The canal, however, needed effective oversight. Bishop, a newspaper editor since 1870 and one who had supported Roosevelt's drive to build the canal, lost out in a newspaper shuffle. This may not have been a great loss as he was appointed in 1905 to become Roosevelt's eyes and ears as executive secretary of the Isthmian Canal Commission in Washington D.C. Later, Bishop even lived in Panama for a period, reporting back to Roosevelt. His experiences led to a book, *The Panama Gateway*.

Joseph Bucklin Bishop

Bishop was put in charge of Roosevelt's reelection campaign in 1904. He also helped lessen the flap that happened when Roosevelt had the audacity to invite Booker T. Washington, the most prominent Black in the country, to dinner at the White House. Bishop and his wife, Harriet, were often guests at the White House as well as Roosevelt's home at Oyster Bay, N.Y. Much press coverage was set in motion by Bishop when Roosevelt received the Nobel Prize for helping to negotiate an end to the 1904–05 Russian–Japanese War. In a bit of presidential trivia, Roosevelt — who disliked the "Teddy" name sometimes used for him — was the first president seen by the public while being driven in an auto. The 1902 event was recorded in Hartford, Connecticut.

Roosevelt was a firm believer in the two-term limit to the presidency. William Howard Taft, a political and personal friend, succeeded Roosevelt as president. But Taft turned out to be much more conservative than Roosevelt and the two were soon bitter opponents. This split led to Roosevelt abandoning the two-term limit and running for president in 1912 on the *Bull Moose* ticket. Bishop served ably but with the Republican Party split, the Democratic candidate, Woodrow Wilson, was voted into office.

Roosevelt is one of four presidents whose head and face grace the Black Hills of South Dakota. After he died in his sleep in 1919 one telling comment was: "Death had to take Roosevelt sleeping, for if he had been awake, there would have been a fight."

***

Among Roosevelt's many quotes:

- To educate a man in mind and not in morals is to educate a menace to society.

- Whenever you are asked if you can do a job, tell 'em, 'Certainly, I can!' Then get busy and find out how to do it.

- Speak softly and carry a big stick; you will go far.

- Far and away the best prize that life offers is the chance to work hard at work worth doing.

- Let us remember that as much has been given us, much will be expected from us.

- Nine-tenths of wisdom is being wise at the right time.

- It is true of the nation, as of the individual, that the greatest doer must also be a great dreamer.

CHAPTER 57. TSARINA ALEXANDRA, ANNA VYRUBOVA, AND GRIGORI RASPUTIN

Anna Vyrubova, who isn't particularly well known, still had an important role in the turbulent period in Russia before and during World War I that led up to the 1917 Russian revolution. She was a trusted friend and confidante to the Tsarina Alexandra. As such she was a conduit leading to Grigori Rasputin, the Siberian mystic, who was accused of having undue influence over the Tsarina and Tsar Nicholas II. The royal pair were the last of the Russian tsars.

The Tsarina, who had a German background, was born in 1872. She had some difficulty in adjusting to Russian court life after her marriage to Nicholas, but she was a strong influence on the Russian ruler.

Vyrubova, who was born in Moscow in 1884 as Anna Taneyeva, came from a well-connected family and was attached to the imperial court at an early age. She was 12 years younger than the empress. Ironically, one of her childhood playmates was Prince Felix Yusupov, one of the nobles who later conspired to kill Rasputin. As it turned out, the German-born Tsarina liked the young Russian girl more than some of the other more distinguished women at the Russian court. She spent a great deal of time with the royal family, which included sailing on the imperial yacht. The two women shared intimacies of their lives. The Tsarina felt uncomfortable with the static nature of court life and Russian culture in general.

Vyrubova later observed that it had been difficult to change any detail in the routine of the Russian court. Showing no ambition for honors or wealth — some said she was naïve — Vyrubova openly and sincerely was devoted to the Tsarina, who was quite appreciative in return.

Royal Martyrs, Tsar Nicholas II of Russia and Family (ROCOR)

Yusupov later wrote: "No one could have foreseen that this unattractive girl would one day become the intimate friend and evil genius of the Tsarina. It was largely due to her that Rasputin owed his amazing rise to favor."

After giving birth to four girls, the Tsarina finally had a boy, Alexei, who automatically became the heir-apparent to her husband. Tragically, the Tsarina was the carrier of hemophilia, which was fatal at the time, as it means that one's blood doesn't clot after a simple bruise or cut. The disease was common to some extent among the royal families of Europe due to their inter-marriages. The

Tsarina sought help from doctors but they had none to offer. She turned then to non-medical sources and Vyrubova may have called the Tsarina's attention to Rasputin and subsequently served as a go-between between the two. The monk had come to St. Petersburg, which was then the Russian capital, from Siberia and established a reputation as a healer of sorts. Vyrobova met Rasputin soon after his arrival. She was greatly impressed with his powers, and soon became a strong advocate for him with the Empress, carrying messages between them.

Tsarina Alexandra

Rasputin's efforts through prayers seemed to be effective with Alexei healing more quickly after any damage to his body. The healer once sent the Tsarina a note with this advice: "Don't let the doctors bother him too much; let him rest." She was a firm believer in prayer. Accordingly, Rasputin's influence with the Tsarina grew immensely. While called a "mad monk" by others, the imperial family considered him their "friend" and a "holy man."

But Rasputin also increasingly behaved in a dissolute fashion, creating a furor with his disreputable activities. It was suggested, falsely, that he was intimate with the Tsarina. But evidently he used his wedge with the Tsarina to elicit favors from ladies of the court seeking preferential treatment for their husbands as far as governmental positions. Rasputin's theme or modus operandi was that one had to first become familiar with sin to overcome it, and evidently he did his share in the former part of the equation. But no matter how scandalous the reports were of Rasputin (which included his sleeping with Vyrobova), his standing stayed fine with the Tsarina as long as Alexei survived. At the same time Vyrubova's role at court remained strong.

The Tsarina was unpopular with the Russian people, but she believed in the divine right of kings and supported autocratic control of the country. During the period that Nicholas went to the front, when World War I broke out (though well back from the actual battlefield), the Tsarina basically ran the nation's affairs.

Vyrubova married a naval officer, Alexander Vyrubov, though she was warned by Rasputin that the marriage wouldn't be a good one. The Tsarina, however, favored the marriage. Rasputin turned out to be right. The couple soon divorced. When interrogated after the revolution, Vyrubova claimed the marriage had never been consummated as her husband was impotent.

Anna Vyrubova

During World War I, Vyrubova served as a Red Cross nurse. She was badly injured in a train accident in 1915 and credited Rasputin with helping to save her life through his prayers. The war went badly for Russia, and even worse for Rasputin. He was finally assassinated in 1916 by a cabal of nobles led by Yusupov, who were fed up with his antics, sexual and otherwise. From most reports it wasn't an easy killing with poison, stabbings, pistol shots, and drowning involved.

Grigori Rasputin

Vyrobova was suspected of having political influence over the royal family. Charges were also levied of sexual improprieties, including sleeping with both Rasputin and the Tsar. She was arrested on the orders of Alexander Kerensky, provisional head of the new government that came into being when the revolution began (before this fledgling authority was overthrown itself by the Lenin-led Bolsheviks). To prove her innocence, she asked for a medical examination — which certified that she was indeed a virgin.

Despite some thought by various groups to rescuing the royal family from their imprisonment by the Bolshevik command, no attempt was made. Finally, the new Bolshevik government had the royal family executed in 1918.

Meanwhile, Vyrubova managed to escape the turmoil in Russia in 1920. A civil war was raging between the "red" Bolsheviks and "white" units who supported the deposed monarchy. She went to Finland, a former Russian duchy that was now independent. Before her departure she had become friends with the famed Russian writer, Maxim Gorky, who urged her to write her recollections of life in the imperial court. Rare and intimate descriptions of the imperial family, as well as many black and white photos, are in her *Memories of the Russian Court*.

Vyrubova lived on for many years, dying in 1964 in Helsinki, the Finnish capital.

Chapter 58. Franz Kafka & Max Brod

One of the greatest acts of friendship can come posthumously. This was the situation between two German-writing Czechs, Franz Kafka and Max Brod. Kafka is a world-famous writer. His writings led to his name becoming an adjective, "Kafkaesque," to describe bizarre happenings.

Kafka and Brod were close friends, and both members of a small group of German artists of the Jewish faith living in Prague that was then part of the Austrian–Hungarian Empire. Kafka read some of the stories he was working on to the group for comments.

Kafka, who died at the early age of forty in 1924 from tuberculosis, was far from sure about his literary talent, despite the encouragement of Brod, already a noted writer and critic. Kafka named Brod as his literary executor. He wrote: "Dear Max, My last request. Everything I leave behind me in the way of diaries, manuscripts, letters (my own and others), sketches, and so on is to be burned unread."

Brod disobeyed and preserved Kafka's works from incineration, claiming subsequently that he had warned his friend of his intention.

The result was the publishing, to continued acclaim and much literary and psychological analysis and interpretation, of such major novels that came out shortly thereafter: *The Trial* in 1925, *The Castle* in 1926, and *Amerika* in 1927. Kafka's *Collected Works* and his diaries and letters, edited by Brod, came out later. Brod also wrote a biography about Kafka.

The two met, only a year apart in age — Kafka was born in 1883, Brod in 1884 — in 1902 when both were students at the Charles-Ferdinand University in Prague. Discovering mutual interests in literature, though their tastes and opinions frequently differed, their friendship grew. Kafka was often a guest at Brod's parents' home, and it was there that he met Felice Brauer, a cousin of Brod's brother-in-law. She worked in Berlin, which led to years of correspondence. The pair had an off-and-on relationship which included an engagement that finally came to an unhappy end in 1917. Kafka actually wrote to Felice's father that she wouldn't be happy with someone like him, as his major interest in life was literature.

Franz Kafka

After graduation Kafka got a job at an insurance agency laboring on workmen's compensation cases. He didn't particularly enjoy the work but it did give him time to write and he worked there until 1922. His first collection of stories came out in 1913. His most famous work, the novella *Metamorphosis*, was published in 1915. Much read since, the tale recounts the experience of a young man who wakes up one morning as a giant insect. Another famous story, *In The Penal Colony*, was published in 1919.

Brod encouraged Kafka to keep a diary, which he did. The two tried to write a travelogue together in 1912 but only got as far as the introduction. Brod married, but they remained close friends and confidants. Life was difficult for Jews in this period in Prague with friction between German- and Czech-speakers as well as anti-Semitism. But during World War I, Kafka received exemption, for health reasons, from military service in the Austrian–Hungarian army.

Kafka, the oldest of six children in a middle-class family, had a troubled relationship with his authoritarian father, who tended to belittle him and to foster notions of inadequacy. Seeking independence from parental influence seemed to be a driving force in his life and fiction. Kafka was diagnosed with tuberculosis in 1917, which altered his thinking and lifestyle (that now included convalescence). Despite assurances from friends like Brod, Kafka feared he came across as unattractive.

Due to unresolved familial difficulties Kafka, already in his thirties, penned a pamphlet-long *Letter to the Father* to explain, if not dissect, their difficulties. In effect, he wanted to declare his final, if belated, independence. Despairing of family life he once wrote, much in the same vein: "I have always looked on my parents as persecutors."

Kafka was greatly valued by his employer, who gave him leaves of absence due to his health. Finally, he retired due to ill health in 1922.

Next year Kafka met a young girl, Dora Diamont, while on vacation at a Baltic Sea resort. He wound up moving to Berlin and living with her, which was another measure of distancing himself from his family's influence. Meanwhile, he continued to write. But his condition worsened and he returned to Prague for treatment, and there he died in 1924.

Brod remained in contact with Kafka during his final years and then performed capably as his literary executor. He and his wife, Elsie, managed to escape the German takeover of Czechoslovakia in 1939. They fled to Palestine with suitcases filled with Kafka's assorted writings. Brod subsequently worked in Tel Aviv publishing Kafka's considerable literary output. He passed away in 1968.

Max Brod plaque, next to the grave of Franz Kafka, in the New Jewish Cemetery in Prague

Scholars and critics in discussing Kafka's works, and such themes as alienation from society as well as irrational societies, have pondered some of Kafka's quotes:

- My fear is my substance, and probably the best part of me.
- My guiding principle is this: guilt is never to be doubted.
- A book must be the ax to break the frozen sea within us.
- Anything that has real and lasting value is always a gift from within.
- Anyone who keeps the ability to see beauty never grows old.
- It is through writing that I keep a hold on life.

CHAPTER 59. RUPERT BROOKE AND DENIS BROWN

Rupert Brooke and Denis Brown were two well-born young, idealistic and artistic Englishmen. Both perished in their twenties during World War I.

Brooke, by far the more famous of the two, was an internationally known poet. He was born in 1887, a year before Brown. However, Brown was a composer, pianist and music critic of note. They met at a public school (prep school) where they became close friends; and then they were reunited at Cambridge University where they took part in stage productions. Brown even asked Brooke, who had already published poems, to write a song for him to be set to music for Easter Day. Brooke obliged, creating *A Song In Praise of Cremation Written To My Lady on Easter Day*.

Subsequently, Brooke had his first collection of poems published in 1911. He also became involved with the Socialist Fabian Society and the Georgian group, a bunch of poets who wanted to expand the interest of the public in poetry. Their initial volume was quite successful. Brooke became well known, and was one of the intellectual stars of his generation. He was also considered quite good looking, with none other than the famed Irish poet W.B. Yeats declaring that Brooke was "the handsomest young man in Britain."

Brown, meanwhile, worked as an organist, teacher and music critic and made a significant name for himself.

Brooke experienced a mental crisis in 1912 due to upsets over his love life. He spent a couple years of extensive travel through "a world grown old and cold and weary," though warmed by a brief affair in Tahiti.

Rupert Brooke

A collection of poems, *1914 & Other Poems*, was published in 1915. This collection included his most famous work, the five *War Sonnets*. *The Soldier*, expressing a chord of idealism in the face of the brutality of war, is the most noted and popular of the sonnets. It has the memorable lines:

> If I should die, think only this of me:
> That there's some corner of a foreign field
> That's forever England.

Sadly, his concern came to pass. He died within a year of the poem's publication.

Both Brooke and Brown volunteered for duty right after World War I broke out in August 1914. Brooke obtained a commission as an officer, but refused to take it unless Brown also received one. This took place in due course — Brooke had a connection to another friend who had access to the First Lord of the Admiralty, Winston Churchill. Both men were duly made Sub-Lieutenants in the newly-formed Royal Naval Division. They were sent to Antwerp to protect the Belgian port, but didn't see any action. It was here that Brooke wrote some of his sonnets. After this short-lived mission, he and Brown were deployed to join the force being assembled for the ill-fated Gallipoli Campaign in Turkish waters.

The reason for this campaign, fostered by Churchill, was to open the narrow strait of the Dardenelles and allow a warm water port through the Black Sea to Russia. Russia was among the Allies while the Dardanelles were controlled by the Turks, still part of the Ottoman Empire, which had sided with the Germans. The overly-ambitious campaign is considered to be the first amphibious operation in modern warfare. It utilized such measures as aerial reconnaissance and photography, steel landing craft, and artificial harbors. The campaign, nonetheless, failed and with heavy casualties. There was plenty of blame all around for the British strategists, with Churchill probably getting the largest share.

Brooke and Brown sailed on the S.S. Grantully Castle to the Dardenelles, and Brown even directed a military band aboard the ship. But then disaster struck. Brooke became increasingly ill from an infected insect bite and died at 28 from blood poisoning while still on the ship. Brown mournfully wrote:

> I sat with Rupert. At 4 o'clock he became weaker, and at 4:46 he died, with the sun shining all around his cabin, and the cool sea breeze blowing through the door and the shaded windows. No one could have wished for a quieter or a calmer end than in that lovely bay, shielded by the mountains and fragrant with sage and thyme.

Brooke personally selected a burial site for his companion on the Greek island of Skyros.

Many tributes were accorded to Brooke by the general public as well as other poets and politicians. Many thought his early poems tended to glorify war, but few doubted the beauty and passion of his verses. After the first flourish of patriotic fervor, the agony of staggering casualties from trench warfare changed the public mood and more realistic war poetry emerged. Brooke's reputation dimmed somewhat but shone again in later years.

Winston Churchill wrote a glowing tribute to the fallen poet/soldier in an obituary published in the Times. His commanding officer, General Ian Hamilton, captured much of Brooke's special appeal in noting that there were many heroes, some of whom had good looks, and a few of whom had some genius; but it was only Brooke that had all three.

Soon thereafter Brown was wounded in the neck. Before he fully recuperated, in Egypt, he hastened to rejoin his unit, only to suffer mortally from multiple wounds in an attack against Turkish trenches. It wasn't feasible to find and evacuate him, and his body was never recovered. He was only 28.

***

Some quotes from Brooke:

- A book may be compared to your neighbor: if it be good, it cannot last too long; if bad, you cannot get rid of it too soon.

- A kiss makes the heart young again and wipes out the years.

- We always love those who admire us; we do not always love those whom we admire.

CHAPTER 60. WOODROW WILSON AND COLONEL EDWARD HOUSE

Woodrow Wilson, the 28th president of the U.S., and Colonel Edward House were political and personal friends before and during World War I. House was the president's chief adviser for many years. But then the two had a major falling out over the President's policies for peace and how they were handled — or mishandled — by House who was the chief negotiator in Europe during the conflict.

The two men, both from the South, were two years apart in age. Wilson, originally from Virginia, was born in 1856, House in 1858 in Texas.

Woodrow Wilson

Colonel House was given his "military rank" as an honorific in his native Texas by a governor whom he had helped get elected. He had no military experience. He also didn't have any foreign policy experience, which still didn't stop him from being tapped as Wilson's foreign policy adviser and personal representative in assorted peace moves in Europe during the war.

Relocating to New York after the turn of the century, House met Wilson, then governor of New Jersey. He gradually became a close friend and confidant. He was instrumental in helping Wilson gain the Democratic Party nomination for the presidency in 1912 and then win the office. Wilson became the first American president with a Ph D degree.

Offered a Cabinet position, House declined, apparently preferring to wield influence as a well-placed adviser. His stature was such that he even had a room at the White House. After Wilson's first wife, Ellen, died in August 1914, his relationship grew even closer with House. The colonel, to some extent, became an alter ego. Wilson declared: "Mr. House is my second personality. He is my independent self. His thoughts and mine are one."

But some observers thought House made an effort to learn in advance what Wilson's opinions were so he could pattern his advice accordingly. The two men, virtually everyone agreed, had different temperaments, with Wilson less disposed to compromises. They did agree, however, on a grand-scale revision of how countries should treat the end of the world war in order to achieve universal and lasting peace.

When Wilson remarried in December 1915, his second wife, Edith, disliked House. This may have been because he reportedly suggested that more time was needed before the President wed again.

Dispatched to Europe to help pave the way to an end to the war, House spent most of the war years dickering in the capitals of the opponents. Some historians believe he exceeded Wilson's policies and was naïvely outmaneuvered by wily European diplomats, especially the British. Others contend he forged useful diplomatic ties while capably coping with the more experienced European leaders. Wilson, as well as House, were faced with secret post-war agreements between the Allies on territorial changes and reparations. House indicated willingness on the part of the U.S. to compromise on some of these matters, believing he was on the right track to achieve Wilson's ultimate purpose; but Wilson felt later that House had gone against his general instructions, possibly not fully understanding all the political ramifications of any agreement or understanding reached with other governments. In effect, Wilson came to believe that House might have damaged his overall policy and possibly his ability to successfully negotiate in constructing a lasting peace after the war ended.

Initially, however, Wilson said he was pleased by House's reports (which may have been read by the British, breaking an overly simplistic code).

President Wilson ran for reelection in 1916 on the platform, "He kept us out of the war." His policy was really one of armed neutrality, but when the Germans began unrestricted submarine warfare, the U.S. finally entered the conflict in 1917 as an associate of the Allies. Wilson and House alike couched the war in terms of a basic struggle between democracy and autocracy. The "associate" distinction was deemed to have value as the U.S. sought a limited victory for the Allies and hardly shared the same war aims as England, France and Italy. The allies, it became increasingly clear, wanted to severely punish Germany. This determination was dramatically revealed during the difficulties at the peace conference. Wilson's and House's notion of an epic "war to end wars" policy was exemplified in the President's altruistic "Fourteen Points" agenda, which was far more liberal than what the allies had in mind. The adjective "Wilsonian" has entered the political/diplomatic vocabulary to denote an idealistic position to spread American concepts about democracy.

Colonel House

Meanwhile, Wilson charged House with responsibility to organize the charter for creation of the *League of Nations*, an organization designed to insure that nations would be able to avoid a future war. When Germany sought an armistice, with the "14 points" in mind, House was also instructed to handle the armistice details. However, the Allies held out for a complete unconditional victory.

When Wilson came to Paris to help draft the Versailles Peace Treaty, and work for implementation of his "14 points," he discovered that some of his plans had been somewhat undermined by compromises House had accepted in his name. Policy disagreements were followed by personality conflicts. Wilson was particularly upset that his concept of a League of Nations was separated from the actual peace treaty. House soon was relegated to the sidelines and their relationship was broken as Wilson struggled to overcome resistance to his 14-point agenda.

Tellingly, the French premier, Georges Clemenceau, quipped that God only had "ten commandments." Wilson, however, did receive the 1919 Nobel Peace Prize.

House, though, was certainly quite right in recommending that Wilson compromise with key senators in the Senate to insure ratification of U.S. membership in the League of Nations. A group of key senators, led by Senator Henry Cabot Lodge, were amenable to ratification with one key amendment that limited American obligations. Wilson refused to compromise, and the League bill failed to pass in the Senate.

Wilson suffered a serious stroke in 1919 and was incapacitated for the rest of his term. His disability was kept from the public while his wife, Edith, served as his unappointed chief of staff. Many thought she was really functioning as a secret president. This situation led later to a revision of the rule about the incapacitation of a sitting president and who should take over the reins of government. Wilson died in 1924. His wife informed House there was no room for him at the funeral.

House published a four-volume work, *The Intimate Papers of Colonel House*, in 1926–28. He lived on to 1938 in time to see another world war coming with its causes clearly traceable to the failures of the Versailles Peace treaty.

Some quotes by Wilson:

- I have enjoyed the friendship and companionship of Republicans because I am by instinct a teacher, and I would like to teach them something.

- At every crisis in one's life, it is absolute salvation to have some sympathetic friend to whom you can think out loud without restraint or misgiving.

- A conservative is a man who just sits and thinks, mostly sits.

- Absolute identity with one's cause is the first and great condition of successful leadership.

- Every man who takes office in Washington either grows or swells, and when I give a man an office, I watch him carefully to see whether he is growing or swelling.

- America was established not to create wealth, but to realize a vision, to realize an ideal — to discover and maintain liberty among men.

CHAPTER 61. LEOPOLD AND LOEB

Friendship can be deadly too, as attested by the tragic saga of Nathan Leopold and Richard Loeb.

The two highly intelligent Chicago-based law students at the University of Chicago were born a year apart — Leopold in 1904 and Loeb in 1905. Both came from wealthy Jewish families, and each had an excellent scholastic record. Tragically, they concocted a plan to kill someone to prove to themselves how bright and superior they were to most people. Just under 20 years old, they developed a homosexual relationship. They were both influenced by the Nietzschean philosophy that generated the "superman" motif in his books *Thus Spoke Zarathustra* and *Beyond Good and Evil* (works which influenced the Nazi movement as well).

In this regard, Leopold wrote to Loeb: "A superman is, on account of certain superior qualities inherent in him, exempted from the ordinary laws which govern men. He is not liable for anything he may do."

The two spent months planning the "perfect" time for their crime including getting rid of the body and any incriminating evidence. Somewhat by chance, their victim turned out to be Bobby Franks, the 14-year-old son of a Chicago millionaire. Franks, walking home from school, was lured in the late afternoon into a rented car driven by Loeb, with Leopold in the backseat.

Franks was nearly killed with chisel blows to his head by Loeb, and was finished off by strangulation. The duo then drove to a remote marshland area near Wolf Lake in nearby Indiana. They removed Frank's clothing and left it at the side of the road, and then poured hydrochloric acid on Franks' body (face and genitals) to make identification difficult. The remains were then shoved into a nearby culvert at the Pennsylvania Railroad tracks.

Leopold (left) and Loeb (center) under arrest

Upon their return to Chicago, one of them called Franks' home with Leopold giving his name as "George Johnson." He told Franks' mother that her son had been kidnapped but was well, and to expect a ransom note to follow by special delivery the next morning. In the ransom note, they asked for $10,000 in different denominations and in old, unmarked bills. Again, they told the Franks family to await further instructions. Meticulous in their planning, they destroyed their blood-splattered clothing after trying to clean bloodstains from the rented car's upholstery. They had used false identities to rent the auto. The money, which was really incidental to them, was supposed to be put into a sealed cereal box and tossed from a moving train at a certain spot where it would be picked up.

With all these tasks finished, the pair spent the rest of the busy evening playing cards.

Before the Franks, who after some hesitation contacted the police, could pay the ransom, their plot fell apart. Franks' body was found. A detective also found a pair of eyeglasses with tortoiseshell frames near the scene that had an unusual hinge mechanism. A check of Chicago optometrists revealed that only three people in Chicago had bought such eyeglasses, and one was Leopold.

Under questioning by the police, Leopold claimed he had lost his glasses while bird watching. Loeb maintained that Leopold was with him at the time of the murder. They both asserted they had picked up two girls in Leopold's car without bothering to learn their last names. None of their alibis worked, especially as it was determined that Leopold's car was in the family garage that night.

Loeb was the first to confess. Each blamed the other. Leopold apparently also pleaded with his friend to admit that he struck the fatal blows: "Mumpsie feels less terrible than she might, thinking you did it, and I'm not going to take that shred of comfort away from her."

Leopold admitted that his attraction to Loeb had greatly influenced his willingness to go along with the plan. His motive, he admitted "to the extent I had one, was to please Dick."

The pair, with the public calling for them to be hanged, had a trial that caught the world's attention. Psychiatrists had a field day analyzing their motives and mental states. Even Sigmund Freud was inveigled to come to Chicago from Europe, but he declined due to poor health.

Noted lawyer Clarence Darrow (only wealthy families were presumably able to pay his fee) was retained to defend the pair. To the surprise of many observers, Darrow entered a guilty plea instead of not guilty, due to insanity. His strategy was to avoid a jury trial, which was likely to end with the death penalty, and instead to have a judge decide the case in a hearing. Darrow was opposed by the prosecutor Robert Crowe, who disdained Darrow's belief that one's life, economic and emotional situation had a lot to be taken into account when assessing guilt and the degree of guilt. Crowe stoutly asserted that criminals were simply responsible for their acts and should be fully punished, which in this case meant hanging.

Darrow's lengthy speech to Judge John Caverly sought mitigation of the supreme penalty — death by hanging. He pleaded the youth of Leopold and Loeb and questioned their capacity to fully understand their actions (though they were certainly responsible and hardly insane). His speech became famous on its own. In part he said: "Is any blame attached because somebody took Nietzsche's philosophy seriously and fashioned his life on it? It is hardly fair to hang a 19-year-old boy for the philosophy that was taught to him at the university."

Darrow succeeded with the judge, who was said to be much moved by his closing argument. The judge issued a life in prison sentence for the murder plus 99 years for the kidnapping.

At the Stateville Penitentiary, Loeb was slashed to death in 1936 at the age of 30 in a shower room by a razor blade wielding former cellmate, 21-year-old James Day. In his defense, Day claimed that Loeb had tried to sexually assault him. Evidence showed Day guilty of murder, but after an inquiry Day's testimony of self-defense was accepted. In Leopold's autobiography, *Life Plus 99 Years*, he wrote that Day's testimony was absurd.

In prison Leopold helped reorganize the prison library, taught classes, worked in the prison hospital, and even volunteered in 1944 to be infected with an experimental vaccine in the Stateville Penitentiary Malaria Study.

Leopold's first crack at parole failed. But after 33 years in prison, Leopold was released on parole in 1958. He attempted, still in 1958, to set up the Leopold

Foundation to help troubled youths. The foundation was supposed to be funded by royalties from his book *Life Plus 99 Years*. The State of Illinois, however, voided the charter for the foundation later that same year on the grounds that it violated the terms of Leopold's parole.

To avoid media attention, Leopold moved to Puerto Rico, where he married a 53-year-old widowed florist and worked as an x-ray technician at the Castaner General Hospital in Adjuntas. He also wrote another book, *The Birds of Puerto Rico*. He considered writing a book, *Snatch For a Halo*, about his life after prison, but decided against it. He tried but failed to block the movie *Compulsion* (one of various cinematic depictions of him and Loeb) on the grounds of invasion of privacy, defamation, and making money from his life story.

In a 1960 interview, Leopold said he was still very much in love with Loeb. Leopold died of a diabetes-related heart attack in 1971 at the age of 66. He donated his corneas, which were promptly put to use with needful recipients. By this time the other notables at the trial were long dead, Darrow in 1938, Judge Caverly in 1939, and Robert Crowe in 1958.

CHAPTER 62. CLARENCE DARROW AND JOHN ALTGELD

Clarence Darrow, undoubtedly one of the most famous trial lawyers in American history, and John Altgeld, governor of Ohio as well as a former judge and owner of a prosperous law firm, were friends who helped each other out at opposing ends of their careers.

Darrow, born in 1857 in Ohio, came to Chicago in 1887 in search of greater opportunities. He had read and been much impressed by a book Altgeld wrote, *On Penal Machinery & Its Victims*. This book held that the justice system favored rich people who could afford better representation and argued for reform of the legal/penal systems.

Darrow got to know Altgeld, who ran a well-known law firm. They became friends, and Darrow landed a job as a staff lawyer in Altgeld's firm. Altgeld served as a mentor of sorts, introducing Darrow to prominent people and providing access to the power center of Chicago. Eventually, through Altgeld, Darrow got involved in Chicago, Illinois, and national politics. He almost became mayor of Chicago.

Subsequently, Altgeld — who was born in Germany in 1847 and came to the U.S. as a child — became a judge. He was elected governor of Illinois in 1892, the first Democratic governor of Illinois in several decades. Very progressive in thought and action, Altgeld was a leader in the Progressive Movement. He signed into legislation stringent rules on workplace safety and child labor.

Governor Altgeld ran into enormous static in 1893 when he pardoned, with Darrow one of his enthusiastic supporters, three of the men convicted in the notorious Haymarket bombing on the grounds there had been a miscarriage of jus-

tice. The riot at Haymarket Square in Chicago in 1886 involved Pinkerton detectives and striking workers. A bomb was thrown, and to this day it isn't known
who threw the bomb. Seven policemen were killed as well as several civilians.
Eight workers were prosecuted for murder. Four were hanged in 1887, and one
committed suicide before being hanged.

Clarence Darrow

Altgeld, himself, was hanged in effigy for issuing this pardon.

Altgeld also faced heavy criticism when he rejected cries calling for federal
force to break up the Pullman workers' strike in 1894. He thought state resources
were sufficient and that force would produce bloodshed. President Grover Cleveland, asserting the federal mantle, still sent in troops — and there was bloodshed.

The pardons he issued effectively dimmed Altgeld's political star. He was called, among other endearments, an anarchist, murderer and socialist. None other than President Theodore Roosevelt fumed at a Chicago rally that Altgeld "condones and encourages the most infamous of murders" and was one who "would substitute for the government of Washington and Lincoln a red welter of lawlessness and dishonesty as fantastic and vicious as the Paris Commune."

Meanwhile, Altgeld helped Darrow secure a well-paying position as a corporate attorney for the Chicago & Northwestern Railway Company. But events soon took a different direction. In 1894, Darrow defended Eugene Debs, head of the American Railway Union, who was prosecuted for his part in the Pullman strike. Darrow had to shed his corporate ties, which involved some financial sacrifice. He succeeded in getting Debs off in one trial. Ultimately, though, he couldn't keep Debs from going to jail on other charges.

Darrow now became a specialist in labor law for nearly 20 years. Due to bribery allegations — he was acquitted in one case with a hung jury in another — he felt obliged to switch legal gears to criminal law. His success ratio was impressive, losing only one murder case out of many he handled. His courtroom eloquence, which was known to produce tearful reactions from juries and a judge or two, was much noted. His 12-hour summation in the Leopold and Loeb case, which helped spare the duo from being hanged and instead secured mitigation with long prison terms, is famous in legal annals. Darrow was a champion of the argument that such elements as psychological make-up and environmental influences can influence a person's criminal behavior more than just a knowing choice between right and wrong.

Darrow's skill in defending hard-to-exonerate defendants earned him the nickname "attorney for the damned."

The 1925 Scopes trial, about teaching Darwin's evolution theory in Tennessee schools, was another famous case. Darrow, in effect, outdueled William Jennings Bryan, who was brought in as a prosecution witness. In addition to being a presidential candidate three times — once with Altgeld on the ticket — Bryan was famous as a strong believer in the Bible. The courtroom drama, made into a notable film, pitted science versus faith. Bryan came out diminished by the power of Darrow's logic. Scopes, the teacher on trial, was fined a nominal $100. The case was appealed, and then dismissed, but the legal drama lives on.

John Altgeld

Another case by Darrow is considered a landmark in the Civil Rights movement. Dr. Ossian Sweet and three members of his family were indicted for murder in Detroit for killing a white man.

Arguing before an all-white jury, Darrow exclaimed in another memorable closing statement: "I insist that there is nothing but prejudice in this case, that if it was reversed and 11 white men had shot and killed a black man while protecting their home and their lives against a mob of blacks, nobody would have dreamed of having them indicted. They would have been given medals instead."

The cases were separated by individual defendants and charges were dismissed after one member of the family was acquitted on the grounds of self-defense.

Meanwhile, Altgeld's fortunes, political and economic, took a turn for the worse. He finally ran and lost in a bid to become Chicago's mayor. Financial losses took a heavy toll on his real estate holdings, which had originally made him a wealthy man. Help came from Darrow who saved him from even more disastrous privations. In an ironic turnabout, Altgeld wound up working in Darrow's law firm.

Altgeld passed away in 1902 when he was only 54. His health had been failing for some time. Darrow provided a moving eulogy, declaring that Altgeld was "one of the rarest souls who ever lived and died" while being "a soldier in the everlasting struggle of the human race for liberty and justice on the earth." Darrow lived on for many more years, and many more legal cases, dying in 1938 when he was nearly 81.

***

Among Darrow's many quotes:

- I am a friend of the working man, and I would rather be his friend than be one.

- Just think of the tragedy of teaching children not to doubt.

- When I was a boy, I was told that anyone could become president. Now I'm beginning to believe it.

- I am an agnostic. I do not pretend to know what many ignorant men are sure of.

- I have never killed a man, but I have read many obituaries with a lot of pleasure.

- With all their faults trade unions have done more for humanity than any other organization of men that ever existed. They have done more for decency, for honesty, for education, for the betterment of the race, for the developing of character in men, than any other association of men.

CHAPTER 63. ERNEST HEMINGWAY, F. SCOTT FITZGERALD, AND ERIC "CHINK" DORMAN-SMITH

Generosity in friendship can be a double-edged sword as suggested by the off-and-on-friendship of two American literary heavyweights: F. Scott Fitzgerald and Ernest Hemingway.

When they first met at the Dingo Bar in Paris in 1925, Fitzgerald was far better known as a writer but he was impressed by Hemingway's macho persona, which included his war experiences during World War I. Only a few years in age separated them; Fitzgerald had been born in 1896 and Hemingway in 1899. *This Side of Paradise* had been published to considerable acclaim when Fitzgerald was just 23 and he had followed up with the less hailed *The Beautiful and the Damned*. *The Great Gatsby*, considered one of the masterpieces of the 20th century by many critics, had just come out earlier that year. Hemingway, at this point, wasn't a well-known name in the U.S. though his book *Three Stories & Ten Poems* had been published in 1923.

This was the heyday of the zany Jazz Age. Fitzgerald and Hemingway, among a covey of other writers and artists, were all part of the American expatriate community in Paris who became integral members of the so-called "Lost Generation." Both went to the famed literary salons of the doyenne Gertrude Stein, who held court in those heady Parisian days and nights. Parties were frequent, with dancing all night, and drinking all night as well. Fitzgerald was with his wife, Zelda, who proved to be a more and more difficult spouse. Meanwhile Hemingway, after his ambulance-driving adventures in Italy during the war, was living with the first of his four wives.

Fitzgerald supplemented his lavish lifestyle by belting out short stories to such magazines as *Esquire* and the *Saturday Evening Post* and selling rights to his novels to Hollywood studios. Hemingway was a foreign correspondent for a Canadian newspaper.

Ernest Hemingway

Though he was more in the limelight, Fitzgerald admired the charisma and adventurous character of Hemingway. He and others in the literary set tried to help Hemingway crack the U.S. market, which Hemingway at first appreciated. Later, he wanted very much to take credit alone for his climb up the literary ladder.

Hemingway also wasn't very supportive of the short story work done by Fitzgerald, which they seemed to agree was a kind of "literary whoring." Still Fitzgerald defended the quality of his short stories, while arguing the pieces enabled him to net solid payments.

Hemingway and Zelda didn't much care for each other. He thought she was daffy, with her antics driving Fitzgerald, who had already shown a tendency toward alcoholism, to drink instead of writing. She thought Hemingway was somewhat of a *poseur*. At one point she even accused her husband of a homosexual relationship with Hemingway.

F. Scott Fitzgerald

All of this didn't do much for their relationship, and they grew apart. Fitzgerald, who wrote very well when sober, flitted around Europe. He provided commentary on Hemingway's *The Sun Also Rises* while Hemingway returned the favor on some of Fitzgerald's writings — as well as his alcoholic habits. Hemingway was less than kind thereafter when discussing Fitzgerald as a person and a writer. Fitzgerald and Zelda spent about two years in Paris, and then they went to Hollywood in 1927 where he received well-paying movie script assignments. Unfortunately Zelda, increasingly unstable, went on to become a schizophrenic and to spend a great deal of time in a sanitarium. Fitzgerald kept writing. *Tender Is The Night* came out in 1934 and he was working on an unfinished book, *The Last Tycoon*, when he died. The novel was published posthumously.

Fitzgerald was based in Los Angeles during the last years of his life, under contract to a Hollywood studio. Never divorced from Zelda, he had some affairs, most notably with Sheila Graham, the noted Hollywood gossip columnist. Their relationship was well treated in her book *Beloved Infidel*. He suffered from bad health and bad habits, such as drinking. In a famous quote, thinking of himself, he said, "There are no second acts in American lives." He died of a heart attack in 1940 in Sheila Graham's apartment when he was only 44.

In parallel to all this, Ernest Hemingway and Eric "Chink" Dorman-Smith had met on the Italian front during World War I. Neither was especially conversant in Italian. Hemingway was a volunteer ambulance driver and Dorman-Smith a British army officer who may have seemed dashing with battlefield tales, a spate of medals, and a sturdy military bearing including a becoming brush mustache.

The two became close friends during the prolonged period when Hemingway was recovering from severe shrapnel wounds. They were just four years apart in age, with Dorman-Smith born in 1895 and Hemingway in 1899. But then they went their separate ways until meeting again in Paris in 1922. Hemingway was now a journalist and aspiring writer while Dorman-Smith was still a career soldier He acquired his "Chink" nickname (which didn't have any connection to a disparaging name for a Chinese person) when a fellow officer noted his resemblance to his regiment's chinkara antelope mascot; the chinkara is a gazelle species found in South Asia.

During these exciting post-war days, Hemingway and his wife Hadley and Dorman-Smith went to Montreux, Switzerland, on a skiing holiday. Deciding to show Hadley one of the cities they had been in during the war, they crossed the St. Bernard Pass on foot, an experience later recounted in Hemingway's posthumous book, *The Moveable Feast*.

The following year Hemingway went to Cologne, on assignment for the *Toronto Star* for whom he worked as a foreign correspondent. Dorman-Smith was posted there as part of the British unit involved in monitoring the smoldering French–German dispute in this crucial area, and they spent some time together.

In 1924 Dorman-Smith was back in Paris and met many of the luminaries of the "Lost Generation" such as James Joyce and Ezra Pound. He also met Gertrude Stein, the literary mother figure. Subsequently, Hemingway dedicated his first book, *In Our Time*, to Dorman-Smith, enriching the narrative with anecdotes from their Italian campaign experiences. Later that same year, Dorman-Smith returned again to Paris to become godfather to Hemingway's eldest son, John.

During this period the duo were part of a group that went to Pamplona, Spain, for the bull-running festival. This experience led to Hemingway's first novel, *The Sun Also Rises*. One of the minor characters, Wilson-Harris, is believed to be based on Dorman-Smith.

Hemingway's great enjoyment of Dorman-Smith's company is spelled out in a 1924 poem *To Chink Whose Trade Is Soldiering*.

They next met in 1926, when Dorman-Smith led an army rugby team to Paris. Changes in Dorman-Smith's postings and Hemingway's growing career as a major writer led to their drifting apart. They didn't meet again until 1950 when Dorman-Smith was touring the United States. Dorman-Smith is also considered to be the model for Col. Richard Cantwell, the hero of Hemingway's *Across The River & Into The Trees*.

Between the wars Dorman-Smith's military career had its ups and downs. He served as an instructor at the Sandhurst Military Academy (the West Point of England), wrote a textbook on military tactics and training, and delivered lectures on tactics he considered outdated (such as any continued military use of horses). He also managed to make some enemies among his fellow officers, who didn't care much for his positions or personality.

During World War II, Dorman-Smith was in the African theater serving as chief of staff to Sir Claude Auchinleck. Opinions differ on whether he was helpful in stemming the German advance under General Rommel on Egypt or his advice was detrimental to the Allied cause. In any event, he was relieved of that post and sent back to England to participate in planning for the invasion of France. Always outspoken, he lectured Prime Minister Churchill — not something that many men succeeded in doing — on military tactics at one luncheon.

After the war Dorman-Smith retired from the army. He spent some time in Ireland where he changed his name to O'Gowan and got involved with the Irish Republican Army (IRA). Unorthodox to the end, he passed away in 1969 at the age of 74.

Hemingway, meanwhile, carved out a great career at a writer who had a major influence on other writers. He was awarded the Nobel Prize for Literature in 1954. Among his seven novels, six short story collections and non-fiction works are several classics in American literature. Along the way he covered wars on different continents and was married four times.

Hemingway described his writing development in this fashion, starting in 1923 in Paris. "I was trying to learn to write, commencing with the simplest things, and one of the simplest things of all and the most fundamental is violent death."

His style came down to reducing things to their basic elements with relatively short but descriptive sentences that carried great impact. Many have tried to imitate his boiled-down style.

In *A Farewell To Arms* (1929) he recounted his wartime experience on the Italo–Austrian front and his romance with an older nurse. In *To Have and Have Not* (1937) he used the Caribbean, where he lived for a time, as a setting. *For Whom the Bell Tolls* 1940) was a stirring story of the Spanish Civil War. He came back to the Caribbean in his 1950 book, *The Old Man & The Sea*, which was awarded the 1952 Pulitzer Prize. Two of his more memorable short stories, both based on his experiences in Africa, are *The Snows of Kilimanjaro* and *The Short Happy Life of Francis Macomber*. Many of his novels and short stories have been used for movies. His *A Moveable Feast*, published posthumously, described his Paris days and nights.

Hemingway's life came to a tragic end. His father had committed suicide, and he was afraid he might, too, once saying, "I'll probably go the same way." Increasingly in poor health and in depression, he did, committing suicide with a shotgun in 1961 when he was 62 years old.

***

Among Hemingway's quotes:

- Always do sober what you said you'd do drunk.

- Never confuse movement with action.

- That is the greatest fallacy, the wisdom of old men. They do not grow wise. They grow careful.

- Happiness in intelligent people is the rarest thing I know.

And from F. Scott Fitzgerald:

- At 18 our convictions are hills from which we look; at 45 they are caves in which we hide.

- Sometimes it's harder to deprive oneself of a pain than a pleasure.

- Action is character.

- The test of a first rate intelligence is the ability to hold two opposed ideas in the mind at the same time, and still retain the ability to function.

- The reason one writes isn't the fact he wants to say something. He writes because he has something to say.

- Show me a hero and I'll show you a tragedy.

Chapter 64. Sergei Rachmaninoff and Vladimir Horowitz

Sergei Rachmaninoff and Vladimir Horowitz were born about 30 years apart — Rachmaninoff in 1873 and Horowitz in 1903 — in Russia and the Ukraine respectively. Both were great musical figures and representative of Russian classical music. Eventually both became American citizens while performing around the world.

Each was a virtuoso on the piano, with both wanting to do more composition. Rachmaninoff was much more successful on this score with three symphonies, four piano concertos, several choral works, etc. Two of his most notable compositions are the *Prelude in C Sharp* and *Rhapsody on a Theme of Paganini*. He also composed over 80 songs.

Rachmaninoff left Russia after the 1917 Revolution and emigrated to the U.S. where he quickly acquired an agent and was given a piano as a gift by the Steinway Company. He played a large number of concerts around the United States. Horowitz left the Ukraine in 1925, stuffing currency notes in his shoes to cover expenses for upcoming performances in Berlin and to avoid Russian laws about taking money over a certain amount out of the country.

The two men met in the basement of Steinway Hall in New York in 1928, several days before Horowitz was scheduled to make his U.S. debut at Carnegie Hall with a performance of Tchaikovsky's *First Piano Concerto*. Rachmaninoff noted that Horowitz had previously played one of his piano concertos very well. Horowitz was much more effusive, declaring that meeting Rachmaninoff was a highlight of his life, and terming the older man as "the musical God of my youth." He added: "This was my real debut."

Sergei Rachmaninoff

While complimentary about Horowitz's performance, Rachmaninoff thought he went through the cadenza too quickly. "He swallowed it whole. He had the courage, the intensity, the daring." Critics largely agreed, though the English conductor, Sir Henry Beecham, also making his Carnegie Hall debit, was much less pleased as he wanted a more sedate tempo than Horowitz's interpretation.

Horowitz acknowledged the criticism and simply continued playing the Tchaikovsky piece at future performances according to his own interpretation.

Rachmaninoff's and Horowitz's friendship continued unabated with both being supportive admirers of the other. Once Horowitz told his manager: "If I am out of town when Rachmaninoff plays in New York, you must telegraph me, and you must let me come back, no matter where I am or what engagement I have."

The duo often performed piano recitals at Rachmaninoff's home in Beverly Hills, a domicile he tried to make as Russian as possible, as he was said to miss his homeland. Horowitz lived nearby. Rachmaninoff also bought a home near Lake Lucerne, in Switzerland, where he spent some summers until 1935, while concentrating on composing. The balance of his time from around the age of 44 shifted somewhat to performing, though he still kept creating music.

Rachmaninoff became an American citizen in 1943, the same year as his last recital. Horowitz, who settled in the U.S. in 1939 after performances in major European cities, became a citizen in 1944.

Rachmaninoff had such confidence in Horowitz's interpretation of his music that he sanctioned a fusion of his *Second Piano Sonata* which combined the 1913 original and a 1931 revision of the piece. After an August 1942 performance of this piece at the Hollywood Bowl, Rachmaninoff enthused: "This is the way I always dreamed my concerto should be played, but I never expected to hear it that way on Earth."

Vladimir Horowitz

Rachmaninoff died in 1943, just four days before his 70th birthday.

Horowitz was at Rachmaninoff's deathbed. Moved by the loss of a great musician and friend — he said, "The man was like a father to me." Horowitz cancelled some scheduled concerts and took on the presidency of a Rachmaninoff Memorial Fund to promote musical talent; the organization only lasted a few years due to insufficient support.

Horowitz, who would live to be 86, kept performing but ran into problems at several intervals with his nerves and depression. He took some years off to recover. Reportedly, despite all the acclaim, he sometimes had to be shoved on stage. He complained of performing too many recitals, and about the strain of his schedule: "I couldn't take the traveling, five days a week, all those trains, all those towns, no sleep, bad food."

However, he came out of this "retirement period" in 1965 and again found enthusiastic critics and crowds. At the 50th anniversary of his U.S. debut he played Rachmaninoff's *Third Piano Concerto*.

Before the performance he said, "I hope I am still a virtuoso; it's nice to be a virtuoso. But I hope they like it because the music is beautiful. It is not easy to play again after 12 years and when you are sixty. Who knows? Maybe I will play like a pig."

He didn't.

Regarding his place in musical history Horowitz commented: "I am a 19th-century romantic. I am the last."

Both men married, Horowitz to Arturo Toscanini's daughter Wanda in 1933. As Horowitz spoke little Italian, and Wanda no Russian, they communicated for a while in French. Some people suspected Horowitz of being a closet homosexual, to which his joking denial was: "There are three kinds of pianists: Jewish pianists, homosexual pianists, and bad pianists."

Horowitz passed away in 1989, a musical legend like his friend, Rachmaninoff.

Quotes from Horowitz:

- I am a general. My soldiers are the piano keys and I have to command them.

- Perfection itself is imperfection.

- My face is my passport.

- If you want me to play only the notes without any specific dynamics, I will never make one mistake.

And from Rachmaninoff:

- Music is enough for a lifetime, but a lifetime is not enough for music.

CHAPTER 65. AL CAPONE AND JOHNNY TORRIO

Scarface and *The Fox* were two of the most significant gangsters in the 1920s in Chicago.

The scar-related facial nickname belonged to Alphonse Capone and the foxy appellation was awarded to his friend and mentor, Johnny Torrio. Capone got his start in the criminal world after dropping out of school at 14. He was taken into the Five Points Gang in New York, and became versed in such rackets as loan sharking and prostitution — and eventually murder. One of his early jobs, however, was as the bouncer at a Coney Island saloon. He had the misfortune of insulting a young lady whose brother promptly slashed the left side of his face. However, Capone forgave the attack and actually hired the man who disfigured his face as a bodyguard when he was in power in Chicago. In the future, Capone would show the right side of his face to photographers while claiming the scars came from shrapnel while fighting in France during World War I. He was actually far removed from the war front, in New York and then Chicago. References to him as "Scarface Capone" invariably brought angry disapproval.

Al Capone

Torrio, known for his clever tactics, moved to Chicago in 1909 to work in the rackets there, especially brothels. Subsequently, he recruited Capone to come work with him in Chicago around 1920. As Prohibition (forbidding the manufacture, transportation and sales of alcohol) became the law of the land, Torrio was quick to recognize the potential for large profits. Capone learned from Torrio the value of appearing like a legitimate businessman as a front while still conducting *sub rosa* activities. However, once he rose in power, Capone was much flashier than Torrio ever was.

It didn't take long before speakeasies as well as casinos and more brothels were spread around the Windy City by the so-called Chicago Outfit. Millions were raked in through bootlegging, gambling, prostitution and opium trafficking. Torrio and his younger sidekick — Torrio was born in 1882 and Capone in 1899 — became rich while trying to pass themselves off as respectable businessmen.

Interviewed by media, Capone cracked, "I'm just a businessman giving the public what they want. If I break the law, my customers — some of the best people in Chicago — are as guilty as me."

In another tell-tale aphorism: "You can get more with a kind word and a gun than you can with a kind word alone."

Capone, to his credit, did try to help people in his fashion — which involved using his wealth. He said: "Many a poor family in Chicago think I'm Santa Claus. If I've given a cent to the poor in this man's town, I'll bet I've given a million dollars. Yes, a million."

During the Prohibition Era, which began in January 1920, Torrio and later, Capone, controlled a substantial part of the Chicago underworld. This ascension to power was accomplished to some extent by killing off and/or intimidating competitors. One estimate is that they accumulated $100 million per year with most of this loot coming from the sale of forbidden liquor. Much of the liquor was smuggled in from Canada with some coming from illegal breweries and moonshine operations. The colorful term, "bootlegging," which the illicit operation was sometimes called, probably came from "boot-leg" — the upper part of a tall boot where a bottle might be hidden.

Such an ample amount of money enabled them to obtain influence, among other benefits, from political and law enforcement quarters. Headquarters were set up at the Lexington Hotel which was nicknamed "Capone's Castle."

Eventually, gang wars broke out as there were territories to be sorted out and enormous profits to be divided in some fashion. The brutal conflict raged for a considerable time, doing little for the image of Chicago. Torrio was almost assassinated. Capone then posted an around-the-clock guard for his friend. Torrio finally decided to retire and return to Italy where he had been born. "It's all yours, Al," Torrio said. "Me? I'm quitting. It's Europe for me."

Capone himself survived attempts against his life. He rode around in a Cadillac with bullet-proof glass, special tires, and a police siren. He dressed and lived ostentatiously, and was often sought out by journalists for a quote or two, which included referrals to his "organization" as "the outfit." Gangsters during this period had something of a perverse romantic aura.

One of the most famous incidents of this intra-crime conflict was the notorious St. Valentine's Day Massacre where seven of Capone's enemies were mowed down in a garage.

The massacre didn't settle the gangland war, but it did heighten federal scrutiny of Capone. FBI man Eliot Ness of television and motion picture fame entered the scene around 1929 and began an investigation of Prohibition violations. These efforts weren't especially effective, though Capone's image and authority had lessened.

Soon, the government took another and more successful tack. They looked into Capone's tax record and discovered that he had never filed a tax return. In short order, Capone was indicted for tax evasion. It was actually Frank Wilson of the Internal Revenue Service, not Ness, who really nailed Capone. He was also hit with violations of the Volstead Act (National Prohibition Act) that was passed as an enforcement measure of the 18th amendment on Prohibition.

Attempts to bribe and intimidate the jury failed, and Capone was convicted of five counts of tax evasion and sentenced to 11 years in prison. At the time this was the longest sentence for tax evasion ever given. Charges of violation of the Volstead Act were dropped, but he was fined $50,000 plus court costs as well as back taxes with interest. Liens were put on his assorted properties, including his mansion in Palm Island, Florida. His appeals were denied. Later, the Treasury Department seized Capone's fortress of a car that was later turned into a limousine for President Roosevelt.

Initially, Capone was placed in the Atlanta Penitentiary in 1932, where he was allowed to have special privileges. But in 1934 he was relocated to Alcatraz Prison, where he was just another prisoner. Prohibition was over and his stature had radically diminished. This reality was harshly established in one incident. Capone cut into a prison line for haircuts. Another inmate, in for 30 years for robbery, objected. When Capone asked if this inmate knew who he was dealing with the man replied, "Yeah, I know who you are, greaseball. And if you don't get back to the end of that . . . line, I'm gonna know who you were."

Capone's health deteriorated. He was diagnosed with syphilis, which he had probably contracted as a youth in New York. In 1939 he was paroled and he went to live at his Florida estate. One report by a psychiatrist who examined him at this time indicated that his mental facilities were no more than those of a 12 year old. He died in 1947.

Johnny Torrio

Meanwhile Torrio, who had come to Chicago for Capone's trial, returned to New York again. Treated as an elder statesman, he told the reigning gang lords to form a national crime syndicate to avoid fighting among themselves. His advice was taken. Later, he became an unofficial adviser to one member of the syndicate, the Genovese crime family. He died of a heart attack in 1957 while sitting in a barber's chair waiting for a haircut.

Both Torrio, and his protégé, Capone — who rose to greater prominence as a criminal celebrity — have been portrayed in many films and television shows. Some travel industry entrepreneurs have even offered tours highlighting places connected with Capone's Chicago.

Some more Capone quotes:

- Vote early and vote often.

- Once in the rackets you're always in it.

- I've been accused of every death except the casualty list of the World War.

Chapter 66. Walt Disney and Ubbe Iwerks

"I only hope that we don't lose sight of one thing — that it was all started by a mouse."

Walt Disney said this in looking back on an illustrious career as a highly creative animator of very popular cartoon characters, a movie director, and a pioneer in theme park design. His career in Hollywood really got started with the creation of Mickey Mouse in 1928, whom he originally wanted to call Mortimer. His mother convinced him that Mickey was a better choice.

Disney, who was born in 1901 in Chicago, grew up in Missouri where as a precocious seven-year-old he sold his first sketch to neighbors. After World War I, where he served as a youthful Red Cross ambulance driver, he returned to Kansas City to begin his career as an advertising cartoonist.

He met Ubbe Iwerks, who was also born in 1901, in 1919 when both worked for the Pesman-Rubin Art Studios in Kansas City. Iwerks shortened his German name to Ub Iwerks. Eventually, the two became friends and formed the short-lived Iwerks-Disney Commercial Artists concern in 1920. After the outfit ended operations, Iwerks became the chief animator when Disney launched his Laugh-O-Gram cartoon series. When this studio failed, Disney decided to relocate to Hollywood, and convinced Iwerks to follow him. Of the two, Disney was more bold and Ubbe more shy and laid back. But both were greatly talented.

Disney began work on a new series called the Alice Comedies, which had live action mixed with animation. When the series ended, Disney asked Iwerks to create a new character. Subsequently, *Oswald the Lucky Rabbit* — animated by Iwerks — came into being and Universal Studios agreed to distribute the series in 1925. But in 1928 Disney lost control of the Oswald character. Many staffers left the Disney studio at this time, but Iwerks stayed loyal.

Walt Disney

It was time for a new character. Sketches of dogs, cats, frogs and other creatures didn't catch on with Disney. Sketches of a pet mouse Disney had back in Kansas City inspired Iwerks to suggest Mickey Mouse and to make the character ready for animation. As one staff member commented: "Iwerks designed Mickey's physical appearance but Walt gave him his soul."

Disney, it should be noted, was Mickey's voice for a considerable time. Thereafter, a bunch of other popular characters emerged including Bugs Bunny, Donald Duck, and Elmer Fudd.

A series of musical shorts, released in 1929, included *The Skeleton Dance* which was drawn and animated by Iwerks. Discord arose as Iwerks kept creating more cartoons and feeling he wasn't getting enough credit for his output that were making the Disney studio very successful. Finally, their friendship and working partnership took a jolt when Iwerks started his own studio in 1930. But his studio never really rivaled that of Disney, and it finally folded in the mid 1930s. After some independent work, Iwerks returned to the Disney fold in 1940, and he's credited with making significant advances in developing new technology in live action animation. He also helped, in later years, in developing many of the Disney theme park attractions. Many people believe Iwerks — who spent most of his working life with Disney — was Disney's oldest friend.

Overall, Iwerks won two Academy Awards as an animator of cartoons. He died in 1971 at the age of 70.

Ubbe Iwerks

Disney in 1938 came out with *Snow White & The Seven Dwarfs*, the first animal feature film in technicolor. Despite some dubious forecasts, the film was a huge success. During the next five years he released such classics as *Pinocchio, Fantasia, Dumbo*, and *Bambi*.

During World War II the Disney studio produced a number of training and propaganda films for the government, with some short cartoon films still released to entertain the public during the strain of the war. Overall, Disney released many feature films including an award-winning True Life Adventure series with such documentaries as *The Living Desert* and *The Vanishing Prairie*.

The *Magic Kingdom of Disneyland* was his greatest non-cinematic production. The famous theme park opened in 1955 and has been visited by well over 300 million people. Similar theme parks, bearing his name, have been erected around the world including ones in Japan and France. With his attention turned on to the nature of urban life, Disney designed an Experimental Prototype Community of Tomorrow or EPCOT as a showcase of American industrial ingenuity. He bought 43 square miles in central Florida and created Walt Disney World, a theme park that opened in 1971. This park was followed by the EPCOT Center in 1982. Subsequently, the Disney Cruise Line was launched to establish a marketing tie-in between land and sea entertainment options.

Disney received many honors including 32 Academy Awards. He died in 1966 at the age of 65, but his name lives on in his cinematic characters, films, theme parks, cruise line, etc.

Among his memorable quotes:

- You're dead if you aim only for kids. Adults are only kids grown up, anyway.
- We are not trying to entertain the critics. I'll take my chances with the public.
- Laughter is America's most important export.
- It's kind of fun to do the impossible.

CHAPTER 67. JOHN STEINBECK AND ED RICKETTS

John Steinbeck was one of the greatest American writers, winning two Pulitzer Prizes and the Nobel Prize for literature in 1962. He wrote 27 books including *The Grapes of Wrath, In Dubious Battle, Tortilla Flat, Of Mice and Men*, and *East of Eden*. Ed Ricketts, a long time friend, was both a companion and collaborator on an ecological book.

John Steinbeck

The Grapes of Wrath, describing the plight of Oklahoma sharecroppers fleeing the Dust Bowl during the 1930s Depression and their subsequent hard scrabble experiences in California, was a controversial best seller. It won the Pulitzer Prize for fiction in 1939. It also had the dubious honor of being kept out of some California libraries for a couple of years due to its language and description of the treatment received by the newcomers. This novel, and several others, were made into movies.

Steinbeck and Ricketts weren't far apart in age with Steinbeck born in 1902 and Ricketts in 1897. Ricketts is credited, and by Steinbeck himself, with being a strong influence on his writing, especially with recurring ecological themes.

Steinbeck and Ricketts met in 1930 in Monterey, California where Ricketts ran the Pacific Biological Laboratories which provided live marine creatures for medical research and college courses. Ricketts was a pioneer in the development of studies in ecology, which wasn't a strong subject at the time. He was particularly involved in intertidal ecology and conducted his own research. He also authored *Between Pacific Tides*, a study of Pacific Coast marine life, in 1939. Carol, Steinbeck's wife at the time, worked part time at Ricketts' laboratory. Steinbeck also spent a good deal of time there learning about marine biology while helping Ricketts work with marine specimens.

Ricketts, who began to live in the laboratory after separating from his wife, was also greatly interested in a large range of philosophical subjects. The pair would have long discussions. Disaster came when a fire in 1936 destroyed the laboratories. Steinbeck came to the rescue, becoming a silent partner in the lab and paying for reconstruction. The two would often take drives along the California coast, permitting Ricketts to do some research while providing Steinbeck with a break from his writing.

In 1940, when Steinbeck was a growing literary success, he and Ricketts went on a chartered fishing boat to collect invertebrates they could use in a co-authored book initially called *Sea of Cortez* (and then *The Log from the Sea of Cortez* when it was republished in 1961). By this time Ricketts was involved with Eleanor "Toni" Jackson who became Steinbeck's secretary while helping to edit their manuscript.

During World War II the two had little contact. Ricketts served as a medical lab technician while Steinbeck, an international figure, had wartime assignments that took him around the world.

Cannery Row, published in 1945, was quite a success. The novel also made Ricketts a celebrity of sorts as he was the model for a key character called "Doc."

Steinbeck had actually let Ricketts read the novel in draft form, and it easily passed muster. In the novel, "Doc" was depicted as a hard-drinking, party-loving intellectual who was just as comfortable with workers on Monterey's cannery row. Steinbeck described his character in this fashion: "He wears a beard and his face is half Christ and half satyr and his face tells the truth." The lab was called Western Biological Laboratories.

Ricketts was not enamored of his portrayal, but he understood it was fiction and with no malice at all involved. Subsequently, Ricketts reappeared to some extent as a character in other novels like "Doc" in *Sweet Thursday*, the sequel to *Cannery Row;* "Friend Ed" in *Burning Bright*, "Doc Burton" in *In Dubious Battle*, "Jim Casey" in *The Grapes of Wrath*, and "Doctor Winter" in *The Moon is Down*.

Ricketts wrote three essays but despite Steinbeck bringing them to the attention of publishers none were published during Ricketts' life. They were later published posthumously.

Bust of Ed Ricketts — Attribution: I, Amadscientist

In 1948 the friends planned a trip to British Columbia with the intent of writing another marine biology book to be called *The Other Shore*. But tragedy drastically changed their plans. Ricketts was badly injured when his car was hit by a freight train. He died within just a few hours, while Steinbeck was rushing back to Monterey. By his own account Steinbeck grieved a long time for his friend of many years, terming him "a part of my brain."

In describing his friend, Steinbeck wrote: "No one who knew him will deny the force and influence of Ed Ricketts. Everyone near him was influenced by him deeply and permanently. Some he taught how to think, others how to see or hear. Children on the beach he taught how to look for and find beautiful animals in worlds they had not suspected were there at all. He taught everyone without seeming to."

Steinbeck handled the disposition of Rickett's laboratory materials, only keeping a microscope they had used on the Sea of Cortez sailing.

Steinbeck passed away in 1968 at the age of 66.

***

Among Steinbeck's quotes:

- Man is the only kind of varmint who sets his own trap, baits it, and then steps on it.

- No one wants advice, just collaboration.

- All war is a symptom of man's failure as a thinking animal.

- If we could learn to like ourselves, even a little, maybe our cruelties and angers might melt away.

- I hate cameras. They are so much more sure than I am about everything.

CHAPTER 68. JEAN COCTEAU AND RAYMOND RADIGUET

Jean Cocteau, who possessed remarkable talent as a poet, playwright, novelist, designer and filmmaker, was also a mentor to a younger talent, Raymond Radiguet. But his young writer friend died at the age of 20 after writing two novels, one published during his life and the other posthumously.

Cocteau, who was born in 1889, was 29 and already famous when he met the youthful Radiguet — who was born in 1903 — in Paris in 1918. His first volume of poems, *Aladdin's Lamp*, was published when he was 19 with a second volume, *The Frivolous Prince*, coming out when he was 22. Moreover, he was working on various projects with such luminaries as Pablo Picasso, the poet Guillaume Apollinaire, and the Russian stage choreographer Sergei Diaghilev. Various collaborations went on with a group of notable composers known as "Les Six." With World War I crimping artistic efforts, Cocteau served as a Red Cross ambulance driver.

So it was no surprise to others in the Parisian artist scene that Cocteau recognized Radiguet's literary promise. The two became close companions, hobnobbing in Cocteau's circle and taking trips together. Influenced by the luminaries, Radiguet even took to wearing a monocle and dressing like a dandy. Cocteau also helped Radiguet avoid getting called into the French army.

Radiguet's first novel, *The Devil In The Flesh*, was considered to be autobiographical to a large extent as it covered an affair between a young married woman whose soldier husband was away at the front and a 16-year-old boy. When Radiguet's faith in his manuscript waned — to the extent of his throwing pages into a fire — Cocteau persuaded him to persevere. Cocteau then promoted the completed book, writing to one publisher: "I am sending you Raymond Radiguet, the adopted son of our group. He has just written a novel which I consider one of the four or five masterpieces of French literature."

Cocteau's efforts led to the novel — which was published in 1923 — being awarded the "Nouveau Monde" literary prize. This success led to Radiguet, with Cocteau serving as a sort of literary agent sans commissions, signing a contract for more novels. He also collaborated with Cocteau on a comic operetta, *Paul and Virginie*.

Jean Cocteau

Cocteau was open about his bisexuality, but claimed his relationship with Radiguet was non-sexual. Radiguet's preference for women was well known.

Tragically, Radiguet came down with a case of typhoid fever during one journey with Cocteau and died in 1923. A second novel, *The Count's Ball*, was published posthumously in 1924.

Cocteau took Radiguet's death hard, even finding it difficult to attend the funeral. He wrote a friend, "I am trying, for my mother's sake, not to die. That's all."

Raymond Radiguet

Some observers opined that Cocteau, saddened by his friend's sudden death, turned to opium in his grief. Cocteau, however, disputed this notion. In the years that he was addicted to opium Cocteau created some of his impressive works including the play *Orphée* in 1926 and the novel *Les Infants Terribles* in 1929. In his 1929 *Opium, Diary of an Addict*, Cocteau candidly describes the experience of his recovery. Despite some visits to detox centers, drugs remained part of Cocteau's life.

One relevant quote Cocteau made about opium was: "Everything one does in life, even love, occurs on an express train racing toward death. To smoke opium is to get out of the train while it is still moving. It is to concern oneself with something other than life or death."

The Blood of a Poet, which appeared in 1930, was Cocteau's first film. *The Infernal Machine*, produced in 1934, is considered by many to be Cocteau's best play.

Myths played a significant part in Cocteau's works in various mediums. On this score, he wrote: "Man seeks to escape himself in myth, and does so by any means at his disposal. Drugs, alcohol, or lies. Unable to withdraw into himself, he disguises himself. Lies and inaccuracy give a few moments of comfort."

Two films, *Beauty and The Beast* (1946) and *Orpheus* (1948) both involved the use of myths.

Cocteau's politics tended to be right-wing. In his diary, he speculated that France might have showed more early respect for Hitler — while evincing some curiosity about Hitler's sexual leanings. At the end of World War II, Cocteau was arraigned on the accusation of collaboration with Germany; but he was cleared of any wrongdoing; and it was noted that he had used his contacts to save some Jewish friends from the clutches of the Nazis.

Until his death in 1963 at the age of 74, Cocteau kept creating, putting together a lifetime of great accomplishments in various artistic fields. He was truly a figure of Renaissance proportions.

Among Cocteau's quotes:

- Film will only become art when its materials are as inexpensive as pencil and paper.

- A film is a petrified fountain of thought.

- Of course I believe in luck. How otherwise to explain the success of some people you detest.

- A true poet does not bother to be poetical. Nor does a nursery gardener scent his roses.

- An artist cannot speak about his art any more than a plant can discuss horticulture.

- Art is the marriage of the conscious and the unconscious.

- Art is not a pastime but a priesthood.

- Art produces ugly things which frequently become more beautiful with time. Fashion, on the other hand, produces beautiful things which always become ugly with time.

CHAPTER 69. HARRY HOPKINS & PRESIDENT ROOSEVELT

President Roosevelt was asked by Wendell Willkie, his Republican opponent in the 1940 presidential election, why he placed such reliance on the opinions of Harry Hopkins. FDR replied that if ever Willkie did become president
(he didn't), "you'll learn what a lonely job it is, and you'll discover the need for
someone like Harry Hopkins who asks for nothing except to serve you."

Hopkins served Roosevelt so well he was often termed "FDR's Deputy President" and as "Roosevelt's own personal foreign office," among other sobriquets.
At one time, before Roosevelt ran for a third term in 1940, Hopkins was even considered a possible presidential candidate. This possibility was discounted after
Hopkins suffered a serious health setback.

For many years Hopkins was one of Roosevelt's closest and most valued ad-
visors. Yet he held a cabinet post — Secretary of Commerce — for only a limited
time, resigning due to poor health. He had a major operation in 1937 which removed part of his stomach. Almost exclusively a non-official and informal advi-
sor he was still credited in some resentful quarters with having undue influence
on domestic matters and more clout in foreign policy than the State Department.
For about three and a half years he lived in the White House. Hopkins' first wife
died in 1937. He married again in 1942 and he and his second wife — displeasing
Roosevelt — moved out of the White House after about a year of living there.
They settled in a new home in Georgetown, near Washington D.C.

Hopkins was born in 1890, eight years after FDR was born in 1882. He
showed his administrative mettle in various social service posts which finally
brought him to the attention of President Roosevelt. Recruited to work in the

new Roosevelt administration, which was confronted by the ravages of the Great Depression, Hopkins ably assisted the President in coming up with and implementing the New Deal policies. The basic premise of the New Deal was to put people back to work through federal programs rather than waiting for the economy to recover and the depression to end. Along with the President's able wife, Eleanor Roosevelt, Hopkins oversaw a vast commitment of federal resources to shore up a badly ailing citizenry. In the process, as a trusted member of the president's so-called "Brain Trust," he became close friends with the First Couple. Not everyone saw eye to eye with his bold and imaginative efforts, and there were intra-administrative battles.

Franklin Delano Roosevelt

As involvement in World War II seemed imminent, and with England faced with possible defeat by the Germans, Hopkins became an all-purpose diplomat and troubleshooter going on fact-finding missions. He was dispatched to London to prepare a first-hand report on the situation facing Great Britain with Germany in control of most of continental Europe. Prime Minister Winston Churchill impressed him, and so did the spirit of the English people. At a dinner party before his departure back to Washington D.C., he made a fateful toast: "I suppose you want to know what I'm going to say to President Roosevelt on my return. Well, I'm going to quote one verse from the Book of Books. 'Whither thou goest, I will go. And where thou lodgest, I will lodge. Thy people shall be my people, and thy God my God.'"

Roosevelt adopted Hopkins' advice, which led to the $50 billion Lend Lease program which helped England fight off the Nazi menace, with more ships bringing more needed items while warding off the German submarine threat. Later, the program was extended to the Soviet Union when Germany attacked Russia, an onslaught which brought the Russians into World War II.

Through the war years Hopkins served as FDR's unofficial emissary to Churchill, who was very complimentary. "He was the most faithful and perfect channel of communication between the President and me." Impressed by Hopkins' no-nonsense and plainspoken manner, Churchill also called him the "Lord Root of the Matter" due to Hopkins' ability to get to the heart of problems.

Hopkins assisted Roosevelt at the major wartime conferences at Cairo, Teheran, Casablanca and Yalta. Unfortunately, neither man was in good health at the last meeting, in Yalta. FDR wanted Hopkins to return with him to Washington D.C. after Yalta, but Hopkins decided he had to rest first, which he did in Marrakech, Morocco. Their parting was cool as Roosevelt felt somewhat deserted. As it happened, the two never saw each other again, though neither suspected it. Hopkins was recuperating at the Mayo Clinic when FDR died in August 1945.

Harry Hopkins

Hopkins tried to leave his role as an unofficial adviser but President Harry Truman, who became president on FDR's death, sent him on another mission to Moscow despite his declining health. Preparations were underway then for the Potsdam Conference, which would be Truman's first meeting with the other Allied leaders. Soon afterwards, Hopkins died in New York in 1946 from stomach cancer at the age of 56.

***

Among Roosevelt's quotes:

- Be sincere, be brief, be seated.

- If you treat people right they will treat you right — ninety percent of the time.

- When you get to the end of your rope, tie a knot, and hang on.

- Repetition does not transform a lie into the truth.

- It's fun to be in the same decade with you. (In World War II correspondence with Winston Churchill)

And from Hopkins:

- They are damn good projects — excellent projects. You know, some people make fun of people who speak a foreign language, and dumb people criticize something they do not understand, and that is what is going on up there (in Washington D.C.) — God damn it!

- We shall tax and tax, and spend and spend, and elect and elect.

CHAPTER 70. BORIS PASTERNAK AND OSIP MANDELSTAM

Boris Pasternak and Osip Mandelstam were two Russian Jewish poets who endured the wrath of the Soviet government during Stalin's oppressive regime. Hounded and reviled, especially after being awarded the Nobel Prize for literature in 1978, Pasternak still survived. Mandelstam, very much an iconoclast critical of the Soviet dictatorship, fared much worse. He died of unknown causes while in a transit camp en route to a Siberian gulag. Born in 1891, Mandelstam was a year younger than Pasternak. At his untimely death in 1938, Mandelstam was only 47.

Pasternak stayed in Russia after the 1917 Revolution that catapulted the Bolsheviks, including Lenin and Stalin, into power. Others in his family, as well as other writers, fled the country. Originally entranced to some extent by the momentous events, he changed his view, and his opinion soured when the harsh policies of the government — especially under Stalin — became increasingly evident.

Mandelstam too was disillusioned, as shown in his work called *Stalin Epigram*. According to reports, he read this work to Pasternak sometime in 1934. During this period when Stalin suspected everyone, Pasternak is said to have replied, "I didn't hear this. You didn't recite it to me. Because, you know, very strange and terrible things are happening now. They've begun to pick people up. I'm afraid the walls have ears and perhaps even these benches on the boulevard here may be able to listen and tell tales. So let's make out that I heard nothing."

Just the next month, Mandelstam was arrested. Pasternak tried to intercede for his friend with the authorities. He also wanted, according to reports about the period, to let everyone know that he had nothing to do with Mandelstam's arrest. Shortly thereafter, according to the memoirs of the poetess Olga Ivinskaya — Pasternak's amour (he never divorced his wife) — Pasternak received a phone call from the Kremlin. Amazed, he heard Stalin himself ask what people in Pasternak's literary circle were saying about the arrest of Mandelstam.

Boris Pasternak

Osip Mandelstam

Pasternak, taken aback by the situation, said there wasn't much of a discussion. When Stalin then asked the pointed question of what Pasternak himself thought of Mandelstam as a poet, Pasternak gave a somewhat evasive answer that distanced himself before finally complimenting his fellow poet. Before hanging up Stalin reportedly delivered a caustic comment, "I see, you just aren't able to stick up for a comrade."

Subsequently, Pasternak had second thoughts about his behavior and tried to reach Stalin by phone but failed to get through. He later wrote to Stalin to explain what he meant and that some injustices had been committed in his name. Possibly, Pasternak did save Mandelstam from the execution list; only to be transferred to the exile roster.

During these dark times in the Soviet Union, Stalin favored what was called Socialist Realism in literary material. Pasternak, who had risen to fame with his poems in *My Sister Life* and *Rupture*, tried to conform but found it difficult. Instead, he turned to translating works of such foreign writers as Shakespeare and

Wolfgang Goethe into Russian. Mandelstam, however, warned: "Your collected works will consist of 12 volumes of translations and only one of your own."

Pasternak had very specific notions about translations, writing, "I am completely opposed to contemporary ideas about translation. I share the 19th century view of translation as a literary exercise demanding insight of a higher kind than that provided by a merely philological approach."

Pasternak began to strike a more defiant stance during the purges that took place in the 1930s. He refused during the "trials" to sign his name, as quite a few writers were asked to do, in support of the death penalty for the defendants. Even his wife appealed to him to kowtow to those placing demands on him. Instead, Pasternak wrote to Stalin that his life was at the leader's disposal, but he wouldn't let himself be the life-and-death judge of others. He expected to be arrested, but it's believed that Stalin crossed his name off the list of those "plotting against the regime." According to Pasternak himself, Stalin commented, "Don't touch this cloud dweller."

Pasternak had a limited role during World War II, serving as an airplane spotter and visiting the troops on the front. With the Soviet Union one of the victors in the conflict, despite suffering horrendous losses, Pasternak was again deeply disillusioned by the post-war period. He wrote: "If, in a bad dream, we had seen all of the horrors in store for us after the war, we should have been sorry not to see Stalin go down together with Hitler. An end to the war in favor of our allies, civilized countries with democratic traditions, would have meant a hundred times less suffering for our people that which Stalin again inflicted on it after his victory."

Olga Ivinskaya was imprisoned in 1953, soon after Stalin's death and Nikita Khrushchev's rise to power. Aghast, Pasternak wrote: "She was put in jail on my account as the person considered by the secret police to be closest to me, and they hoped that by means of a grueling interrogation and threats they could extract enough evidence from her to put me on trial. I owe my life and the fact that they did not touch me in those years to her heroism and endurance."

About the two Soviet leaders, Pasternak commented: "For so long we were ruled over by a madman and a murderer, and now by a fool and a pig."

Pasternak's major work, *Doctor Zhivago*, relating the end of Tsarist Russia and the formation of the Soviet Union through the eyes of a physician/poet, achieved a worldwide success (and became the basis for a noted movie). However, he was forced by the authorities to decline the Nobel Prize for literature. The Union of Soviet Writers came out against Pasternak, asking that the Politburo strip him of his citizenship and impose other dire penalties. It was noted, though, that no one at the Union had read the novel, which had been spirited out of Russia to Milan where it was printed (Ivinskaya was suspected of being involved in the process). This led to a joke that made the circuit: "I did not read Pasternak, but I condemn him."

Pasternak appealed personally to Khrushchev, writing: "Leaving the motherland will equal death for me. I am tied to Russia by birth, by life and work." Khrushchev relented. Pasternak stayed in Russia, never going to Stockholm to claim his prize — though the world gave him credit anyway for the accomplishment.

In 1959, American cartoonist Bill Mauldin won a Pulitzer Prize for his cartoon in which Pasternak and another gulag prisoner are chopping trees in the tundra and Pasternak says, "I won the Nobel Prize for literature. What was your offense?"

He died of lung cancer in 1960 at the age of 70.

***

Some quotes from Pasternak:

- In every generation there has to be some fool who will speak the truth as he sees it.

- Man is born to live, not to prepare for life.

- What is laid down, ordered, factual, is never enough to embrace the whole truth: life always spills over the rim of every cup.

Chapter 71. E.E. Cummings and William Slater Brown

Edward Estlin Cummings (a name shortened to E.E. Cummings) and William Slater Brown were two young American writers — two years apart in age with Cummings born in 1894 and Brown in 1896 — who volunteered for the Norton-Harjes Ambulance Corps in 1917 during World War I before the U.S. entered the fray. They met aboard the ship bound for France. A mix-up in assignments led to the pair first spending five weeks together in Paris. They became good friends during this period. Then they were finally sent to an ambulance unit on the front.

Both men were rather outspoken, at least as far as their letters home. French censors reading their letters determined that they held anti-war views that made them suspect of espionage as well. Cummings' indication of a lack of hatred of Germans doubtless did little to improve the French impression.

Cummings also wrote that the French themselves had doubts about the war, while Brown was even stronger in his comments, writing: "Everyone is sick of war here and I look forward to a revolution in France soon. The French soldiers are all despondent and none of them believe that Germany will ever be defeated. They maintain the war just as they hold onto the Church or marriage or a senescent institution."

They were imprisoned in September 1917 at a detention camp at Orne. The experience led to Cummings' famous 1922 novel, *The Enormous Room*, that combined a large amount of autobiography as well as poetic touches. Brown became the character "B" in the novel. The pair, the book relates, were placed in one large room with a motley collection of other "undesirables" of various nationalities, all controlled by corrupt guards.

E.E. Cummings

After failing to get his son released through diplomatic channels, Cummings' father wrote directly to President Wilson. Cummings was released in December 1917. However, Brown was transferred to another detention camp and not released for another couple of months. He sailed to New York for a reunion with Cummings. They shared an apartment in Greenwich Village for a time. In 1920, they even contemplated traveling to Asia or South America. The following year, in Paris, they went on a bicycle journey to Italy.

Both men then went on to notable literary careers. Cummings, far better known, was a poet, playwright, painter and essayist. He's best known for his poetry and his distinctive style, using the lower case and not bothering with conventional grammar and syntax. He produced 2,900 poems in 11 volumes, two autobiographical novels, four plays, and some fairy tales for his daughter.

Cummings began writing poetry early, and in an unconventional style, as witnessed by this poem at the age of six:

FATHER DEAR, BE, YOUR FATHER — GOOD AND GOOD,
HE IS GOOD NOW, IT IS NOT GOOD TO SEE IT RAIN,
FATHER DEAR IS, IT, DEAR, NO FATHER DEAR,
LOVE, YOU DEAR,

ESTLIN

In a mature example of his style in the *Buffalo Bill's* poem (1920):
Buffalo Bill 's
defunct
who used to
ride a watersmooth-silver
stallion
and break onetwothreefourfive pigeonsjustlikethat

Jesus

he was a handsome man
and what i want to know is
how do you like your blueeyed boy
Mister Death

Cummings' volume of poems *Tulips and Chimneys* came out in 1923 and received mixed reviews. But Brown, reviewing the book in *Broom*, a magazine of the day, related Cummings' poetic style to his paintings and wrote: "Cummings seldom attempts to achieve momentum through the utilization of mass. The violent and often painful impact of his poems is the active manifestation of speed;

their formal beauty has the quality common to racing cars, aeroplanes, and to those birds surviving because of their swift wings."

Another volume, *XLI*, was published in 1925. After a trip to the Soviet Union in 1931, he gave a diaristic version of his less than pleasurable experiences in *Eimi*. One of his comments: "I feel that whatever's been hitherto told or sung concerning Russia's revolution is bunk."

William Slater Brown

A play, *Him*, was better liked by audiences than critics. Getting published, however, wasn't always easy and he did have to publish some early volumes at his own expense. Satirically, he cited 14 publishers who rejected his 1935 manuscript of *No Thanks* in the volume itself. He added reference to his mother in *Thanks* for financing its publication.

Some of Cummings' poems on themes of prejudice, in which he used derogatory terms for Blacks and Jews to make his point, caused controversy. One representative comment: "The Hebraic they — it permeates everything, like a gas or smell. It has no pride — any more than a snake has legs."

One of his last collections was the 1950 *Xaipe: Seventy-One Poems*. He died in 1962 at the age of 67.

Meanwhile, Brown stayed for a while in the bohemian group of artists and writers in Greenwich Village in New York. Later, he moved to a less urban area. He wrote extensively as a novelist, biographer, and translator of French literature. His novels include *The Burning Wheel* in 1943 and *Ethan Allen & The Green Mountain Boys* in 1956. He passed away in 1997 at the age of 100.

***

Two of Cummings's many quotes:

- It takes courage to grow up and become who you really are.

- The most wasted of all days is one without laughter.

- May my heart always be open to little birds who are the secrets of living.

- Once we believe in ourselves we can risk curiosity, wonder, spontaneous delight, or any experience that reveals the human spirit.

- To be nobody but yourself in a world which is doing its best day and night to make you like everybody else means to fight the hardest battle which a human being can fight and never stop fighting.

- I'm living so far beyond my income that we may almost be said to be living apart.

- Life's not a paragraph And death I think is no parenthesis.

Chapter 72. Harry S. Truman and Eddie Jacobson

It isn't often that a friendship can be instrumental in creating a new country. But this is the case due to the enduring friendship between Harry Truman, the 33rd president of the United States, and his World War I buddy and post war business partner, Eddie Jacobson.

Jacobson, who was Jewish, was asked by Jewish leaders to help convince Truman to support creation of Israel. At this time in early 1948, the British mandate over Palestine was due to shortly end, and there was great uncertainty over what would transpire. The State Department was opposed to creation of a Jewish state, arguing that it would rupture relations with the Arab countries in the region, imperil the supply of oil, and that such a Jewish state would have indefensible borders.

But Jacobson, who was allowed easy access to the Oval Office, managed to convince Truman to see Dr. Chaim Weizmann, head of the World Jewish Organization. This meeting was held over the objections of the State Department. One tactic Jacobson employed was to somehow compare Weizmann, someone he looked up to, with one of Truman's heroes — Andrew Jackson. As the forthright seventh president, Jackson was famed for knowing what he wanted to do and then doing it despite any obstacles.

Jacobson appealed to Truman by letter and in person. In one note, he wrote: "I think if I am one of the few who actually knows and realizes what terrible heavy burdens you are carrying on your shoulders during these hectic days. I should, therefore, be the last to add to them; but I feel you will forgive me for doing so, because tens of thousands of lives depend on words from your mouth and heart."

In person, at the White House, Jacobson said, "Harry, all your life you have had a hero. You are probably the best-read man in America on the life of Andrew Jackson. I remember when we had our store together and you were always reading books and papers on this great American. Well, Harry, I too have a hero, a man I never met, but who is, I think, the greatest Jew who ever lived."

Harry S. Truman

Truman finally gave in and agreed to meet Weizmann, with this choice comment: "You win, you baldheaded son of a bitch. I will see him."

Truman wrestled with the Palestine/Israel issue, balancing domestic politics with international geopolitics — besides the sheer moral issue involved. After considerable soul-searching he decided to recognize Israel, and the U.S. was the first country to do so; and it happened just 11 minutes after Israel declared itself a sovereign nation. The brand new nation went on to defend its "indefensible borders" successfully against the combined Arab armies attacking it from different directions.

Truman wrote about the situation: "Hitler had been murdering Jews right and left. I saw it, and I dream about it even to this day. The Jews needed some place where they could go. It is my attitude that the American government couldn't stand idly by while the victims of Hitler's madness are not allowed to build new lives."

Truman also told Arab delegates that he had to answer to many people eager for establishment of a Jewish homeland while he didn't have that many Arab constituents.

Truman, who was born in 1884, was seven years old than Jacobson. The two had met in Kansas City, Missouri when Jacobson was a stock boy and Truman worked at a bank. They found themselves together in 1917 when they reported for basic training at Camp Doniphon (now Fort Sill) near Lawton, Oklahoma in an artillery unit. Jacobson was a private and Truman a first lieutenant. Together they managed a canteen for troops awaiting deployment to Europe. The canteen was a popular and business success, which helped both in the eyes of their superiors. Impressed by Jacobson's sound business approach, Truman confided in a letter to his girlfriend, Bess Wallace: "I have a Jew in charge of the canteen by the name of Jacobson and he is a crackerjack."

On the other side of the ledger, some officers called him "Trumanheimer."

Eventually, Jacobson and Truman were separated on the battlefront. Truman saw considerable combat, and was promoted to captain. His military record helped in his later political career.

After World War I ended Truman and Jacobson went into business together, opening a haberdashery store in Kansas City in 1919. There was no contract between them. They operated on trust. Truman was responsible primarily for the bookkeeping, while Jacobson concentrated on the inventory. Initially the business did well enough, but a 1921 recession dampened sales and they might have been hurt by an overstocked inventory. In a telling commentary, Truman later wrote: "Jacobson and I went to bed one night with a $35,000 inventory and awoke the next day with a $25,000 shortage. This brought bills payable and bank notes due at such a rapid rate we went out of business."

Jacobson declared bankruptcy in 1925. Truman finally settled his debts when he paid off the last bank loan at a deep discount in 1935. It helped that he had become a U.S. Senator from Missouri a year before.

Despite the business debacle, the two remained close friends. Truman, joining the Pendergast political machine in Kansas City, ascended the political ladder in the Democratic Party. He went from county administrator to senator, and then to vice president in 1944. In April 1945, he became president when Franklin Delano Roosevelt suddenly died less than three months into his fourth term. Truman finished out Roosevelt's term; and then in a stunning upset over Thomas Dewey, the favored Republican opponent in the 1948 election, won the presidency in his own right. One newspaper (the *Chicago Tribune*) made a famously embarrassing and premature assumption before the final election returns were in. Its large boldface headline read: *Dewey Defeats Truman*.

Jacobson worked as a traveling salesman in the clothing field during the 1922–1945 period, which brought him to Washington D.C. sometimes. He was able to get together with Truman, who was very much a down-to-earth personality with great respect for his roots. They also maintained a steady correspondence. Doubtless, the Nazi persecution of Jews in Germany after Hitler came to power in the early 30s, and then the spreading reports of the Holocaust, was a subject they discussed. Jacobson did finally open his own clothing store in 1945.

After Truman's presidency the two resumed frequent walks and lunches in Kansas City. In 1955 they discussed the possibility of a trip to Europe where Truman would be seeing various dignitaries and receiving various honors. But Jacobson died in October of that year. Truman lived on to 1972.

Jacobson received a great deal of recognition for his efforts on behalf of the creation of Israel, and he lived long enough to gain satisfaction from seeing his friend get elected on his own — to everyone's surprise — in the 1948 election. Truman delivered a eulogy for Jacobson, later writing that Jacobson was "as fine a man as ever walked."

***

Quotes from Truman:

- If you can't convince them, confuse them.
- It's amazing what you can accomplish if you don't care who gets the credit.
- It's a recession when your neighbor loses his job; it's a depression when you lose yours.
- I never did give them hell. I just told the truth, and they thought it was hell.

Chapter 73. John F. Kennedy & Kirk DeMoyne Billings (Lem and Jack)

Being one of the best friends of a U.S. president brings benefits as well as challenges, as Kirk Lemoyne Billings discovered.

Billings and Kennedy were roommates at the elite Choate School in Wallingford, Connecticut. They were close in age with Kennedy born in 1917 and Billings in 1916. Both were fun-loving, with a similar sense of humor; both disliked some of the disciplinary aspects of life at Choate, and each had an older brother who were the stars of their respective families. They began using the nicknames of Lem and Jack as part of a group of prank-loving boys in a "Muckers Club" which played tricks on fellow students as well as faculty and administrators.

Both boys, roommates for two years, barely escaped expulsion from the unappreciative school. At graduation, however, Kennedy was selected as the most likely to succeed and Billings, the son of a Pittsburgh physician, as the most good natured. Kennedy had health problems — later diagnosed as Addison's disease which involves insufficient production of hormones by the adrenal glands. After tests at the Mayo Clinic, Kennedy confided to Billings, "I'm still eating peas and corn for food, and I had an enema given by a beautiful blonde. That, my sweet, is the height of cheap thrills."

John F. Kennedy

Their friendship lasted a lifetime. Billings was often the guest of Kennedy at the family home in Hyannis Port and also at Palm

Beach, Florida. The pair went on double dates and caroused in New York at the Stork Club and other high-living places. They also took a two-month grand tour of France, Germany, Italy and England in the summer of 1937, sharing adventures and misadventures. Both developed a considerable alarm over Germany's mounting aggressions. Neither were they impressed by any of the speeches they heard by Il Duce, Benito Mussolini, Italy's fascist leader; nor did they form a good impression of Germany under Adolph Hitler.

Subsequently, Kennedy did some newspaper work in London for Hearst newspapers while Billings worked as a junior executive for the Coca Cola Company in Bridgeport, Connecticut. But the two remained in contact through correspondence, with young Kennedy sharing candid rundowns of his love life as a very active bachelor. Billings was also good friends with Kennedy's sister, Kathy.

As his father was the ambassador to Great Britain, Kennedy spent some time in London during this turbulent period which led to his insightful book *Why England Slept*, which came out in 1940. Some writing and editing help was provided young Kennedy, but it isn't known how much. The basis for the book was his senior thesis at Harvard, titled *Appeasement In Munich*, which discussed the implications of the famed meeting between Hitler and British Prime Minister Neville Chamberlain.

When World War II came, both men wanted to enlist, but they each had medical problems and were rejected for military service. Kennedy, from a famous family with connections, secured a commission as an ensign in the Naval Reserves. He worked at the office of Naval Intelligence in D.C., writing and editing bulletins. He had an affair with a Danish journalist which led to notations in a FBI file about suspicions of her being a spy. Billings, 4F, got into the American Field Service, a paramilitary ambulance unit. Soon he was in North Africa, with Allied forces facing the German army led by General Erwin Rommel.

Kennedy, itching for more active service, finally got into patrol boat training in 1943 and was soon posted to the South Pacific as an officer. His bravery in saving the crew of PT109 after a Japanese destroyer sheared the patrol boat in two is famous — albeit exaggerated. Kennedy wrote Lem about his heroism: "We had a bad time — a week on a Jáp island — but finally got picked up — and have got another boat. It really makes me wonder if most success is merely a great deal of fortuitous accidents. I imagine I would agree with you that it was lucky the whole thing happened — if the two fellows had not been killed which rather spoils the whole thing for me."

Meanwhile, Billings received minor shrapnel wounds during the decisive battle of El Alamein that gave the Allies control of North Africa.

In the immediate post war period, Kennedy set his sights on a political career, especially after his older brother, Joe, groomed to become president, died during the war. He ran in 1946 and won a congressional seat representing his home state of Massachusetts. Billings helped in his various election campaigns.

Of his entry into politics, Billings commented: "I think a lot of people say that if Joe hadn't died, Jack might never have gone into politics. I don't believe this. Nothing could have kept Jack out of politics. I think this is what he had in him, and it just would have come out."

Kennedy also won a Pulitzer Prize for his book *Profiles In Courage*, which is widely reputed to have received considerable help from other writers/editors. Subsequently, he ran in a senatorial race and won again. After various affairs, Kennedy married Jacqueline Bouvier when he was 36 and she was 24. His bride was warned about Kennedy's well-known flings and affairs, with Billings also providing some advice on this touchy score. The glamorous couple had two children who survived to adulthood. Though he dated often, including celebrities, Billings remained a bachelor.

After graduating from the Harvard School of Business Administration in 1948 Billings went on to become a vice president of a pharmaceutical company in Baltimore. Later, he became a vice president of a New York advertising agency.

Lem and Jack

As Kennedy's star rose, Billings was cautioned by Kennedy's father to be less familiar with his son in public, such as calling him by his first name or his school nickname. Still friends, Billings recognized that some changes in their relationship were inevitable, especially in the public arena.

Kennedy, after a run to be the Democratic vice presidential nominee in the 1956 presidential election, ran for the presidency in 1960. A pivotal moment came when he decided to run in the West Virginia primary; his religion as a Catholic was a major factor in a heavily Protestant state. But Kennedy was forthright in overcoming this issue, paving the way for his nomination. He squeezed out a narrow victory over Richard Nixon, who had been vice president in the outgoing Eisenhower administration, and became the first Catholic president of the United States.

Billings was then offered some governmental positions, including the ambassadorship to Denmark, which he declined. Later, he did accept a position as a founding trustee of the National Cultural Center, which later became the Kennedy Center for the Performing Arts. A frequent visitor to the White House, where he often stayed in his own room, Billings was provided a code name by the Secret Service. Fond of practical jokes, perhaps recalling Choate days, Kennedy enjoyed such pranks as introducing Billings as a senator or general at some functions.

Of their friendship Billings wrote: "Jack was the closest person to me in the world for thirty years. I've often wondered why, you know, all through the years we continued to be such close friends, because I never kept up on politics and all the things that interested him. What he really wanted to do, on weekends, was to get away from anything that had to do with the White House."

Billings survived the tragic death of Kennedy, though he often relived their many years of friendship in various interviews and discussions with friends. He died in 1981.

***

Some quotes by Kennedy:

- Forgive your enemies, but never forget their names.
- I would rather be accused of breaking precedents than breaking promises.
- The time to repair the roof is when the sun is shining.
- We must use time as a tool, not as a crutch.
- When we got into office, the thing that surprised me the most was that things were as bad as we'd been saying they were.
- The only reason to give a speech is to change the world.

Chapter 74. J. Edgar Hoover and Clyde Tolson

Whether J. Edgar Hoover, the controversial head of the Federal Bureau of Investigation for nearly half a century, and Clyde Tolson, his second-in-command for much of this time, were lovers will probably never be known for certain. They never acknowledged having any sort of romantic relationship. Hoover was accused of being a homosexual but this was never proven, and some observers believe he would have been too afraid of any scandal hurting or ending his career. But what is well established is that the pair of lawmen were close friends and kindred spirits for many years with their closeness going well beyond office hours.

Clyde Tolson

The two dined together twice a day usually, socialized together at night, went as a duo to sports events and racetracks, and vacationed together. On work days Tolson would be picked up and go to the FBI offices with Hoover in his limousine. Similarly, they were known to frequent the Stork Club in New York at times and spend time with such luminaries as the fighter Jack Dempsey and the author Damon Runyon. Often the two were recognized as a couple of sorts. This worked out that when

Hoover was invited to a dinner party or like event, Tolson would be invited as well.

The pair sometimes wound up in the famed column of newspaper columnist Walter Winchell who reported gossip and the goings on of celebrities. Both men were life-long bachelors, with Hoover senior to Olson by five years. Hoover was born in 1895 and Tolson in 1900. When Tolson's parents died, Hoover accompanied Tolson to their funerals.

They worked closely together, with Tolson involved with Hoover in some major successful hunts for gangsters in the 30's. Tolson also had responsibilities for maintaining the bureau's personnel and the general subject of staff discipline and deportment. Hoover called Tolson his alter ego.

After Hoover died, Tolson was named executor and chief beneficiary of Hoover's estate, getting in excess of $500,000 as well as his house, where he lived for the rest of his life. He moved into Hoover's house shortly after his death. Tolson was also the beneficiary of Hoover's life insurance policy. In his will he made arrangements to be buried near Hoover at the Congressional Cemetery.

The two met in 1927 when Olson was 27. Hoover invited Tolson to join the FBI the following year in 1928. Both men had earned law degrees at night school and found their personalities were very compatible. Tolson rose quickly in the ranks and was named associate director in 1947. He had special access to Hoover. When the television show, *The FBI* began, he was entrusted with script supervision.

Hoover himself also paid a great deal of attention to how the FBI was depicted. Throughout his career Hoover showed a strong and meticulous desire to reap positive publicity for himself and the FBI. It's believed he harbored ambitions that included appointment to the Supreme Court or even the presidency. He tried but failed to secure control of intelligence operations on both the domestic and international fronts, and wasn't pleased with the creation of the Central Intelligence Agency which handled the latter.

Tolson had a stroke in 1964 and suffered from poor health from that point on. Even though he was past retirement age Hoover made sure he stayed in his post.

When Hoover died in 1972 Tolson became acting head of the bureau for a day. President Nixon ordered Patrick Gray, who he quickly named acting head of the FBI, to seize Hoover's secret files. It was well known that Hoover, over the years, had accumulated potentially damaging information about many figures of the day including presidents, politicians, show business luminaries, and such Civil Rights leaders as Martin Luther King Jr. The existence of this material, some of it salacious, helped keep Hoover in power despite the preference of a couple of presidents to ease him out of his high office. Today, the term of office of a FBI director is limited to 10 years, a policy doubtless adopted due to Hoover's secret files.

Tolson, however, refused to turn over the files. Instead he ordered Hoover's executive secretary, who had been with Hoover for decades, to destroy these personal files and thus preserve his sterling image. As it turned out Hoover had left instructions for this destruction himself. Once the task was done Tolson submitted his formal letter of resignation.

He died a few years later, in 1975, still living in Hoover's house.

Among Hoover's quotes:

- No amount of law enforcement can solve a problem that goes back to the family.

- The cure for crime is not the electric chair, but the high chair.

- Justice is incidental to law and order.

- Just the minute the FBI begins making recommendations on what should be done with its information, it becomes a Gestapo.

CHAPTER 75. CHRISTOPHER BOYCE AND ANDREW DAULTON LEE

Christopher Boyce and Andrew Daulton Lee, two friends with a relatively upscale Southern California background, had their lives go horribly astray when they became involved in espionage and selling military secrets to the Soviet Union. Both are still alive at this writing. Their story has been written about a great deal, with the book and subsequent movie, *The Falcon & The Snowman*, read and seen respectively worldwide.

The boys — born only a year apart, Boyce in 1953 and Lee in 1952 — went to Catholic school together where they bonded as best friends. They were both altar boys at the local church. Boyce took up the hobby of falconry that Lee also practiced with him.

The Vietnam War was raging at this time with war footage being shown daily on television. Boyce developed a distaste for American involvement in Vietnam, and his view of the country overall became further jaundiced by the Watergate debacle. He also suffered a crisis of religious faith. Meanwhile, Lee — who was shorter (about 5 feet, two inches) and less prepossessing — had turned to using and selling marijuana and cocaine, in part to gain more popularity with girls and more money.

Boyce, through his father (who used to work for the FBI), got a low level job at the age of 21 as a clerk with the Santa Monica-based TRW Defense Space Systems Group, a private company that handled sensitive spy satellite work for the government. His starting salary was $140 a week. Having taken a security pledge, Boyce worked in the Material Control section. He also received clearance from assorted federal agencies that allowed him access to a special room called the "Black Vault" which contained top-secret material.

Increasingly dismayed by what he considered U.S. duplicity in events worldwide — the Salvador Allende coup in Chile was one factor — Boyce's disillusionment led to concoction of a plan to sell material to the Soviet Union. Money was one motive but it may not have been the primary one.

Boyce enlisted the aid of Lee, whose life had devolved into one of crime and drug-dealing. He started as a runner for dealers and graduated to being a pusher himself. Then his specialty became the lucrative sale of heroin/cocaine which led to his nickname as "The Snowman."

The method they used was for Boyce to smuggle material out of the Black Vault — he also took photos eventually (at the request of their Russian handlers) — and Lee to serve as a courier to the Soviet Embassy in Mexico City. Initially, Lee made contact with this embassy, which showed interest. Lee managed, with an example of what Boyce had to offer, to convince the Russians that he had useful information. Lee received their first modest payment, and the two were given the code names of "Luis" and "The Snowman." Boyce, at first, was unidentified to the Russians, though that changed later when Lee disclosed his name under a combination of Russian pressure and ample vodka.

As the collaboration between the friends grew, tensions came to the fore. Boyce wasn't sure that Lee was giving him his full share of money received. While Lee was heavily involved with dope, Boyce may have gotten more of a high from being a spy, and a successful one to boot — at least so far. Lee also had more grandiose plans, including selling material to China; and he asked Russian assistance to transport drugs from South America to Mexico, from where they could get them into the U.S. market. Seeking a big score, Lee might have had images of a well-heeled and youthful retirement in Costa Rica or another safe haven.

As it turned out, two years of delivering spy material sales netted Boyce only about $20,000. He may have been disillusioned by this relatively paltry amount and ready to call it quits. One report has it that the Russians paid $77,000 before the pair were caught.

Later, Boyce wrote: "I knew from the beginning that I would eventually be caught. There was no escape from it. After all, I'm an amateur, 21 years old, and the Central Intelligence Agency had been in business a lot longer than I had."

Their fall started when Lee was caught dropping some material over the gates of the Russian Embassy by the Mexican police instead of employing the usual system of placing marks at designated places in the Mexican capital. The police didn't buy his explanation, which included a claim he was working for the CIA and providing disinformation to the Russians. A search revealed film with

"Top Secret" on it. An American consular officer who came to the police station also saw the incriminating material, which soon brought the FBI onto the scene.

After some less than gentle prodding by the Mexican police, Lee confessed. His treason to the U.S. was obvious. He was given a choice by the Mexicans: to be deported to the Soviet Union or to the United States. He chose the United States. Soon thereafter, Boyce was arrested in January 1977. He confessed, repudiating Lee's CIA claims.

Separate trials were run. One concern on the part of the government was the possibility of having to turn over sensitive material to the defense attorneys which would then likely surface at trial.

In Boyce's trial he claimed the material he turned over was outdated and of little value, and that Lee had threatened blackmail if he didn't continue the espionage. After less than four hours of deliberation, Boyce was found guilty and subsequently sentenced to 40 years in jail.

Lee's trial went on much longer. A sole juror held out against guilty. Finally, she gave in. Lee, given his criminal record, was sentenced to life imprisonment.

Both men were sent to Lompoc Prison in California. Lee successfully withdrew from drugs in prison. Boyce, more the intellectual traitor, might have found adjustment to prison life more difficult. Regardless, he very cleverly managed to escape from prison in January 1980, greatly assisted by watching *Escape From Alcatraz*, a movie that surprisingly was shown to the convicts. In the film, actor Clint Eastwood escapes by making a dummy to lie in his cot to give him enough time to make his get-away. Boyce followed suit, placing a *papier-mâché* dummy in his cot.

When Boyce escaped from prison, Lee was sent to another facility, which effectively cut off any communication.

On the loose for less than two years, Boyce robbed several banks in the Pacific Northwest, took flight lessons, and entered a relationship with a woman who shielded him as a fugitive. Finally, he was captured and sentenced to three extra years beyond his original sentence. His practice was to refuse media interviews, but finally he relented with an Australian television show similar to *Sixty Minutes* in the United States

He said: "I have no problem with the label 'traitor,' if you qualify what it's to. I think that eventually the U.S. government is going to involve the world in the next world war. And being a traitor to that, I have absolutely no problem with that whatsoever."

He also admitted that "Espionage was a cruel wound to inflict on a father who loved me."

Lee was released from prison on parole in 1998 at the age of 46. He was hired as a personal assistant by actor Sean Penn who played him in the movie, *The*

Falcon and The Snowman. His partner in crime Boyce, paroled in 2003 at the age of 50, subsequently married Cait Mills. Both men have been out of the news since. How much damage their espionage did to American security has never been fully established.

BIBLIOGRAPHY

Ainger, Michael, *Gilbert and Sullivan, A Dual Biography*, New York, Oxford University Press, 2002

Anderson, Wayne, *The Youth of Cezanne and Zola*, Boston, Editions Febriart, 2003

Arvin, Newton, *Herman Melville*, New York, Grove Press, 1950

Ashton, Rosemary, *The Life of Samuel Taylor Coleridge*, Cambridge, MA, Blackwell, 1996

Baatz, Simon, *For The Thrill Of It: Leopold, Loeb & The Murder That Shocked Chicago*, New York, Harper Collins, 2008

Bakewell, Sarah, *A Life of Montaigne* New York, Other Press, 2010

Barker, Juliet, *Wordsworth: A Life*, New York, HarperCollins, 2000

Barra, Allen, *Inventing Wyatt Earp*, New York, Carroll & Graf, 1998

Bergreen, Laurence, *Capone: The Man and the Era*, New York, Simon & Schuster, 1994

Bishop, Chip, *The Lion and the Journalist*, Guilford, CT, Globe Pequot, 2012

Black, Conrad, *Franklin Delano Roosevelt: Champion of Freedom*, New York, Public Affairs, 2003

Bloom Harold, *Samuel T. Coleridge*, Broomall, PA, Chelsea House, 2001

Bloom, Harold, *Lord Byron*, Broomall, PA, Chelsea House, 2004

Bloom, Harold, *Poets of World War I*, Broomall, PA, Chelsea House, 2003

Bosco, Ronald and Murphy, Jillmairie, *Hawthorne In His Own Time*, Iowa City, University of Iowa Press, 2007

Bosco, Ronald and Myerson, Joel, *Emerson In His Own Time*, Iowa City, University of Iowa Press, 2003

Bostridge, Mark, *Florence Nightingale: The Making of an Icon*, New York, Farrar, Straus & Giroux, 2008

Boswell, James, *The Life of Samuel Johnson*, New York, Penguin, 1791/2008

Bowen, Catherine and von Meck, Barbara, *"Beloved Friends": The Story of Tchaikovsky and Nadejda von Meck*, New York, Random House, 1904

Brinkley, Alan, *John. F. Kennedy*, New York, Henry Holt, & Co., 2012

Brombert, Beth, *Eduarde Manet: Rebel In A Frock Coat*, Chicago, University of Chicago Press, 1997

Brown, Frederic, *An Impersonation of Angels, A Biography of Jean Cocteau*, New York, Viking Press, 1968

Brown, Frederick, *Flaubert*, New York, Little & Brown, 2006

Brown, Frederick, *Zola: A Life*, New York, Farrar, Straus & Giroux, 1995

Brown, Jonathon, *Claude Debussy*, London, Pavilion Books, 1996

Bruccoli, Matthew, *Some Sort of Epic Grandeur: The Life of F. Scott Fitzgerald*, New York, Harcourt Brace Jovanovich, 1981

Buchan, James, *The Authentic Adam Smith*, New York, Norton, 2006

Burgess, Glyn, *The Song of Roland*, New York, Penguin Books, 1990

Cate, Curtis, *Friedrich Nietzsche*, New York, Overlook Press, 2005

Collier, James, *The Susan Anthony You Never Knew*, New York, Children's Press, 2004

Colman, Penny, *Elizabeth Cady Stanton & Susan B. Anthony*, New York, Henry Holt, 2011

Cooper, John, *Woodrow Wilson: A Biography*, New York, Knopf, 2009

Coventry, Angela, *Hume: A Guide For the Perplexed*, New York, Continuum, 2007

Craft, Robert, *Stravinsky: Glimpses of a Life*, New York, St. Martin's Press, 1992

Cramer, Jeffrey, *The Quotable Thoreau*, Princeton, N.J., Princeton University Press, 2011

Daiches, David, *James Boswell and His World*, New York, Scriber, 1976

Dallek, Robert, *Harry S. Truman*, New York, Times Books, 2008

Damrosch, David, *The Buried Book: The Loss & Rediscovery of the Great Epic of Gilgamesh*, New York, Henry Holt, 2007

Damrosch, Leo, *Jean-Jacques Rousseau: Restless Genius*, New York, Houghton Mifflin, 2005

Daniel, Lucy, *Gertrude Stein*, London, Reaktion Books, 2009

Danielson, Dennis, *The First Copernican*, New York, Walker & Company, 2006

Davidson, Ian, *Voltaire: A Life*, London, Profile Books, 2010

Davie, John, *Horace: Satires and Epistles*, New York, Oxford University Press, 2011

Delbanco, Andrew, *Herman Melville: His Life and Work*, New York, Knopf, 2000

Dodge, Walter Phelps, *Piers Gaveston: A Chapter of Early Constitutional History*, New York, B. Blom, 1971

Donaldson, Scott, *Fitzgerald & Hemingway*, New York, Columbia University Press, 2009

Durant,Will, *Heroes Of History*, New York, Simon & Schuster, 2001

Farrell, John, *Clarence Darrow, Attorney For The Damned*, N.Y., Doubleday, 2011

Feist, Peter, *Renoir*, Cologne, Taschen, 2004

Fellows, Otis, *Diderot*, Boston, Twayne, 1989

Ferguson, Diana, *Greek Myths & Legends*, London, Collins & Brown, 2000

Ferry, David, *The Epistles of Horace*, New York, Farrar, Straus & Giroux, 2001

Fontana, Biancamaria, *Montaigne's Politics*, Princeton, N.J., Princeton University Press, 2008

Fox, Christopher, *The Cambridge Companion to Jonathan Swift*, New York, Cambridge University Press, 2003

Freeman, Philip, *Alexander The Great*, New York, Simon & Schuster, 2011

Freeman, Philip, *Oh, My Gods: A Modern Retellings of Greek & Roman Myths*, New York, Simon & Schuster, 2012

Fried, Michael, *Manet's Modernism*, Chicago, University of Chicago Press, 1996

Fulcher, Jane, *Debussy and His World*, Princeton, N.J., Princeton University Press, 2001

Furbank, P.N., *Diderot: A Critical Biography*, New York, Knopf, 1992

Furbank, P.N. *Italo Svevo: The Man and the Writer*, Berkeley, University of California Press, 1966

Gabler, Neal, *Walt Disney, The Triumph of the American Imagination*, New York, Knopf, 2006

Gara, Larry, *The Presidency of Franklin Pierce*, Lawrence, KA, University Press of Kansas, 1991

Garrett, Martin, *George Gordon, Lord Byron*, New York, Oxford University Press, 2001

George, Alexander and Juliette, *Woodrow Wilson & Colonel House*, New York, John Day & Co., 1956

Gibbs Christopher, *The Life of Schubert*, Cambridge, U.K, Cambridge University Press, 2000

Gigante, Denise, *The Keats Brothers*, Cambridge, MA, Harvard University Press, 2011

Gill, Gillian, *Nightingales*, New York, Random House, 2005

Gillam, Scott, *Andrew Carnegie*, Edina, MN, ABDO Publishing, 2009

Ginzberg, Lori, *Elizabeth Cady Stanton*, New York, Hill & Wang, 2009

Glendinning, Victoria, *Jonathan Swift*, New York, Henry Holt & Co., 1998

Goldman, Martin, *John F. Kennedy: Portrait of a President*, New York, Facts On File, 1995

Gorrell, Gena, *Heart and Soul, The Story of Florence Nightingale*, Toronto, Tundra Books, 2000

Grey, Thomas, *Richard Wagner and His World*, Princeton, N.J., University of Princeton Press, 2009

Gibbs, Christopher, *Schubert*, New York, Cambridge University Press, 1997

Richard Gutman, Robert, *Mozart: A Cultural Biography*, New York, Harcourt Brace, 2000

Hack, Richard, *Puppetmaster: The Secret Life of J. Edgar Hoover*, Beverly Hills, New Millennium Press, 2004

Harrison, Max, *Rachmaninoff*, New York, Continuum, 2005

Harrison, Stephan, *The Cambridge Companion to Horace*, New York, Cambridge University Press, 2007

Hayman, Ronald, *Kafka*, London, Weidenfelt & Nicolson, 1981

Hemmings, F.W.J., *Alexandre Dumas: The King of Romance*, New York, Scribner, 1979

Herrmann, Dorothy, *Helen Keller: A Life*, Chicago, University of Chicago Press, 1998

Hiller, Bevis, *The Wit & Wisdom of G.K. Chesterton*, New York, Continuum, 2010

Hodgson, Godfrey, *Woodrow Wilson's Right Hand Man: The Life of Colonel Edward M. House*, New Haven, Yale University Press, 2006

Holden, Anthony, *Tchaikovsky: A Biography*, New York, Random House, 1995

Holt, Michael, *Franklin Pierce*, New York, Henry Holt, 2010

Hunt, Tri-Star, *Marx's General: The Revolutionary Life of Friedrich Engels*, New York, Henry Holt, 2009

Hyman, Robert, *K: A Biography of Kafka*, London, Phoenix Press, 2001

Irving, William, *John Gay: Favorite of the Wits*, Durham, N.C., Duke University Press, 1940

James, Carolyn Curtis, *The Gospel of Ruth*, Grand Rapids, Michigan, Zondervan, 2008

James, David, *Hegel: A Guide For The Perplexed*, New York, Continuum, 2007

Joannides, Paul, *Renoir: Life and Works*, Nashville, Sourcebooks, 2000

Jones, David Wyn, *The Life Of Haydn*, New York, Oxford University Press, 2009

Josephson. Judith, *Walt Disney: Genius of Entertainment*, Berkeley Heights, N.J., Enslow Publishers, 2006

Junker, Klaus, *Interpreting The Images of Greek Myths*, New York, Cambridge University Press, 2012

Kainz, Howard, *G.W.F. Hegel*, New York, Twayne, 1996

Kersten, Andrew, *Clarence Darrow: American Iconoclast*, New York, Hill & Wang, 2011

Kiernan, V.G., *Horace: Poetics and Politics*, New York, St. Martin's Press, 1999

Kohler, Joachim, *Richard Wagner: Last of the Titans*, New Haven, CT, Yale University Press, 2004

Krass, Peter, *Carnegie*, New York, Wiley, 2002

Kritzman, Lawrence, *The Fabulous Imagination: Montaigne's Essays*, New York, Columbia University Press, 2009

Lash, Joseph, *Helen and Teacher: The Story of Helen Keller and Anne Sullivan Macy*, New York, AFB Press, 1997

Laskowsky, William, *Rupert Brooke*, New York, Macmillan, 1994

Lever, Maurice, *Beaumarchais: A Biography*, New York, Farrar, Straus & Giroux, 2009

Lindsay, Jack, *Cezanne: His Life & Art*, N.Y., Graphic Society, 1969

Lindsay, Robert, *The Falcon and The Snowman*, Guilford, CT., Lyons Press, 2002

Linzie, Anna, *The True Story of Alice B. Toklas*, Iowa City, Iowa, University of Iowa Press, 2006

Lloyd, Rosemary, *Baudelaire's World*, Ithaca, N.Y., Cornell University Press, 2002

Mack, Maynard, *Alexander Pope*, New York, Norton, 1986

Malcolm, Janet, *Two Lives: Gertrude & Alice*, New London, Yale University Press, 2007

Maney, Patrick, *The Roosevelt Presence*, Berkeley, CA, University of California Press, 1992

Marschall, Rick, *Bully! Life & Times of Theodore Roosevelt*, Washington, D.C., Regnery Publishing, 2011

Martin, Peter, *A Life Of James Boswell*, London, Weidenfeld & Nicolson, 1999

Martin, Peter, *Samuel Johnson*, London, Weidenfeld & Nicolson, 2008

Masterson, W.B. (Bat), *Famous Gunfighters of the Western Frontier*, Mineola, N.Y., Dover Publications, 2009

Mawer, Deborah, *Ravel*, New York, Cambridge University Press, 2000

Mellow, James, *Hemingway: A Life Without Consequences*, New York, Houghton Mifflin, 1992

Meltzer, Milton, *Up Close: John Steinbeck*, New York, Penguin, 2008

Millgram, Hillel, *Four Biblical Heroines and the Case for Female Authorship*, Jefferson, N.C., McFarland & Co., 2008

Morris, Edmund, *Beethoven: The Universal Composer*, New York, HarperCollins, 2005

Morton, Timothy, *Shelley*, New York, Cambridge University Press, 2006

Mossner, Ernest, *The Life of David Hume*, New York, Oxford University Press, 1980

Motion, Andrew, *Keats*, Chicago, University of Chicago Press, 1997

Murray, Nicholas, *Kafka*, New Haven, CT, Yale University Press, 2004

Nichols, Roger, *Ravel*, New Haven, Yale University Press, 2011

Nielson, Kim, *Beyond The Miracle Worker*, Boston, Beacon Press, 2009

Nokes, David, *Samuel Johnson: A Life*, New York, Henry Holt, 2010

Nokes, David, *Swift: A Hypocrite Reversed*, New York, Oxford University Press, 1985

Norris, Geoffrey, *Rachmaninoff*, New York, Schirmer Books, 1993

O'Brien, Edna, *James Joyce: A Life*, New York, Penguin, 1999

Oliphant, Margaret, *The Atlas of the Ancient World*, New York, Barnes & Noble, 1992

Olson, Steven, *Henry David Thoreau*. New York, Rosen Publishing, 2006

Orel, Harold, *Gilbert and Sullivan*, Iowa City, University of Iowa Press, 1994

Payne, Robert, *The Three Worlds of Boris Pasternak*, New York, Coward-McCann, 1961

Pearson, Roger, *Voltaire Almighty*, New York, Bloomsbury, 2005

Peters, Angie & Richards, Larry, *The Life Of David*, Nashville, Thomas Nelson, 2008

Pointer, Larry, *In Search Of Butch Cassidy*, Norman, OK, University of Oklahoma Press, 1977

Phillipson, N.T., *Adam Smith: An Enlightened Life*, New Haven, Yale University Press, 2010

Plaskin, Glenn, *Horowitz*, New York, Morrow, 1983

Plumly, Stanley, *Posthumous Keats*, New York, Norton, 2008

Potter, Philip, *Gothic Kings of Britain: The Lives of 31 Medieval Rulers, 1016-1399*, Jefferson, N.C., B. Blom, 1971

Radosh, Allis and Ronald, *A Safe Haven: Harry S. Truman And The Founding Of Israel*, New York, HarperCollins, 2009

Read, Mike, *Forever England: The Life of Rupert Brooke*, Edinburgh, Scotland, Mainstream Publishing, 1997

Reef, Catherine, *E.E. Cummings: a Poet's Life*, New York, Houghton Mifflin, 2006

Reef, Catherine, *Ernest Hemingway: A Writer's Life*, Clarion Books, 2009

Reavey, George, *The Poetry of Boris Pasternak*, New York, G.P. Putnam, 1959

Reinach, Salomon, *Orpheus: The History of Religions*, New York, Liveright, 1930

Repcheck, Jack, *Copernicus' Secret: How The Scientific Revolution Began*, New York, Simon & Schuster, 2007

Reynolds, Larry, *Nathaniel Hawthorne*, New York, Oxford University Press, 2001

Richardson, Joanna, *Baudelaire*, New York, St. Martin's Press, 1994

Rogers, Pat, *Cambridge Companion to Alexander Pope*, New York, Cambridge University Press, 2007

Rose, David, *Hegel's Philosophy of Right*, New York, Continuum, 2007

Rousseau, Jean-Jacques, *Confessions of Jean-Jacques Rousseau*, Bibliobazaar, 2008

Sadie, Stanley, *Verdi and His Operas*, New York, St. Martin's Press, 2000

Salisbury, Cynthia, *Elizabeth Cady Stanton*, Berkeley Heights, N.J., Enslow, 2002

Sawyer-Laucanno, Christopher, *E.E. Cummings*, Naperville, IL, Sourcebooks, 2004

Schmitt, Richard, *Introduction to Marx and Engels*, Boulder, CO, Westview Press, 1997

Schom, Alan, *Emile Zola*, New York, Henry Holt, 1987

Schonbert, Harold, *Horowitz: His Life and Music*, New York, Simon & Schuster, 1992

Schopp, Claude, *Alexandre Dumas: Genius of Life*, New York, Franklin Watts, 1988

Schreiner, Samuel, *The Concord Quartet*, Hoboken, N.H., Wiley & Sons, 2006

Suerr, Ruth, *Voltaire's Memoirs*, London, Hesperus Press, 2007

Simpson, Matthew, *Rousseau: A Guide For The Perplexed*, New York, Continuum, 2007

Sisman, Adam, *The Friendship: Wordsworth & Coleridge*, New York, Penguin, 2006

Sisman, Elaine, *Haydn and His World*, Princeton, N.J., Princeton University Press, 1997

Sisson, C.H., *The Song of Roland*, Manchester, England, Carcanet Press, 1983

Solomon, Maynard, *Beethoven*, New York, Schirmer Books, 1998

Spate, Virginia, *Claude Monet: The Color of Time*, New York, Thames & Hudson, 1992

Sullivan, K.E., *Greek Myths & Legends*, London, Brockhampton Press, 1998

Summers, Anthony, *The Secret Life of J. Edgar Hoover*, New York, Putnam, 1993

Svevo, Livia, *Memoir of Italo Svevo*, Marlboro, VT., Marlboro Press, 1990

Tsumura, David Toshio, *The First Book of Samuel*, Grand Rapids, Michigan, Erdmans Publishing Co., 2007

Unger, Harlow, *Improbable Patriot*, Lebanon, N.H., University Press of New England, 2011

Urban, William, *Wyatt Earp*, New York, Rosen Publishing Group, 2003

Vyrubovna, Anna, *Romanov Family Album*, New York, Vendome Press, 1982

Wall, Geoffrey, *Flaubert: A Life*, Farrar, Straus & Giroux, 2001

Webster, James & Georg Feder, *Haydn*, New York, Macmillan, 2002

Whelen, Francis, *Karl Marx: A Life*, New York, Norton, 2000

Whiting, Jim, *The Life and Times of Giuseppe Verdi*, Hockessin, Delaware, Mitchell Lane, 2005

Wells, H.G., *The Outline of History*, New York, Doubleday & Co., 1949

Wineapple, Brenda, *Hawthorne: A Life*, New York, Knopf, 2003

Woolhouse, R.S., *Locke: A Biography*, New York, Cambridge University Press, 2007

Wray, T.J., *Good Girls, Bad Girls: The Enduring Lessons of Twelve Women of the Old Testament*, New York, Rowman & Littlefield, 2008

Yenne, Bill, *Alexander The Great*, New York, Macmillan, 2010

Zannos, Susan, *Life and Times of Felix Mendelssohn*, Hockessin, Delaware, Mitchell Lane, 2004